TIME TO MARKET

Reducing Product Lead Time

By
Cyril (Cy) Charney

Philip E. Mitchell
Publication Administrator

Published by

Society of Manufacturing Engineers
Publications Development Department
One SME Drive
P.O. Box 930
Dearborn, Michigan 48121

TIME TO MARKET

Reducing Product Lead Time

Copyright © 1991
Society of Manufacturing Engineers

First Edition
Second Printing

Library of Congress Catalog Number: 90-072145
International Standard Book Number: 0-87263-396-9
Manufactured in the United States of America

To the people who matter most to me,

Rhona, my wife, for her friendship,
my children,
Daneal for her enterprise,
Thalia for her originality, and
Davin for his eternal optimism.

PREFACE

The word speed is described in most dictionaries in terms of swiftness or rapidity. It is derived from the German word *Spowan* which means to succeed. And that is what this book will help you to do—to succeed. *Time To Market* is a system that utilizes speed as a key to reducing product lead time. It will not only inform you about the importance of speed to your organization, but how it can impact on your success. It will share with you many examples of how the leading companies have turned their customer responsiveness from spluttering four cylinder engines to high-speed turbo machines. And, most importantly, it will give you the tools to get started. Then the rest will be up to you. Because being good just isn't good enough. Being the best—by a long shot —will differentiate you in the marketplace.

While we believe that being quick will be the dominant operating strategy of the 90s we do not suggest that everything else is unimportant. Quality, the most important strategy of the 90s and will continue to be important, as will cost effectiveness.

HOW TO USE THIS BOOK

This book is designed for managers at all levels. It provides a conceptual, strategic view of the importance of time, for senior managers, and it provides a how-to for middle and front line managers, and support staff. It also goes beyond education. It helps the user to diagnose strengths and weaknesses in terms of major concepts so that they can take corrective action. And for those readers who are going to run training sessions, it provides exercises after each chapter to enable participants to internalize and then apply key concepts.

THANKS

The author wants to thank the many people who gave him encouragement, help, and advice to make this into the useful book that it is designed to be.

The people of Northern Telecom were most helpful. Robert Badelt, Assistant Vice President, Manufacturing, reviewed the text and gave me useful feed back. Marwan Shishakly and his enthusiastic team at the Switching Division in Calgary, Alberta, allowed me to see and document their democratic management process in action. Mike Ennis, General Manager of the Business Products Division, where the Norstar product is manufactured, allowed me to delve into all aspects of their product development process. John R. Lawler, Director of Communications in Mississauga, Ontario, facilitated my visits to various parts of Northern Telecom. Bob Miller and Sam Barnes at NT Corporate allowed me to try out much of my new knowledge in a new product design, increasing my confidence in the power of Time To Market techniques.

Treat Hull, President of the Canadian Supplier Institute, probably Canada's most knowledgeable consultant in the Quality arena, for his insights into the potency of reducing design time by doing things right the first time. Many of Treat's ideas were used to complete Chapter Two.

Warren Vandal and Dave Scheel of Cadworks in Toronto, Ontario, provided valuable help from their vast practical knowledge of CAD/CAM applications contained in Chapter Five. Suzanne Park enhanced my knowledge of Time To Market design teams by showing how the Meyer-Briggs Type Indicator© could be used to make most effective use of a variety of talents.

Special thanks to Dr. Klaus Blache of the General Motors Technical Center in Warren, Michigan, and Dr. William Spurgeon of the University of Michigan-Dearborn in Dearborn, Michigan, for their valued input on Chapter Five.

Pat Tondreau, Professor of Industrial Engineering at Conestoga College, Kitchener, Ontario, whose knowledge of advance manufacturing techniques influenced Chapter Seven.

Bill Craig, whose patience and courtesy in editing my work made my task much easier.

Thanks to David A. Smith of Smith and Associates of Monroe, Michigan, for his work on the section on Quick Die Change. Thank you to Dr. Nancy Hyer of Hewlett-Packard in Santa Rosa, California, for her valuable review of the section on Group Technology. Dr. Spurgeon also reviewed some of the material in Chapter Seven.

And lastly, but not least importantly, my assistant, secretary, accountant, office manager, and friend, Rosemary Kercz, whose skills on the computer made our production of endless rewrites almost pleasant!

Cyril (Cy) Charney

CONTENTS

chapter 1

Background

Looking back at North American business trends, it seems that strategies have changed. "How to do more" was emphasized in the 60s. "How to do it cheaper" became important in the 70s. "How to do it better" was certainly the theme of the 80s. But "How to do it quicker" will be key in the 90s. This is not to say that doing more, doing it for less per-unit cost and doing it better do not apply any more. They still do. But meeting the increasing time demands of customers will become paramount. Time needs will be *the* strategic focus for at least the next decade.

Time — the number of seconds, minutes, days, months or years — is the yardstick by which we increasingly judge those around us — particularly organizations providing services. As evidence, note:

- That about one in every three meals in North America is eaten outside of the home. People value their time. Many cannot be bothered to waste it in activities that add little or no value to the quality of their lives.
- The proliferation of services focusing on speed. The auto lubrication business is increasingly being dominated by the fastest serving lubrication shops. Note the name of one of the most successful: Hurry Lube.
- Instant printing shops are a similar phenomenon, taking an increasing amount of business away from traditional printers.
- The habit of motorists to get into every gap of more than one car length to gain a time advantage. People are even shooting at each other on the freeways of Los Angeles, as a means of discouraging others from doing likewise.
- The design of modern electronic watches includes, as almost standard items, stop-watch capability and count-down systems. This reflects an awareness that consumers want to monitor time in a variety of ways.

- The proliferation of instant banking machines is an attempt to placate an increasingly angry population that detests spending endless time in lines. The organizations that profit from the increasing obsession with time have not done so by accident. They have made time a cornerstone of their competitive strategy. They have sought to differentiate themselves in the market by being the quickest. Just two examples:
- McDonald's — who are probably the fastest in the so-called fast food business.
- Michigan-based Domino's Pizza, whose guarantee of "30 minutes delivery or you don't pay" has enabled them to expand into the largest pizza network in the U. S. Pizza Pizza, a Toronto-based chain, boasts a similar strategy and is Canada's largest pizza franchise operation.

THE STATE OF THE NATION

This is in an exciting and frightening time. Exciting because changes are so widespread and dramatic. Frightening in the sense that the changes are happening so quickly that it is becoming almost impossible to keep up. Futurists predict that our technological information base will double every 24 months by the end of the century. In fact, the only constant we are facing is change itself.

The same is true of consumers. North American buyers are becoming increasingly fickle and demanding. As the world economy brings greater choice, buyers are more informed and spend their dollars on quality and features. Clearly, organizations that bring new products to market quicker enjoy a great advantage as market life-cycles are shrinking at a rapid rate. Telecommunication equipment, for example, has a product life of less than two years as compared to 20 years for some earlier models. Moreover, constantly improving features and benefits help to keep products in the forefront of consumer attention.

It does not take a genius to realize that North America has not kept up with other nations, particularly those of the Pacific Rim. Since the early 1960s, "Made in America" has been disappearing as overseas manufacturers dominate increasing shares of our traditional markets. For example, in 1969 the U. S. produced 82% of the nation's TV sets, 88% of its cars and 90% of machine tools. Today, hardly any TVs are produced locally, half the machine tool market has been given away, while more than 30% of the auto market has passed into foreign hands.

There are many reasons for losing market share. Shoddy products are an important reason. Equally important is the fact that the products are old-fashioned before they hit the market. It takes so much longer to bring products to the market than the competition that the "new" features are often obsolete. "In North America, the average replacement period per automotive model is 9. 2 years. In Japan, it's 4. 2 years. Design time is typically 60 months as opposed to 47 months in Japan. "[1]

---

[1] The Globe and Mail, Wednesday, April 18,1990, p. B22, "Detroit Makers Will Need Lean Manufacturing to Survive the 1990s" (reprinted from the *Economist*).

A closer study of organizations reveals the reason for the relatively slow Time To Market. Put simply, we spend too much time administering the process. Decision making is clumsy and bureaucratic. The result? Actual manufacturing takes only 10% or even less of the total time to get a product to the market.

Reversing this trend will not be easy. The harder we try, the harder our competition seem to try, which creates an ever wider gap. Example: faced with a 100% revaluation of the Yen, Japanese automotive producers increased productivity by 64% in 1987/88.

So much seems misdirected. Daniel Whitney sees the challenge in terms of better design rather than driving down labor dollars. "If manufacturers used to think a 5% improvement was good, they now face competition that is dramatically reducing the number of components and subassemblies for products and achieving a 50% or more reduction in direct cost of manufacture. And even greater reductions are coming, owing to new materials and material-processing techniques. Direct labor, even lower-cost labor, accounts for so little of the total picture that companies still focusing on this factor are still misleading themselves not only about improv-ing products, but also about how foreign competitors have gained so much advantage. "[2]

STRATEGIES FOR SURVIVAL

So what can you do? At most companies, strategic choices seem to include only three options;

1. **Work with competitors.** This strategy appears to result from fear — the fear of losing. It assumes that when you get closer to your rivals, you can understand them better and learn to live with them more comfortably. The auto industry has produced many American-Japanese joint ventures. Ford, with a 25% stake in Mazda Motor Corporation, has developed the Probe. Chrysler's relationship with Mitsubishi has had less success with the Colt. The benefits of these relationships are hard to find. Market share for General Motors, Ford and Chrysler continues to slip. This strategic choice is seldom stable, since competitors refuse to stay put, let alone cooperate.

2. **Run from competitors**. Many companies choose this course. The business press fills its pages with accounts of companies in retreat. They consolidate plants, re-focus their operations, move into outsourcing, divest, pull out of markets, or move upscale.

    The United States steel industry is a prime example. From employing over 100,000 people in the 1960s, the industry employs about 30,000 today. Many plants have closed.

3. **Attack competitors**. The direct attack involves classic confrontation — cut price and capacity, create head-on competition. Indirect attack re-

---

[2]Daniel E. Whitney, "Manufacturing By Design," *Harvard Business Review*, July-August 1988, p.83.

quires surprise. Competitors either do not understand the strategies being used against them, or they do understand but cannot respond — sometimes because of the speed of the attack, sometimes because of their inability to mount a response.

Organizations such as Xerox and Motorola have taken on their competitors head to head. Motorola has gone into Japan with high-quality, well-priced cellular telephones and beaten the locals at their own game.

Of the three options, only an attack creates the opportunity for real growth. Direct attack demands superior resources; it is always expensive and potentially disastrous. Indirect attack promises the most gain for the least cost.

Time-based strategy offers a powerful new approach for successful indirect attacks against larger, established competitors.

Does fast mean working harder? No. It's probably the worst thing to do! Workers will simply burn out and become resentful. Should we introduce an employee involvement program or Just In Time Manufacturing? Or what about a dose of Management By Objectives? While each of these programs has merit, we know too well why they never realize their full potential. The trouble is that these programs are seldom implemented as a truly strategic initiative, with the full backing, support; and involvement of senior management.

Making time a key corporate strategy does not mean neglecting other issues. Rosabeth Moss-Kanter[3], a professor of business administration at Harvard Business School, believes that organizations need to be fast, flexible, friendly and focused. Notice she puts fast first. Time To Market (TTM) is a concept that includes all of these. It starts at the drawing board and continues right to the point of sale.

An excellent example of an integrated approach is that of General Electric Company. Once a laggard in a variety of businesses, GE became more focused in the 1980s. Starting with some 350 major product lines, it has shed many of its slow-growth businesses to concentrate on high- growth technology and service. Many of GE's businesses have sliced layers from management to reduce bureaucracy and improve response time. Chairman and C. E. O. , John F. Welch, Jr., provided employees with a compelling vision. Besides focused and fast, Welch believes in simplicity. He noted that the tendency to over-complicate matters is an attempt to deal with personal insecurities, not solve matters. Business is simple, "not rocket science," says Welch. So decisions should be made quickly and be put in the hands of those best qualified to make them, often front line-people.

Commitment to Time To Market strategy has become more commonplace. The numbers are astonishing. General Electric, for example, has cut its delivery time of custom-made circuit breaker boxes from three weeks to three days. AT&T has reduced design time on its telephones by half. Motorola used to make electronic pagers in three weeks from order. It now does so in two hours.

---

[3]Rosabeth Moss-Kanter, *When Giants Learn to Dance*, Simon & Shuster, Inc., New York, 1989.

Northern Telecom has reduced delivery time on its popular DMS switching systems by half.

What does this mean to the bottom line? According to McKinsey & Co.[4], a U.S. based international management consultant, a high-tech product that reaches the market six months late, even on budget, will earn 33% less profit over over five years. On the other hand, finishing on time, but 50% over budget, will reduce a company's profit by only 4%.

AN INTEGRATED APPROACH

To make a time-based strategy work, it must be integrated. Its component parts are 1) planning and evaluation, 2) goal setting, 3) simultaneous engineering, 4) reduced bureaucracy, 5) world class manufacturing, and 6) the use of computers in design and manufacturing (see *Figure 1-1*).

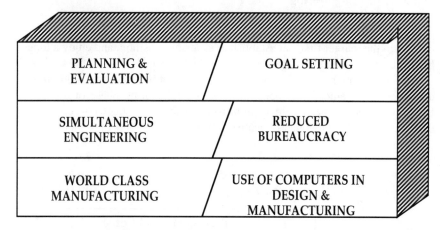

Figure 1-1. Components of a Time-based Strategy.

Each of these components is vital. Taking out one can affect the benefits of any or all of the others. Examine each briefly.

Planning and Evaluation

To develop any meaningful change in business strategy, senior management needs to evaluate:

- Where it wants to be;
- Where it is now, and
- What the gap is, so it can plan to close the gap.
  A useful way of determining where it wants to be is to:
- Ask customers about their satisfaction with the goods and services provided;

---

[4]Chistopher Musselwhite, "Time-Based Innovation: The New Competitive Advantage," *Training and Development Journal*, January 1990, p.55

- Study competitors, and
- Evaluate growth in relation to the market.

Goal Setting

To have key players pulling in the same direction, it is important that each identifies with the same goals. Good goals are characterized by being:
- Specific,
- Attainable,
- Measurable,
- Challenging, and
- Desirable.

Details of how this can be done are set out in Chapter 9.

Simultaneous Engineering

Typically, 80-90% of the time-to-market equation is absorbed in the design phase. Significant profits can flow from a reduction of this time, since products that get to the market first can establish a leadership position, and enjoy a longer life cycle before technology makes the product obsolete.

An analysis of business spending over the last few decades would show a disproportionate amount of spending in the manufacturing phase of a product. Little attention has been paid to improvement at the product conception and design phases, which together typically will influence the bulk of final costs. *(see Table 1-1)*.

Table 1-1.
Comparison of Key Steps for Cost and Time To Market of New Products.

	Percent of Total Costs*	
	Incurred	**Committed**
Conception	3-5%	40-60%
Design Engineers	5-8%	60-80%
Testing	8-10%	80-90%
Process Planning	10-15%	90-95%
Production	15-100%	95-100%

*Cumulative
Data: Computer-Aided Manufacturing International Inc.
Business Week, McGraw Publications, April 30,1990, p.110

Simultaneous engineering provides for the active participation of all interested parties — manufacturing, design, purchasing, finance, vendors and customers — in design. They work where necessary with a common database. The sharing of information and ideas helps to reduce territorialism, and increases energy directed

at common goals. Simultaneous engineering can reduce design time by:
- Involving all key decision makers in the design function;
- Providing for instant communications and feedback using a common database;
- Avoiding time spent on bickering about "territorial" issues;
- Dealing directly with key people instead of following formal organizational lines.

Reduced Bureaucracy

Decision making in most organizations takes much longer than needed due to:
- Multi-layered management which prevents decision makers from having access to knowledge at all need-to-know levels;
- Conflict among departments;
- Unwillingness of managers to trust lower level people to make decisions regarding things that they are knowledgeable about.

Today's successful organizations are redesigning their structures and re-examining values. They empower lower level people to make more decisions. Other supervision roles are changing radically, too. In fact, many new organizations are opting for self-managed work teams. Team members are encouraged to take responsibility for carrying out managerial duties such as scheduling, training, hiring and discipline, to name a few.

Methods of reducing bureaucracy and improving responsiveness are discussed in greater detail in Chapter 8.

World-Class Manufacturing Techniques

A total competitor requires a variety of techniques. Two of these, with large time-saving components, are the Just In Time concept and Statistical Process Control. Just-In-Time techniques reduce waste, space, storage, work in process, and cycle times. Statistical Process Control provides the measurements to track changes and ensures that time is spent making the product right the first time. It reduces or eliminates time wasted on inspection, rework, retrieval from customers and investigation. Note, however, that neither technique works without a heavy emphasis on extensive employee involvement. They are more fully described in Chapters 6 and 7.

The Use of Computers in Design and Manufacturing

The use of computers in design and manufacturing, while not new, remains an under-utilized tool. Through a linked database, people in the organization have instant access to design during and after the process. Design changes can be made quickly. Involving manufacturing ideas during the design phase leads to products that are more easily and rapidly manufactured.

QUESTIONNAIRE

Answer the following questions ranking your answers from 1 to 5. It will provide a good test of your company's Time To Market ability.

Evaluation and Planning
1. Do you regularly survey your customer's needs?

   1 = never   4 = quite regularly

   2 = seldom   5 = regularly

   3 = sometimes

2. Are your customer concerns dealt with quickly?

   1 = they are low priority

   2 = they get dealt with when we get around to it

   3 = fairly quickly

   4 = quickly

   5 = urgently

3. Has the Time To Market for your new products changed materially in the last three to five years?

   1 = not at all   4 = quicker

   2 = a little quicker   5 = much faster

   3 = somewhat

4. Is continuous improvement an integral part of your management process?

   1 = change is discouraged

   2 = we make small changes with difficulty

   3 = we change somewhat over time

   4 = change is relatively easy

   5 = we make changes all the time with little disruption

5. Is your organization proactive or reactive?

   1 = constant fire fighting   4 = some planning

   2 = frequent fire fighting   5 = most often, plan for future

   3 = reasonable

6. Does top management monitor Time To Market statistics?

   1 = never   4 = quite often

   2 = infrequently   5 = always

   3 = sometimes

7. Are your plans documented?

   1 = no   4 = most

   2 = few   5 = almost all

   3 = some

Goals
1. Do you measure and monitor design time?

   1 = never   4 = often

   2 = infrequently   5 = always

   3 = sometimes

2. Do you measure your manufacturing cycle time?
   1 = never   4 = often
   2 = infrequently   5 = always
   3 = sometimes
3. Do you have goals for reducing the TimeTo Market of your products?
   1 = no   3 = yes but unclear   5 = yes
4. Do your key people meet regularly to evaluate progress in meeting your goals?
   1 = never   4 = quite often
   2 = infrequently   5 = often
   3 = sometimes
5. Do you have specific, measurable TimeTo Market goals?
   1 = no   3 = somewhat   5 = yes
6. Are the goals known to all people who can impact their achievement?
   1 = no   4 = most
   2 = few   5 = all
   3 = some
7. Are the goals documented?
   1 = no   4 = most
   2 = few   5 = all
   3 = some
8. Are the goals set with the involvement of the people who are responsible for their achievement?
   1 = never   4 = often
   2 = infrequently   5 = always
   3 = sometimes
9. Are your goals prioritized to avoid getting into trivial performance issues?
   1 = never   4 = mostly
   2 = infrequently   5 = always
   3 = sometimes
10. Does management reward goal achievement?
   1 = never   4 = often
   2 = infrequently   5 = almost always
   3 = sometimes

In relation to the elements of Evaluation and Planning, and Goals:
- A score of 17 to 30 indicates that your organization is Poor.
- A score of 31 to 42 indicates that your organization is Weak.
- A score of 43 to 63 indicates that your organization is Reasonable.
- A score of 64 to 76 indicates that your organization is Good.
- A score in excess of 77 indicates that your organization is Excellent!

CONCLUSION

A strategy focused on the customer must integrate sales, design, manufacturing, finance, and distribution. Few ideas can pull these resources together faster and more efficiently than the idea of a Time to Market strategy.

As a strategic weapon, time is as important as a low-cost structure, unique products or cash in the bank. It can mean the difference between success and failure, holding one's own, or growth.

Getting things done quickly benefits everyone. It requires that people at all levels are involved in decisions, and that they work collaboratively. It demands fast decisions and elimination of bureaucracy. It works best when people have a clear time to market mission. And it produces a real sense of purpose — a feeling of pride.

Case Study

How General Electric's Circuit Breaker Business Became a Winner.

In the early 1980s, six domestic G. E. plants faced a stagnant market for circuit breakers, with ever increasing competition from Westinghouse, Siemens, and others.

Unless something different was done, the circuit breaker division would die an agonizing and slow death. Management committed itself to a lead position in the marketplace. Delivery times would be a key component of their strategy to acquire a bigger share of the market. They set a target to reduce delivery times for customer orders from 21 to three days!

G. E. 's first step was to assemble a team from manufacturing, design, and marketing.

After initial study, the team believed that nothing less than a radical restructuring of design and manufacturing would help them reach the goal. Mere automation wasn't the answer.

They adopted a five-pronged attack. Their strategy was:

1. **Rationalize the Manufacturing Facilities**
   From a start of six plants, one was chosen to specialize in circuit breakers. The plant in Salisbury, N C was improved with the most modern manufacturing equipment and systems available.

2. **Standardize on Parts**
   From a start of 28, 000 different parts, many parts were made interchangeable, reducing them to 1, 275. This didn't detract from customer ability to mix and match. They still had 40, 000 different sizes, shapes, and box configurations from which to choose.

3. **Cut Out Manual Design Engineering**
   A sophisticated computer system in the corporate offices in Connecticut permits salespeople to enter their needs into the system and have that data

flow directly to the factory in Salisbury.

4. **Reduce Bureaucracy**

Getting decisions made quickly in the plant was key. But this was difficult, given the traditional hierarchical management structure. The answer? Reduce the levels between shop floor and plant management from three to one.

5. **Develop a Team Approach on the Shop Floor**

A key strategy was to change the way people worked on the shop floor. Instead of working on single tasks, people were formed into teams, each team having total responsibility to manage its own quality and productivity. Supervisors were no longer needed. Each person on the shop floor was trained to work together and make decisions. This approach brought out the creative genius of people, allowing them the opportunity to contribute meaningfully to their work area. To help workers meet timing objectives, management provided feed-back on performance. Giant electronic signs tell workers the manfacturing time of each box; expectations for the day and units to date. In this, way workers can pace themselves without having supervision on their backs.

chapter 2

Toward A Revolution In Design

INTRODUCTION

In their famed book, *In Search of Excellence,* Peters and Waterman emphasized the importance of "getting close to the customer" or "focusing on the customer." This is an important insight, but with today's sophisticated products and complex organizations, such a philosophy is difficult to implement in practice without a structured methodology or system.

During the last five years, a number of leading North American companies have begun to adopt a new product-planning methodology called *Quality Function Deployment* (QFD). QFD is a customer-driven planning approach incorporating the "voice of the customer," all the way from product development to the production floor. By ensuring that new product designs are done right the first time and truly capture customer wants, QFD not only results in better products and wider customer acceptance, but also in products which can be brought to market faster, and at a lower cost.

QFD Began in Japan

QFD was originally developed by Mitsubishi's shipyard in Kobe, Japan in 1972. In 1977, it was adopted by Toyota and has guided the development of new products launched since that time. The major auto manufacturers such as Ford and General Motors were the first North American QFD users, beginning in the mid-1980s. Since then, the approach has spread to other sectors and companies such as aircraft (Boeing, McDonnell-Douglas), computers (Digital Equipment, Hewlett-Packard), and consumer products (Procter & Gamble).

The 1980s will probably be remembered as the decade when manufacturing changed from a traditional quality paradigm based on defect detection to one based on defect prevention. Within the traditional approach, inputs are transformed through a work process into outputs, with quality as a distinct, after-the-fact activity which serves to verify whether output conforms to requirements. This approach is intrinsically wasteful: if non-conformities are detected in the output stream, waste results in the form of either scrap (materials, labor, facilities, etc.) or rework (labor, facilities, etc.). In addition to being wasteful, detection activity is rarely fully effective: if non-conformities are present in the output stream, some will almost invariably slip through to the customer. During the 1980s, many companies, therefore, moved to implement manufacturing approaches such as Statistical Process Control (SPC). Through carefully controlling key inputs and work processes, SPC offered manufacturers the opportunity to prevent defects, not only improving quality but eliminating waste and reducing cost.

Quality Concepts are Rarely Applied to Design in North America
In many instances, the concept of defect prevention was limited to production activities. At the same time, the traditional model of defect detection often remains the quality approach employed in the rest of the company's activities and work processes. This is especially important because the earlier in the product development process and engineering process that prevention concepts can be applied, the greater the gains which can be realized in saving time, costs, and greater consumer satisfaction.

This helps to explain a discrepancy in the focus of quality activity which was observed by American automakers in the mid-1980s when they began to closely study their Japanese competitors (*Figure 2-1*).[1] The popular stereotype was that the Japanese attained superior quality levels because of a fanatical devotion to detail in manufacturing. In fact, American executives found that the way the Japanese competition assigned their resources was almost a mirror image of traditional American practice; the Japanese approach emphasized quality activity early in the product development process, as opposed to the heavy North American emphasis on defect prevention in manufacturing.

Moving the focus of quality activity upstream has dramatic effects, not only in improving customer satisfaction, but also in reducing waste and in improving Time To Market through what has been referred to as "quality leverage."[2] *Figure 2-2* illustrates the high level of waste which occurs when a design deficiency is detected through activities such as SPC in production.

If the same quality effort could have been applied at the engineering stage, the need to purge inventories, revise procedures, retrain employees, re-issue draw-

---

[1]Reproduced with permission of Treat Hull, *Canadian Supplier Institute*, Mississauga, Ontario (Refers to *Figures 2-1* to *2-6*).

[2]W. Eureka, N. Ryan, *The Customer-Driven Company*, Dearborn, MI, ASI Press, 1988.

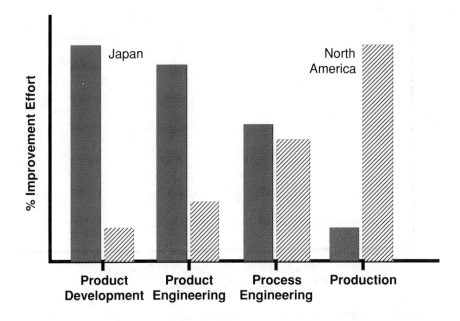

Figure 2-1. Allocation of Quality Effort.

ings, and re-tool suppliers could have been eliminated. Similarly, if the deficiency could have been avoided in product development, additional savings could be realized in the elimination of design revisions and unnecessary proto-type builds. Design improvement late in the development cycle results in waste of resources, not the least of which is time and, therefore: Time To Market.

Simultaneous Engineering Must Incorporate the Voice of the Customer

Concurrent or simultaneous engineering practices can contribute to moving the focus of quality activity upstream and eliminating waste by ensuring that concerns about manufacturability and process capability are addressed early in the design process. Without a strong customer focus, however, the risk remains that the development process will be driven primarily by the internal technical experts and their interpretation of what the customer wants, rather than by what the customer **really** wants. This risk is particularly high in consumer markets where customer wants are often subtle and ambiguous ("convenient to use," "fits right," "rides well") or in industrial markets, which have to simultaneously satisfy complex requirements emanating from multiple user groups.

QFD provides a vehicle to minimize this risk by focusing the entire develop-ment and manufacturing process on the "voice of the customer." It provides a vehicle to shift the emphasis of quality activity from manufacturing upstream to design, and in doing so, changes the nature and content of quality activity. Manufacturing quality control is concerned with physical products which can be touched and measured. It is concerned with "doing things right."

15

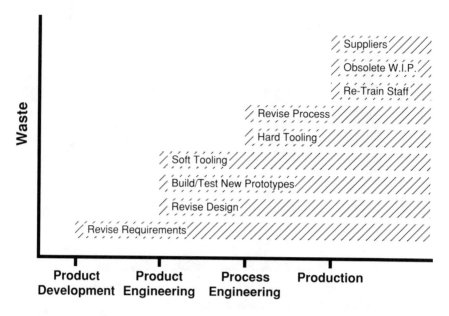

Figure 2-2. Improvement Timing Versus Waste.

Design quality control, on the other hand, is concerned with "doing the right things," assuring that products possess the appropriate features which will lead to customer satisfaction.

Relating Product Features to Customer Satisfaction

This raises an interesting question, namely, "how do different types of product features contribute to customer satisfaction?" The foremost work in this area has been done by the Japanese expert Dr. N. Kano, who developed a model (*Figure 2-3*) which relates customer satisfaction to the degree in which different types of product features are achieved.[3] These fall into three types of features: basic, performance, and excitement.

Basic features are expected. These include fundamental functions which must be present, along with safety and reliability considerations. These features act as dissatisfiers, not satisfiers. For example, airlines are expected to transport their passengers safely and cars are expected to start. If a product fails to satisfy a customer's basic expectations, dissatisfaction results. But if all the basic features are present, customer satisfaction is not only created, dissatisfaction is eliminated. (For those with an interest in motivational psychology, these basic features are analogous to hygiene factors in Hertberg's theory.)

Because they are expected as a condition of doing business, customers will not normally volunteer information about basic features in routine market research.

---

[3] Treat Hull, "New Quality Capabilities for Auto Parts Suppliers," *Financial Post Auto Executives Conference,* October 1989.

Successfully identifying basic product features requires that research and development people generate a clear understanding of the customer and the conditions of the actual product.[4]

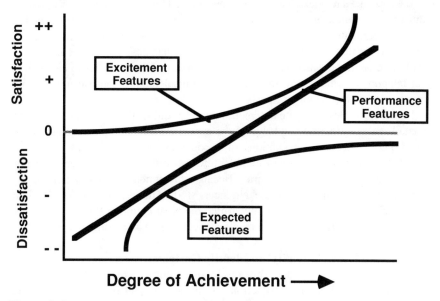

Figure 2-3. Kano's Model of Customer Satisfaction.

Performance features are those where the degree of satisfaction or dissatisfaction is directly related to product performance. These features can create satisfaction if the customer's expectations are exceeded, and dissatisfaction if they fall short. Examples of performance features include the degree to which an airline meets its schedule, or the acceleration of an automobile intended for the youth market.

Because customers will often volunteer their opinions on performance features, this is commonly the subject of market research. As will be seen, however, considerable probing is often required to move from initial customer responses to an understanding of what the customer truly wants. Faced with the customers wanting "good acceleration," the natural response of a designer might be to develop a vehicle with a low 0-60 mph time. The customer, however, might rarely accelerate directly from a standstill to 60 mph. If they drove primarily in city traffic, "good acceleration" might mean minimizing the 0-20 mph time for "jackrabbit" starts from stop lights.

Excitement features are innovations where the customer is not even aware that they can be achieved within the existing technology. Even seemingly minor

---

[4] Treat Hull, "New Quality Capabilities for Auto Parts Suppliers," *Financial Post Auto Executives Conference,* October 1989.

items which customers perceive as superior value can represent a major competitive opportunity. (Example: an especially high level of service or courtesy during an air flight.)

Because they are unexpected innovations, market research will normally provide limited information on excitement features. At the same time, efforts aimed at technical innovation which are not based on an intimate knowledge of customer product usage may result in dissatisfaction rather than customer excitement. The field of consumer electronics is littered with products from VCRs to calculators and telephones which were loaded with technical features but difficult, if not impossible, for the customer to use.

Successfully developing excitement features requires that technical staff have a detailed and intimate knowledge of the customer, the fundamental function of the product, and actual conditions of product usage. In the mid-1970s, for example, one Japanese camera manufacturer set out to make fundamental improvements in the 35-mm camera. Because the fundamental function of the camera was to take a good picture, engineers studied thousands of rolls of film at commercial development labs to determine the most common flaw in consumer snapshots. The innovation which resulted was the built-in automatic flash.

Using The "House of Quality" to Identify Customer Needs

QFD provides a method to shift the focus of quality concern from avoiding dissatisfaction to creating satisfaction. It shifts the field of quality from one which is limited within operations to one which includes strategic marketing and positioning issues. The central tool of the QFD process is a planning matrix usually referred to as the "House of Quality" because of the roof-like structure on top.

A completed "House of Quality" represents the culmination of months of work and contains a potentially intimidating amount of information *(Figure 2-4)*. In fact, when broken down into its separate rooms, the QFD chart is not difficult to understand and use.

QFD starts with a listing of objectives of what has to be accomplished. In the context of developing a new product, this is a list of the customer requirements, and is often called the "Voice of the Customer." These customers' wants are usually very general, vague, and difficult to implement without further detailed definition. One such item in an auto might be "good ride," which means different things to different people, or "easy to re-seal," for a consumer package. The example given is a small subset of a QFD study of the characteristics of a good car door. Where a typical application would include 30 or more customer wants, only four are shown here, all relating to the ease of use of the door locks: "inside lock knob easy to use," "key inserts easily," "key operates easily," and "lock does not freeze in cold weather."

Accurate information on these customer requirements is critical. Surveys, clinics, focus groups, and other conventional market research techniques may be employed. In addition, there is no substitute for direct contact between engineers and customers to understand what lies behind potentially vague customer wants

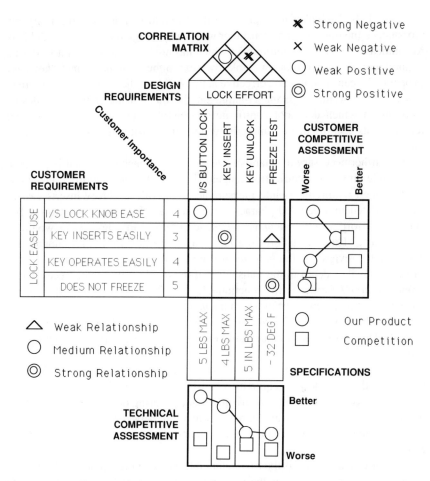

Figure 2-4. "House of Quality:" A Planning Matrix.
Reproduced with permission of Treat Hull, *Canadian Supplier Institute*, Mississauga, Ontario

such as "good ride," "easy to use," etc.

The "House of Quality" starts with the key customer requirements (expressed in their own words) as the *what's* on the left-hand side. These customer requirements, however, are often ambiguous and must be translated into measurable product design requirements, or *how's*. "Key inserts easily" might be translated into measurable characteristics such as "key insertion effort" and "meets freeze test requirement."

The relationship between *what's* and *how's* is potentially complex since one *what* may require several *how's* to implement it, and one *how* may have a bearing on several *what's*. Therefore, the relationship matrix shows the connection between *what's* and *how's* using different symbols to designate weak, medium, and strong relationships.

The method permits very complex relationships to be easily pictured and interpreted. It also makes it simple to verify the quality of the design activity and cross-check the translation of consumer wants into design requirements. A blank row indicates a customer requirement which has not been translated into a design requirement. In the example, a blank row next to the customer want: "key easy to operate" means that unless corrective action is taken, the design will not satisfy this customer want. A blank column, on the other hand, indicates a design requirement which does not contribute to satisfying any of the key customer requirements identified, i.e., an activity potentially without value for the customer.

It is further necessary to establish a *how much* for each *how;* that is to say, a measurable target or specification range. These are the engineering translations of the design requirements into measurable target values. "Key inserts easily" was translated into detailed characteristics such as "key insertion effort." The "insertion effort" would be a *how,* and its measurement in pounds force would be a *how much.* This translation from *how's* to *how much's* provides another opportunity for review. If the *how much's* are not measurable, then there is not a sufficient level of detail in the translation of the *how's.* It is often necessary to refine the *how's* further until an actionable level of detail is obtained. This is done by creating a new chart in which the *how's* of the previous chart become the *what's* of the new chart. The *how much* values are carried along to the next chart as well. This process is continued until each objective is refined to an actionable level.

In the product development process, this means taking the customer requirements and defining design requirements. These are carried to the next chart as necessary to establish part characteristics, manufacturing operations, and production requirements. In this way, there is a direct link between the wants expressed by the consumer and quality plans for the control of critical production parameters.

The correlation matrix is the triangular table added at the top of the "House" in *Figure 2-4,* which establishes the relationship between each of the *how's.* Different symbols identify the direction and strength of the relationship. Positive correlations are those where the implementation of one *how* assists the implementation of another. Resource efficiencies can sometimes be gained in this way by avoiding duplication of efforts. Likewise, a positive relationship between two *how's* shows that an action which adversely affects one *how* will have a degrading effect on the other.

Negative correlations are those in which the achievement of one *how* adversely affects the achievement of another. Negative correlations (conflicts) are very important because they indicate situations where the design intent and technology are in conflict. Trade-offs which are not identified and resolved will often lead to unfulfilled customer requirements, even though everyone individually has done their best. Where key design requirements have a negative correlation (conflict) and trade-offs are not viable, then technical innovation will be required to eliminate the conflict. *Figure 2-4,* for example, shows a negative correlation between "key insertion effort equals four pounds force maximum" and "passes freeze test at minus 32 degrees Fahrenheit."

Careful review of negative correlations is especially important when the responsibility for implementing the conflicting *how's* lies in different parts of an organization, for example, in the design of complex systems such as aircraft. In this case, individual functions may work to implement their responsibility without realizing that it is compromising another aspect of the product. Similarly, the correlation matrix can help to avoid the situation where a "fix" is adopted to cure a recognized problem without realizing that this action itself will create new problems.

Customer importance ratings have been included in the example next to the original customer requirements. These are based on surveys to establish the relative importance of the original customer wants, and typically range from not very important (1) to very important (5). In combination with the competitive assessment, these importance ratings can evaluate the competitive strengths and weaknesses of a product as compared to the competition.

The competitive assessment includes a pair of graphs which depict item for item how leading competitors' products compare with our product. The assessment of the *what's,* or customer requirements, is often called a customer competitive assessment, and uses customer and market research feedback to compare our product against the competition for each key customer requirement. The resulting graph shown at the right hand side of the "House" is sometimes called a "perceptual map," which can be used to diagnose the market impact of action on different customer requirements.

In the example, our product is rated poorly for "key easy to operate," while the competition rates very well. This suggests that even significant improvement would offer little opportunity for differentiation, since it will only bring us up to the level of the competition. A strategy of imitation rather than innovation is therefore suggested. However, for the customer want "lock does not freeze," no one is doing well, according to the customers. At the same time, the importance rating (5) indicates that this is an important customer want. Technical innovation should be concentrated here to differentiate our product from the competition and create an excitement feature. This illustrates how QFD can be used to move the scope of quality thinking from avoidance of dissatisfaction in manufacturing to the creation of satisfaction in design.

The competitive assessment of the *how's* is often called a *technical competitive assessment.* Sometimes called "tear down analysis," it compares our product and our best competitors' on the basis of conformance to the targets and specifications (*how much's*) previously established for each of the design requirements. It provides another review of engineering judgement, since if the design requirements and specifications have been accurately translated from the customer requirements, the customer assessment and the technical assessment should be consistent.

Customers rated our product poorly, compared to the competition, for the requirement "inside lock knob easy to use," yet at the same time, our product seemed appreciably better than the competition when measured against the design requirement identified to implement that customer want ("inside lock button effort equals five pounds force maximum"). Such discrepancies between customer and technical competitive assessments may indicate a poor translation from *what's* to *how's*, inappropriate target values for the *how much's*, or inappropriate test methods. Comparison of the competitive assessments thus provides a mechanism to "calibrate" internal test standards and methods to the marketplace. To summarize the use of the "House of Quality" planning process:

- The *how's* are related to each other and the *correlations* are established.
- This suggests trade-offs which will be reflected in the values of the *how much's*.
- Trade-off decisions are made using judgement and analysis, assisted by the *competitive assessment* and *importance ratings*.

Review and cross-checking occurs throughout the process, to ensure that customer wants are adequately translated into the final product.

QFD is Easily Applied

QFD is a low-technology, highly detailed approach with documented results to show that it is worth the effort to invest in quality planning right at the start of the project.

The QFD process leads the participants through a detailed thought process, pictorially documenting their approach. The results of graphic and integrated thinking will lead to the preservation of technical knowledge, minimizing the knowledge loss from retirements and personnel transfers. It also helps transfer knowledge to new employees, starting them higher on the learning curve. It can help the company avoid making the same mistakes over and over as new employees are hired. Once a QFD study has been completed on a product, its insights can often be generalized to other products or future versions of similar products.

Benefits of QFD

Obviously, one of the most significant benefits of QFD lies in its impact on customer satisfaction. Prior to using QFD, one major auto manufacturer experienced a customary surge in product problems and customer complaints with each new product launch, as unanticipated problems were discovered in production or in the field.[5] After implementing QFD, the general level of problems was reduced, while the surge of unanticipated problems on start up disappeared (*Figure 2-5*). QFD helped to eliminate it by identifying problems before they happened, thus allowing true preventive action to be taken, instead of corrective action.

Another benefit offered by QFD is significant reduction in new product start-up costs and lead times. Part of this reduction is the result of when product design changes occur (*Figure 2-6*). A study of "engineering change orders" associated

---

[5] L.P. Sullivan, "Quality Function Deployment," *Quality Progress*, June 1986.

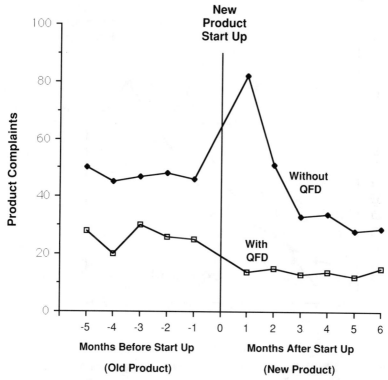

Figure 2-5. Start Up Problems Compared With Product Complaints.

with the development of similar new products was recently conducted on two companies, one which used QFD and the other did not.[6]

For the company which did not use QFD, the number of changes increased as time progressed and problems were brought to the surface through testing and prototype trials. Following a design freeze just before production, further changes were experienced after start up as new problems came to the surface in production. For the company with QFD, there was a reduction of more than 60% in the number of engineering changes. Even more significant is the timing of these changes: over 90% were made more than a year before production start up. Such changes are less expensive, because they are made on paper, preventing problems instead of reacting to them.

In summary, QFD "focuses and coordinates skills within an organization, first to design, then to manufacture and market goods that customers want to purchase and will continue to purchase." [7]

---

[6]L.P.Sullivan,"Quality Function Deployment,"*Quality Progress*, June 1986.

[7]J.R.Hauser and D.Clausing,"The House of Quality,"*Harvard Business Review*,May-June 1988.

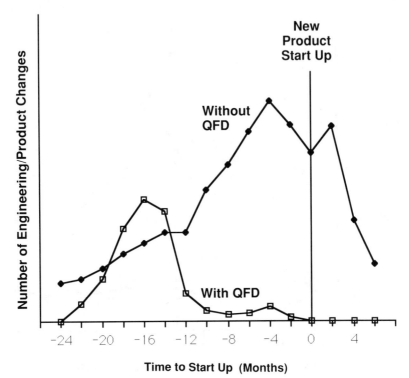

Figure 2-6. The Relationship of Engineering Changes and New Product Start Up.

USING A LINEAR APPROACH TO DESIGN

Getting a product to market quickly gives any company a competitive advantage. The organization is seen as responsive, committed, and pioneering by customers and competitors alike. And there is a bonus: the faster the product gets to the market, the longer the company can "stretch" the stream of income before technological obsolescence catches up.

So what causes the long delays? Consider the sequence from conception of an idea to delivery. It appears to be a linear process (see *Figure 2-7*).

This linear process is reinforced by any organization structure based on functions.

Each of these functions has some common objectives and others that differ. Their common objective is to make the organization as profitable as possible through the provision of the best product, in the right place at the right price. In reality it does not work that way. Marketing people want a product that appeals aesthetically. Design people, on the other hand, will want to do away with the "bells and whistles" to ensure that the design has fewer parts that can break or malfunction. Quality people want the best parts, but financial people want the cheapest. And at the end of the line, manufacturing people want a process that is simple to use.

Concept → Design → Manufacturing → Distribution → Sale

Figure 2-7. Typical Linear Approach to Bringing New Products to Market.

The segmented structure produces the equivalence of a relay race. It starts off with research or marketing people who pass on the idea to the design department. At this stage, the baton is dropped on the relative importance of their viewpoint. Design people make a physical model of the product, or design a prototype on a CAD system, and then pass the baton to manufacturing. At this stage, the baton is likely to be dropped again. The challenge of producing the item is often overwhelming and impractical so that the plans are sent back to design for modification. And a new game is started: Ping Pong. Ideas and designs pass back and forth between the two groups until a compromise is reached. The players then get back on track and pass the baton to purchasing. Buying the necessary materials, parts and/or equipment without forewarning and involvement will typically lead to further delays of weeks, months, or even years. And any rethinking by manufacturing or design people will cause further delays. Buying from the vendor who will supply the quickest can lead to problems, too. Costs will invariably be higher and quality could also suffer.

When manufacturing eventually starts, operators are bound to find easier ways of producing the product, requiring changes in design and documentation.

Few organizations can boast a process that does not encourage rivalry between areas. In fact, in most organizations, the differences between areas and departments often overshadow their common objectives. People spend more time fighting one another than they do battling the competition. This fruitless energy leads to long-time delays. When people don't trust each other, time is wasted on:

- Focusing communication on differences rather than common objectives.
- Writing formal communications instead of taking part in one-on-one problem solving.
- Ignoring one another's needs because of differing priorities.
- Defending a narrow viewpoint instead of looking at problems from a global perspective.

The linear approach to engineering is horrifyingly expensive. Data from Dataquest Inc., points to a 10-fold increase in costs as design changes are made (see *Table 2-1*).

The North American automotive industry takes much longer to design products than its major competitors (see *Table 2-2*).

An excellent illustration of time-delayed bureaucracy is given by Daniel Whitney from Charles Stark Draper Laboratory in Cambridge, MA. He cites the case of the problems of an engineering manager responsible for the design of a single automobile part—a process involving 350 steps. Each job needed to be signed off—350 different times. So, in a five-year design, signatures are required every 3.5 days for minor parts.

25

Table 2-1.
Typical Costs of Design Changes of a Major Electronics Product

When design changes are made	Costs
DURING DESIGN	$1,000
DURING DESIGN TESTING	$10,000
DURING PROCESS PLANNING	$100,000
DURING TEST PRODUCTION	$1,000,000
DURING FINAL PRODUCTION	$10,000,000

Data: Dataquest Inc.
As reported in *Business Week, " A Smarter Way to Manufacture,"* McGraw-Hill, Inc., April 30, 1990 p. 110.

Table 2-2.
Comparison of Time To Market Capabilities of Selected Auto Manufacturers [8]

Company	Time To Market (years)
General Motors	6
Ford	5
Toyota	4
Honda	3

While the design process of local auto manufacturers has moved away from linear design, the effectiveness of the alternative approach—simultaneous design—has yet to have its full impact on design time.

SIMULTANEOUS ENGINEERING

By far, the most effective means of speeding up the design is to involve all key players and have them work together. This is a parallel approach as opposed to the linear approach (see *Figure 2-8*).

Design itself does not ensure consumer acceptance. Quality, cost, and repeatability are important, too. These features can be brought about only by a coordinated approach, one that ensures that product, tools, fixtures, and material flow are all designed as a coordinated system to promote harmony between design and manufacturing.

Simultaneous engineering is a process that promotes manufacturability. Using computer technologies, common databases and networking design, and manufac-

[8] George Peterson, "The Competitive Background," by *Auto Pacific Group*, Newport Beach, CA.

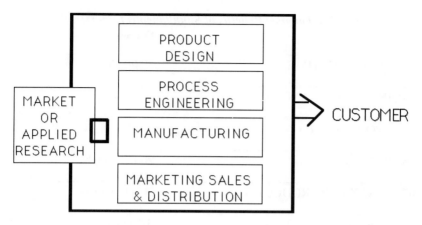

Figure 2-8. Simultaneous Engineering Using Parallel Approach.

turing, people can work together so that problems can be overcome as the design unfolds. It ensures that at the end of the design process, the part is ready for production and its manufacturability does not have to be "sold" to the people on the shop floor.

The payback on simultaneous engineering can be staggering (see *Table 2-3*).

Ford Motor Company has made significant strides to improve networking. It has standardized two Computer-Aided Design (CAD) and Computer-Aided Manufacturing (CAM) programs for product design: Product Design Graphics System (PDGS), Ford's own development product, and Computervision's CADDS software. Ford's CAD/CAM manager of Car Product Development, Wayne Harmann, reported that the CAD system has brought about significant cost reduction in tooling and reduced production time by half.

Networking of Ford's CAD system is facilitated by common software that allows 1700 workstations to design car and truck bodies, chassis, electrical wiring harnesses and schematics, interiors, and instrument panels. "These stations also manufacture and assemble applications to design and build sheet metal stamping, dies, and assembly fixtures in numerical control milling, blank nesting of sheet metal parts, layout of plants, process planning, and quality control," says Harmann.[9]

CAD is a growing phenomenon, but has a long way to go before it replaces the paper and pencil method preferred by most designers. CAD systems linked to manufacturing at the shop floor are even more rare. Difficulties in making a system that meets the needs of all players continue. For example, if one were designing an object that needed a hole, the system would tell the designer what size hole is required based on the size of the drill bits available in the shop. This kind of system is beyond the capability of current microcomputer systems. The ability of a system to recognize holes and other shapes, such as grooves, bevels, and notches is known as "feature recognition." Most feature-based systems are

---

[9] CAD/CAM and Robotics. A. Kerwell Publications, April 1989, p. 44.

Table 2-3 The Tangible Benefits of Simultaneous Engineering.

	Percent
DEVELOPMENT TIME	30-70 less
ENGINEERING CHANGES	65-90 fewer
TIME TO MARKET	20-90 less
OVERALL QUALITY	200-600 higher
WHITE-COLLAR PRODUCTIVITY	20-110 higher
DOLLAR SALES	5-50 higher
RETURN ON ASSETS	20-120 higher

Data: National Institute of Standards & Technology, Thomas Group Inc., Institute for Defense Analyses. As reported in *Business Week*, "A Smarter Way to Manufacture," McGraw-Hill, Inc., April 30, 1990 p. 110.

still in the R&D stage, or first generation working prototypes. But feature technology is cited as the primary means of bringing manufacturing and design people together.

Typical improvements from simultaneous engineering include:
• Using snap-on parts as opposed to screw-ons,
• reducing number of parts,
• achieving maximum symmetry,
• preventing tangling,
• avoiding hard to handle, delicate, or sticky parts,
• avoiding jamming during insertion,
• avoiding separate fasteners when not absolutely necessary, and
• assembling from above.

Dramatic improvements in assembly time result from these considerations.

SETTING UP MULTI-FUNCTIONAL TEAMS

Probably the biggest impediment to getting the product to the market quickly is the inordinate amount of time spent on:
• Getting **a meeting of the minds** between design and manufacturing;
• defending a design,
• rationalizing why the design is impractical, and cannot be manufactured; and
• explaining why one group or the other cannot support an idea because of the existence of other priorities.

Many of these issues can be addressed by involving key people who have an interest in the product. In most organizations, they are responsible for:

- design engineering,
- test engineering,
- manufacturing engineering,
- manufacturing management,
- shop operators,
- vendors,
- purchasing,
- cost management,
- marketing, and
- field sales.

A joint effort through frequent meetings and simultaneous data sharing will produce two key benefits:

1. Everyone gets the same information at the same time.
2. Everyone works towards a common goal.

While this idea may appear new in North America, it has been happening for so long in Japan that most people there cannot remember a different way to design a product.

This consensus approach to design might appear to be cumbersome, especially when teams might include anything from four to 20 people; but the overall time saved can be dramatic (see *Figure 2-9*).

Not only is there a savings in time, but costly mistakes made by not using the best ideas are avoided.

Hewlett-Packard, long a leader in management practice, used a multi-functional team to develop its high-performing super mini-computers at its Cupertino, CA facility. The benefits were significant, and there were rarely failures at the testing phase of the product. To HP engineers, the results were astounding. They had been accustomed to failure rates of 20-30%.

Another example of the benefits derived from simultaneous engineering was experienced by NCR Engineering and Manufacturing of Cambridge, OH [10] In the production of their 2060 terminal, aimed for the hospitality industry, the multidisciplinary team focused on manufacturability before production. The motto, "Do it Right the First Time," paid off. Parts were reduced from 117 to 16. Vendors were reduced by 80%. Morale of the engineering team soared as communications among all players improved. The bottom line was impacted by:

- **Faster production**. Fewer functions were required. Also, producing three-dimensional drawings on a computer helped vendors to produce parts much quicker than before.
- **Lower cost.** All parts were designed to be "snap-on." Tooling was reduced to a minimum.
- **Improved functionability.** Looking at each part from the customers' viewpoint led to improvements in design.

---

[10] The Quick Change Advantage, Videotape by North Carolina State University, 1988. Distributed by the Society of Manufacturing Engineers, Dearborn, MI.

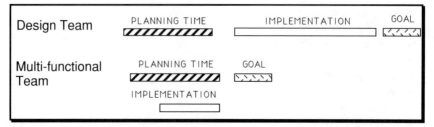

Figure 2-9. Impact of Single Team Versus Multi-functional Team On Time To Market.

CASE STUDY

MOTOROLA—A FLEET-FOOTED GIANT [11]

Few people realize that Motorola's roots can be traced back to 1928, when present Chairman Robert W. Gavin's father began selling car radios. And most people see the organization as hugely successful today— which it is— but the same people forget the problems of the recent past.

In the early and mid-1980s Motorola was overstaffed and was slowly taken apart by cheaper and better Japanese imported products. Its traditional lock on the pager and cellular phones disappeared. Its Semiconductor Products Sector, based in Phoenix, was forced out of the largest sector of the chip business, dynamic random access memories (DRAMs). In no time, Motorola slipped from the number-two player, to shadow NEC, Toshiba, Hitachi, and the American company, Texas Instruments.

Things have now changed. The company has undertaken a major overhaul of itself. Its very culture has changed. Motorola has pared itself down to fighting weight—2500 people have disappeared off the payroll. The bottom line benefits of a reduced work force could add as much as $100 million to the bottom line in the future. But one should not get the impression that Motorola does not believe in its people. On the contrary. Significant expenditures ($60 million in 1989) were made to upgrade the talents of Motorola's 100,000-plus people. [12]

More importantly, the company has committed itself to the customer. Getting innovative products to the market quickly has been a core strategy. And key to the time-based focus has been quality. Defects of around 3000 per million have been reduced to less than 200. But the goal is far more ambitious. Plans to get

---

[11] *The Quick Change Advantage*, Videotape by North Carolina State University, 1988. Distributed by the Society of Manufacturing Engineers, Dearborn, MI.
[12] *Business Week,* McGraw-Hill, Inc., November 13, 1989, "The Rival Japan Respects," p. 109.

this number down to near perfection (about three to four defects per million) are projected for 1991. Design engineering has claimed its share of the bouquets, too. Through teamwork with other areas of the new company, cellular phones are expected off the production lines six months after the design phase begins. It used to take three years.

How Motorola Builds A Better Paging Product, Faster

Motorola's Paging Products Division, based at Boynton Beach, FL introduced a new pager, code named Bandit, in 18 months. Without adoption of some simple Time To Market strategies, it would otherwise have taken five years to do the same thing, say company executives. This is what they did to make the change:

Number 1. Abolished the "Not Invented Here" Syndrome.

Motorola borrowed or bought technology wherever they could find it—inside or outside of the company. The idea was simple: use existing technology, improve it, refine it, adapt it. Executives felt they did not have the time to re-invent the pager. Accordingly, a decision was based on time, cost, risk, and performance. Motorola would design and build pagers based on existing surface-mount technology configured with some 15 components fewer than a standard paging unit. The largest component was an AA battery cell.

The decision to go with such a technology gave Motorola the potential of a limitless number of variations in manufacturing—in short, the ability to produce lot sizes of one at a planned profit. Contributing to this breakthrough, too, was the company's combining of computers, robots, process engineering, top quality raw materials, and components.

Everything manufactured would be based on customer input: colors, labels, vibration signals, frequency, and others, with the options translated by computer to instruct assembly operators or robots. As a way to limit errors and much of the paperwork associated with "normal" manufacturing, the company also strategically placed workstation touchscreen terminals to give operators assembly diagrams and troubleshooting instructions. Screen menus give operators immediate fingertip access to capacity data, product status, operation or maintenance procedures on any or all of the machines.

Number 2. Used A Multi-functional Team

Every group that could contribute to the product's success was allowed to do so. These included:
- product development engineers,
- process development engineers,
- manufacturing engineers,
- quality specialists,
- computer specialists,
- materials sourcing specialists,
- financial experts, and
- vendors.

Motorola's procurement team decided early they would work closely with suppliers and did so by sharing proprietary information with vendors as a means of gaining concessions and commitments. The move worked. The company reports that the 18-month target launch of Bandit otherwise would be stretched to five years.

Number 3. Reduced Vendor Numbers

Initially the project started with 300 suppliers. This number was reduced to 22 after a certification process incorporating high standards was instituted. Motorola realized early that this step was the only way to reach a Six-Sigma (or 3.4 defects per million parts) quality standard. So successful is the finely tuned procurement procedure now that vendors participate as partners with Motorola. One computer provider, for instance, so intent on meeting specifications, scored a major victory by pointing out in plain language that Motorola executives were making arbitrary decisions not in the stated and mutually agreed plan.

The company also created interdisciplinary teams, careful to marry engineering, manufacturing, operations, and design people at each stage of the process. As well, the teams were encouraged to set seemingly impossible time and production goals. In turn, the company instituted a risk-taking and quality-gain reward system that now amounts to 3% of Motorola's total payroll.

Summary

Motorola's success with its Bandit project is attributed by management to its adherence to the axiom that plants and equipment don't design and build superior products—people do. So, too, does the strictly adhered to philosophy that anyone associated with a project should be given a chance to talk about it, regardless of position in the company. And that includes vendors.

The company has the obligation to make the best product it can, commensurate with what customers need now and will need in the future. The obligation extends to manufacturing at a profit, with a work force that is well rewarded and that shares in the process.

Motorola is now number one in the United States, and number four in the world in its market. It is a reflection of the firm's 19% of revenue reinvestment in research, development, training, and capital improvement.

CASE STUDY

FORD MOTOR COMPANY

A major gamble of $3 billion and five years of work paid off big when the Taurus came onto the market. In a short period of time, Ford achieved record profits. Its Taurus and Sable accounted for two-thirds of the increase in Ford's U.S. market share. The cars had a combined average share of the mid-sized auto market of 28%—almost twice that held by the cars that they replaced, which were the Mercury Marquis and the LTD. Many feel that this was Ford's greatest success since the Mustang first appeared in 1964.

The Taurus did more than just add to Ford's bottom line. It rekindled a sense of pride among its people.

Key to Taurus Success—Teamwork

Ford's success went beyond design. It changed the very heart of the company's operating culture. Prior to Taurus, the company's vehicles were designed in a linear fashion with little or no cooperative involvement of each party with those at the next step of the process.

Ford made effective use of its *shop floor people*. It empowered them to take responsibility for quality themselves (as compared to the responsibility imposed by an outside inspector) and authorized them to shut down the line if they felt that quality was unacceptable. Another aspect of a very successful employee involvement effort was a suggestion program. More than 1400 recommendations were submitted, of which more than half were actually adopted and implemented by the Taurus/Sable team.

Other inside sources that contributed were Ford's *marketers and dealers*. Dealers gave advice on how a car could be made more user-friendly and adaptable to the customer. They based their comments on real-life eyeball-to-eyeball consumer sales situations.

Ford also got legal input.

Representatives from Allstate, State Farm, and other automotive insurance companies were consulted to find out how to design a car that minimized expenses following an accident.

Team Taurus developed an improved relationships with its *suppliers*. Instead of following the traditional method of finding the lowest bidder, Ford identified the highest quality supplier and committed themselves, where possible, to that one supplier. Ford even took a car to each supplier so that they could see the parts, where they fit, and how they were integral to the vehicle's performance. Feedback was also solicited from the employees of the selected suppliers. This dedicated linkage with supplier companies became vital as time-based strategies developed into the organizational strategy. Programs such as JIT depend on a committed and reliable supplier. Suppliers were shown exactly how their contributions dovetailed. Each was made a partner of the process.

Ford also solicited customers' ideas. They used customer comments in the initial stage of the design process to find the ideal and most desired characteristics of a car. Ford had learned not to try to impose their design and performance ideas on the car-buying public.

Team Taurus completed its project under the proposed budget. When the Taurus project ended, the team process was hailed a grand success by Ford's top management, and this is now the model for future Ford new product development.

With Taurus, representatives of all interested parties (see *Table 2-4*) and their customers worked together. Since these disjointed groups were involved from the start, problems were resolved early and major crises were avoided.

Table 2-4. Ford Company Functions and Customers.

Department	Customer
Sales	Car Buyer
Legal	D.O.T.
Purchasing	Suppliers
Service	Insurance Companies
Manufacturing	Assembly Plant
Component Engineering	Corporate Management

The Customer Comes First

Team Taurus was determined to produce an exceptional product. They knew that they would have to meet customers' needs like never before. The team did an enormous amount of market research. First, they "reverse engineered" 50 vehicles of major competitors to see if they could improve the best features or simply copy them. Typical of their research findings was that:
- the Audi 5000 had the best accelerator pedal feel;
- the Toyota Supra had the best fuel gauge accuracy; and
- the BMW 528E had the best tire and jack storage.

They identified major customer groups and key needs of each group. For example, the insurance companies wanted repair to be done as quickly and cheaply as possible; corporate management wanted the vehicle to be as saleable as possible; and the plant wanted assembly as simple as possible. This prompted the team to aim to be the best in their class for key items. This number, based on customer focus, group input, and other expert opinions, was narrowed down to 12 categories (see *Table 2-5*).

Within these categories, the team narrowed thousands of items to a short list of 400.

Team Organization

Four hundred project teams were set up, consisting of members from different parts of the organization, suppliers, and customers. Each team developed its own mission as a statement of intention. They also had a budget and schedule of milestones and completion dates. Being the best in their class required tangible evidence that this was achieved. So each group had to find ways of measuring their performance. For example, people working on the heating system measured their time to heat to a specified temperature.

Typical of the many achievements of Team Taurus were these:

- The ease of raising the hood angle which promoted accessibility—measured in degrees.
- Easy access to the oil filter—measured on FDSD scale.
- Higher trunk storage height—measured in inches.

- A superior window turning mechanism—measured in number of turns.
- A shorter braking distance at 70 mph—measured in feet.
- A superior steering wheel "feel"—measured as a comparison with other types of vehicles.
- Low wind noise—measured in decibels at 70 mph.

Table 2-5. 12 Categories of Key Result Areas.

- Ride,
- performance,
- steering,
- driveability,
- handling,
- brakes,
- power transmission,
- operational comfort,
- power transmission smoothness,
- seat performance,
- body chassis, and
- climate control.

And the teams provided some "tremendous trifles" too. A rope netting in the trunk allows buyers to pack groceries and then take them out after a trip without falling all over. Another was an oversized accelerator pedal to increase driver comfort. And better windshield wipers allow for a greater than normal surface area percentage to be cleaned.

The team was so proud of its efforts that they sent a Taurus and a Sable in two vans around the country for viewing at Ford facilities and supplier plants. In this way, they were able to show to both managers and workers how they contributed to the final product. The "caravans" reached 110 Ford and supplier plants in U.S. and Canadian cities, exposing the vehicles to more than half a million company and supplier employees.

Team Taurus really was a team. For the four years before launch of the new cars, teams of managers, designers, and engineers made 14 visits to the selected manufacturing plant at Atlanta. There, the teams actually asked line employees for ideas—a move unheard of and seldom practiced by any other North American auto maker.

During this period, more than 1400 recommendations were made by employees. Over half of these were adopted in the design of Taurus/Sable, or incorporated in the planning of a $250 million expansion and modernization of manufacturing facilities.

Realization that employees were a major untapped resource led to several major time, cost, and quality improvements:

- A body shop supervisor wondered why three separate welding guns were needed to attach the fire wall. Engineers came up with a single gun.
- A line employee said that if the six side and door opening panels could

be reduced in number, it would save assembly time and permit a better fit and finish. Engineers redesigned it and came up with a two-panel side assembly.

- Employees pointed out that the headlight assemblies didn't match the smooth lines of the design. The design was changed.
- Virtually every workstation, conveyor line, or other operation in the redesigned two to three million square foot Atlanta plant would work there. The team concept now embraced by Ford is not as arcane as it might sound to some senior management ears. Ford determined right at the beginning that everyone involved with Taurus/Sable would be listened to before a single decision could be made by anyone. Further, the new car would have quality second to none, that product integrity would never be compromised, and that customers would define quality for Taurus/Sable. The initial return on investment target for Taurus/Sable was 8%. Within a little more than two years, it was 11%.

CASE STUDY

SIMULTANEOUS ENGINEERING MAKES A BIG DIFFERENCE FOR CADILLAC MOTOR CAR DIVISION OF GENERAL MOTORS CORPORATION AT DETROIT

Cadillac's use of simultaneous engineering started in the mid 1980s follow ing a reorganization in the automotive division.

The process started with a directive from senior management to improve the design process through a team approach. The next stage was training. Team members learned how to work together, plan projects, run meetings, and communicate without being over-territorial.

The team restyled the 1980 Cadillac El Dorado in 55 weeks—a record for the group.

Other teams, using a similar process, improved the quality, reliability, and durability of the product.

Cadillac learned that the bottom line benefitted from the approach. Typical among these were:
- Reduced Time To Market,
- improved quality, and
- lower costs.

But the "psychic income" of team members was great, too. Positive feed-back led to feelings of euphoria. Self-esteem soared. They felt empowered to take risks and adapt a more innovative approach.

Cadillac's organizational structure is designed as follows *(Figure 2-10)* :

The role of top management in the simultaneous engineering process was to:
- sanction the process,
- set policies, and

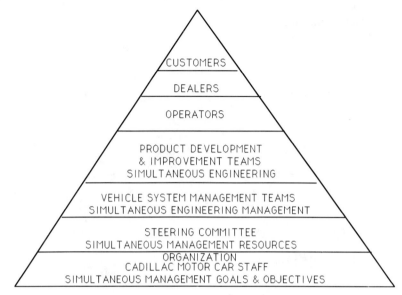

Figure 2-10. Cadillac's Organization Structure.

- provide the environment for the process to be successful.

The steering committee was comprised of people reporting directly to the executive staff. They:

- define policy and direction,
- provide the necessary resources,
- encourage growth of the process throughout the organization; and
- allocate resources.

The vehicle teams were comprised of disciplines from the various parts of the organization *(Figure 2-11)*.

The vehicle team's role was to:

- define the strategy, including defining the product target market and demographics,
- establish the goals required to meet the strategy,
- manage the content,
- manage the timing,
- ensure profitability, and
- ensure continuous improvement of vehicles, quality, reliability, dependability, and performance.

Each was produced by six Vehicle System Management Teams *(Figure 2-12)*.

The Product Development and Improvement Teams (PDITS) were comprised of people from:

- vehicle engineering,
- manufacturing,
- reliability and testing,

- suppliers,
- materials management, and
- design staff.

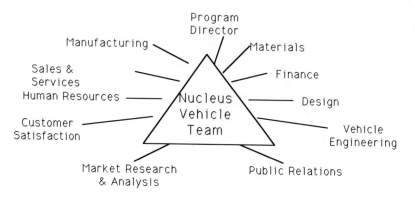

Figure 2-11. Vehicle Teams.

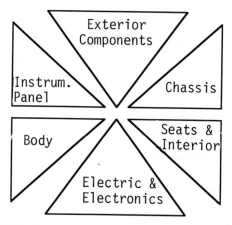

Figure 2-12. Vehicle System Management Teams.

The members of the team had overall responsibility for their parts of the vehicle, specifically, its
- quality
- timing
- reliability
- cost
- technology
- profitability

Cadillac currently has 60 of these teams with an average membership of eight people. The operators are union members who are involved in providing information to the PDITs through suggestions from the shop and their visitations to local dealerships.

The benefits that Cadillac has derived from simultaneous engineering are:

- quicker response to the market,
- better value for the customer, and
- lower costs.

Source: Simultaneous Engineering. Society of Manufacturing Engineers, Videotape 1989.

chapter *3*

Running A Successful Multi-Functional Team

In most organizations, there is a continuous struggle to facilitate decision making. Should decisions be made by one person? Or by a group? Neither is ideal. While individuals can make a fast decision they usually spend time gaining acceptance from those who must implement the idea. Time is often wasted placating angry people whose needs were not taken into account. Conflict ensues and additional time is wasted finding someone to blame.

A multi-functional team, all contributing to one goal can save time on a product design by:

- Working parallel, getting things done simultaneously rather than in a linear fashion.
- Providing the best overall input into a design, avoiding or reducing needless revisions.
- Reducing lost time caused by communication breakdowns. Since multi-functional teams have the same objectives, they strive to be more open and available to input from one another. In a linear process, the team is divided. Communications tend to be less frequent and more formalized. Having a design engineer share an office with a manufacturing counterpart will save time.
- Avoiding adjustments made to accommodate changes wanted by the customer who has had no input until it's too late.
- Reducing the learning curve. (A multi-functional group can help each other get up to speed quickly).

41

- Focusing on a common goal instead of conflicting departmental goals.
- Saving time spent in needless conflict.
- Bringing concentrated resources to bear on the task.

For a multi-functional team (see *Figure 3-1*) to achieve its goal—time reduction—it needs to be structured properly and managed effectively. The design and structure of the group is a senior management function, while the day-to-day running of the team involves people at different levels.

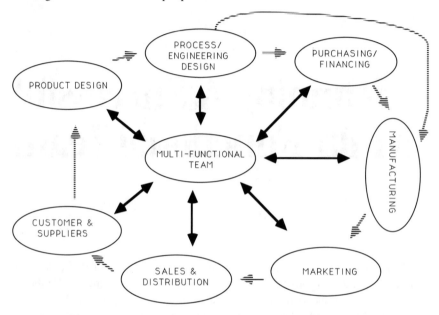

Figure 3-1. A Multi-functional Design Team.

BENEFITS OF TEAMWORK

Many people avoid joining committees because of the frustration of poorly run teams. Ask people about the teams they belong to and most will tell you about bickering, nothing getting done, and meetings dominated by a few people.

The benefits of an effective team, on the other hand, are:
- High-Quality Solutions.
  A team is composed of a number of members with a variety of strengths, interests, knowledge, and talents. Together they can arrive at far better solutions than can individuals.
- More Creative Solutions.
  Using the talents of all members, the group can generate new and innovative solutions to problems.
- Things Get Done Quickly.
  If decisions are made by consensus, there is a stronger commitment to action than when decisions are made by a minority.

Running a successful multi-functional team is no easy task. Lack of success results when the coordinator:

- Does not have line authority over members.
- Does not control or have the ability to reward the members.
- May be dealing with volunteers, as in the case of distributors and customers.
- May have people who until this time have been in conflict with one another.
- Is dealing with people from different levels in the organization.
- Has members who may perceive that their objectives are not as those of the other members of the team.

The skills to be used in the team may be more organizational and interpersonal than technical. People who have good process skills will be far more effective as coordinators than people who are on the team for their technical skills.

Poorly managed teams are often characterized by:

- bickering,
- low morale,
- low commitment,
- work done by one or a few,
- domination by few,
- withdrawal by some members,
- low attendance at meetings, and
- little creativity.

THE CHANGING DYNAMICS OF A TEAM

Teams are dynamic, just like people. But teams are much more complex. It is important for the coordinator to understand the psyche of the group to meet constantly changing needs. Most people agree that groups go through four stages before they become really productive. These stages are:

Stage 1 - FORM

Getting acquainted, exploring mutual expectations. Some degree of anxiety and insecurity about the group structure is experienced. People are tentative, testing limits, wondering whether they will be accepted.

Stage 2 - STORM

Increased anxiety and defensiveness. Anxiety grows out of the fear of letting others see oneself on a level beyond the public image. Some testing and challenging of the group leader can be expected. Members are torn between wanting to stay safe and wanting to go beyond safety, and risk getting involved. Negative comments and criticism increase.

Stage 3 - CONFORM

Some cohesion begins to show. Risk taking becomes more frequent. Members begin to challenge each other. More action results. The sharing of common experiences binds the group together. Trust develops. Empathy and caring surface. Joint commitment to change is made.

Stage 4 - PERFORM

Full trust develops. Members express themselves fully. Cohesiveness leads to mutual innovation. The group will challenge itself to perform at higher levels.

Clearly, the storm stage is the most difficult. If the team fails to mature to stage three, it will simply fall apart, continue to drift, or become dominated by a few individuals who will do most of the work.

Any group trapped in the storm stage will need an effective intervention, to get them to meet their obligations and then move to the performance stage.

STRATEGIES TO HELP MULTI-FUNCTIONAL TEAMS WORK SMOOTHLY AND QUICKLY

A group of people put together for a task will not automatically be successful. At a conscious level, many things need to be done to get them working effectively together so that they do a quality job quickly. Among the most important strategies senior management can use are the following.

Provide the Team with a Clear Mandate

Teams that have a clear idea about what they have to accomplish, how they will go about it, and the deadlines involved will be more successful than those without clear direction. An example of a clear mandate would be:

"To develop a new six-cylinder car design, with manufacturing costs of under $10, 500 for the family car owner, by July, 1990. Development costs are not to exceed $15 million."

An example of an unclear mandate would be:
"To develop a nice car that has wide appeal, as soon as possible."

Not only is it important for the core team to have a clear mandate, but each support team must do likewise. For example, the purchasing team's mandate might be:

"To reduce the number of vendors by 80%, and to assure that all vendors are able to supply parts on a Just In Time basis."

The quality engineering team's mandate might be:
"To reduce the cost of manufacturing by 25% per unit by eliminating inspection by a third party."

The design and manufacturing engineers might have the following mandate:
"To reduce the number of parts by 80%, to avoid fasteners altogether, and to reduce manufacturing cycle time by 60%."

Give Consistent Support

Any radical change in the way people do things presents a danger of having the process reverting to its original state without constant monitoring. Through words and actions senior management needs to reinforce the importance of the teams.

Give the Team "Teeth"

To get things done, the team needs clout. They need to have the power to use resource people, money, and equipment. They need to be able to make decisions and take action.

Referring to other people or committees is enormously time-consuming.

Provide a Leader from Senior Ranks

Power makes things happen in organizations. Forming a group composed of middle and lower-level managers will severely inhibit their credibility and decision-making ability.

What a difference a name or rank makes! A call from a vice president will get things moving far quicker than will the same message from a newly graduated design engineer.

Ensure that the Leader is a "Champion"

An "ordinary" manager is not going to make significant gains. The group should be headed up by a "champion." Research into the characteristics of people who have made significant changes in organizations find that they are people who:

- Are persistent;
- Have a clear vision about what they are trying to do;
- Are able to establish effective networks with other influential people; and
- Are able to bring about a sense of team spirit.

An effective coordinator will ensure that the group process follows these key guidelines:

1. The group is organized. Members' talents are utilized fully. The workload is shared. Each person knows what is expected and all members are contributing. Systems and procedures are known and are being followed.

2. Decisions are made by consensus. When major decisions are made and they impact all people, there must be general agreement on the issue. The decisions are ones that all members can live with. Consensus decisions are not easily achieved. They are generally the result of thorough debate and analysis of the facts, and a willingness to listen to the views of others.

3. Conflict is confined to the issues and does not affect relationships. Members should feel free to disagree with each other and fight for their ideas. However, when issues become personal and individuals fall victim to verbal attack, the group begins to run downhill, commitment wanes, and decision making becomes protracted. All too often, dictatorial decisions begin to be made, resulting in increased isolation by certain members.

4. Leadership is democratic. The old concept of "strong" leadership may be ineffective in a multi-functional team. Leadership should be seen as a joint responsibility with all members having the ability to influence the outcome. This responsibility is particularly important in those areas where individual members are expert. A democratic style of leadership will ensure greater involvement and participation by all members. In turn, this will increase members willingness to contribute.

Keep the Group Size Manageable

Groups that are too large become ineffective. They cannot keep everyone involved. As a consequence, members lose the feeling of commitment to decisions. The group should make decisions by consensus. As the numbers grow, this becomes increasingly difficult. As a consequence, because of this, decisions tend to be made by majority—a simple vote—causing polarization to take place.

The ideal size for a core team is six to 12. If this is not practical, because of the size of the projects, subcommittees might be needed, also of reasonable size. The overall team can meet periodically, on a monthly basis for example, for information rather than problem-solving or decision-making purposes.

Encourage Risk Taking

There is an old saying used in banking, "When in doubt, don't." There are many uncertainties in organizations. Think of how long it would take to get anything done if we stopped at each moment of doubt.

Teams need to know that they need to take risks. They are working in an uncertain environment where nothing is guaranteed. Management can encourage risk taking in three ways.

1. Accept the fact that mistakes will be made.
2. Reward and recognize risk taking.
3. Treat mistakes as a learning experience.

Keep the Team Physically Together

People working in the same area interact more frequently. The closer their offices, the more time they will spend getting to know each other. The more they know each other, the greater the trust established and the less time spent bickering about trivial issues. Some organizations have "forced" design and manufacturing to work together by having them use common facilities such as a coffee machine.

People who work together cannot develop the traditional head office or ivory tower psychoses, accusing everyone not located at the same physical site of having no idea how things really are in the "real world."

Give the Team the Skills Needed

People most often join teams with the best intentions. Because their expectations, skills, background, and perspectives differ, it is extremely difficult for them to work cohesively. Since the value of what they are doing is significant, it is

cost-effective to train members in how to perform at a high level. Specifically, the team needs to learn how to:
- manage projects,
- run and participate in meetings,
- solve problems,
- make decisions by consensus and identify when they should be done,
- manage conflict,
- plan,
- promote creativity, and
- influence people who are not part of the group, but whose help they are dependent upon.

Help the Group Understand Each Other, and Use Each Other's Strengths

Whenever a group of individuals who are specialist in their fields are brought together, differences are bound to erupt. Rather than being viewed as a threat, these differences can be embraced as the route to superior products and working relationships. If recognized, understood, and dealt with appropriately, differences can enhance both the output and team spirit of the group.

An effective team is like a peak performance symphony orchestra: a diverse group of specialists creating an inspirational performance through a mutually satisfactory process.

Like an orchestra, a work team is a collection of specialists brought together to achieve a common goal. Differences arise from two sources as work takes place; functional specialty is a predictable source of conflict, while personality differences are less predictable and often very subtle. This makes relating style differences more difficult to identify and address.

Functional differences will always exist and often challenge work teams to consider what is best for the organization, not just their division or department. This can result in superior decisions and more creative solutions and/or outcomes. Increasing everyone's understanding of the roles, responsibilities, and interrelationships of the various functional groups can result in better decision-making.

Understanding relational style differences is a complex process. A number of tools can help teams appreciate and maximize team members' relating style strengths and differences. One of the most popular is the Myers-Briggs Type Indicator™ which outlines 16 relating style profiles. The profiles describe how individuals prefer to perceive or take in the world around them, how they make decisions about the data they take in, and how they interact with others.

The original work on relating styles was conducted by Carl Jung, a Swiss physician and psychologist. He was interested in helping people understand themselves. His career was devoted to helping people improve their self-awareness. The result of his work and the subsequent work of Isabel Briggs Myers was the development of the Myers-Briggs Type Indicator.™ The instrument is intended as a template against which individuals can examine the richness of their personal preferences and appreciate the preferences of others. His intention was very emphatically not to stereotype or label people. A team facilitator can use this information to improve understanding between team members so that they can contract with one another around desirable and undesirable behavior, resulting in a caring and productive workplace.

There are four major areas where team members may have different preferences. They may prefer:
- talking or reflecting,
- planning or adapting,
- specializing or visioning, or
- thinking or feeling.

Talkers and Reflectors

The first area of potential difference is what could be called the reflectors and the talkers. Reflectors like to ponder ideas and problems and are not eager to share them until they have been well-thought through. They like to think before acting. They may not share their ideas with others if they have already been presented or if they judge them not fully developed. When they do share their ideas they are usually short and to the point. In meetings, reflectors will share polished ideas and expect others to do the same.

Talkers prefer to generate and discuss ideas with others. Brainstorming is an ideal medium for them. They also enjoy discussion and describing their ideas at great length; they may repeat themselves or what others have already said. They come to meetings expecting to have their own ideas revised and are not shy about challenging the ideas others present—even the polished ideas of the reflectors. Talkers like action and have been known to act first and think it through later. Talkers may appear insensitive to others when talking and interrupting, but their intentions are usually honorable.

Talkers and reflectors must establish special understandings with one another to ensure that their strengths enhance rather than hinder the team. For instance, a reflector might agree with a talker that they have heard enough, they've got the message, and will inform the talker. A talker might tell a reflector when they are unclear, ask where the reflector stands on an issue, and will request more information. Rather than being annoyed by this kind of behavior, contracting helps team members understand one another by discussing problem behaviors and fosters solutions mutually arrived at.

Planners and Adaptors

The second major difference encountered in relating styles is that some people prefer to live their lives in a planned and orderly fashion, while others prefer a more spontaneous, adaptive, go-with-the-flow style. Those who prefer a planned approach want to plan their days and have them go according to plan. They want closure. Let's get through this meeting's agenda. Let's stick to the project time-lines. Once planners have made decisions they like to stick to them and may reject or discount new information so that they can reach closure on an issue. They may, regrettably, jump to conclusions and/or action.

Those who prefer a more spontaneous approach are much more open to new data. They will consider all information and may delay making a final decision or committing themselves or their resources too soon. They tend to be comfortable with last minute changes and welcome new ideas even at a late date in the project. Adaptors may be too open to new information. The possibility of getting additional data later may result in procrastination and decision delay.

Detail Specialists and Visionaries

Team members tend to prefer one of two necessary but often opposite methods of perceiving the world around them. The detail specialists like to give and receive factual data when they communicate. They can be relied upon to secure or seek out concrete facts. Detail specialists are interested in information that can be seen, counted, or measured, and reflects the current reality. They are unlikely to approve or align themselves behind a proposal which has not been well researched and carefully documented—according to their standards. They will ask, "Have I got the complete picture?" To get a detail specialist on board, it is important to present information in a concise and deliberate manner that focuses the bulk of comments on the immediate effects rather than upon potential future benefits.

The visionaries or possibility thinkers on a team will gather data and quickly move to establish patterns and relationships within that data. They will ask, "so what?" when presented with factual data. They want to make meaning and see possibilities—both positive and negative—of specific information. They are less concerned with digging deeply into or verifying the specifics of the data and may see possibilities which are hard to justify with the amount of data available.

The visionaries on a team may accuse the detail specialists of "raining on their parade" when they get sent back to gather more data to justify their grand schemes. To get a visionary to cooperate, the leader must permit them to "blue-sky" ideas without questioning them as to how it will work or by pointing out potential dangers. When one is presenting data to them, it is most effective if the big picture is provided first and the specifics later. All facts presented should relate to an understanding of the big picture.

Thinkers and Feelers

The last preference that team members may exhibit is how they prefer to make decisions. Some may prefer "thinking." This will be evidenced by the to-the-point and seemingly unfeeling manner in which they make and announce their decisions. Thinkers tend to consider the issue at hand, weigh all the pros and cons and make what they consider to be a fair or just decision. They ask and answer this question—"Given the facts, what is the best business decision in this case?" Thinkers are ready and willing to defend their decisions and are not scared off by confrontation—some, in fact, welcome and enjoy a heated discussion and giving constructive criticism.

"Feelers" prefer a more subjective or value-based process of making decisions. They are passionate about what they believe in, but this should not be mistaken for compassion. Feeling decision makers can make some ruthless decisions when they feel their own or the values of others have been violated. An example might be a manager who, when faced with the decision to trim staff, releases the employee he dislikes even if that employee is highly skilled, competent, and cooperative.

Organizations tend to favor "thinking" decision making, so most corporately successful feelers have learned to justify their gut responses with hard facts. "Feelers" will often strive for cooperation and harmonious working conditions and will be sensitive to others. Whether they act upon sensitivity depends upon the corporate culture in which they reside.

The business world is full of "thinking" managers and it is important to talk their language. Thus, feelers must learn to minimize their encouraging, harmony-seeking behavior and continually prepare themselves to justify and show just cause for their actions and decisions.

When dealing with feelers, thinkers need to soften their stance so that they will be heard. A wise strategy is to summarize common agreements and then move on to more contentious issues. Both feelers and thinkers will benefit from negotiating discussion ground rules.

Using Myers-Briggs™ in a Multi-functional Team

The Myers-Briggs Type indicator™ can be a powerful tool for an effective team if used under the following conditions:

- No one is excluded from the team because of their personality type.

- All members are considered to have equal value to the team.

- People's strengths are used whenever appropriate.

- Diversity strengthens a team rather than detracting from its effectiveness.

- Different types can make unique contributions to different stages of the design process. For example, visionaries or intuitive types may have a valuable role to play at the product definition phase. They are able to picture the future and view the product's potential. Thinkers, who make logical decisions based on facts, are able to help decide which concept may be best when evaluating a variety of alternatives. And finally, the detail specialists, or sensing people can contribute effectively with the practical necessity of ensuring that the product will actually work!

Undertake Team Building as Needed

Managing a project on time and within budget is a challenging task. But project management is beyond the scope of this book. Rather, it will focus on techniques to keep the group moving forward—teamwork skills.

Getting to know and appreciate each other will help the team perform well. But the group will become bogged down from time to time. When the leader detects a problem, there are a variety of team building techniques to get them back on track again. Some effective methods are:

Technique Number 1. Negotiate a Code of Conduct with Team Members

Team members can brainstorm for items that will help them to work effectively as a team. Examples are:

- No one is more important than anyone else.
- Make sure that everyone has a chance to participate.
- There is no such thing as a stupid question.
- Listen to and be prepared to be influenced by the ideas of others.
- Avoid disruptive behavior.
- Attend meetings on time.
- Do all assignments on schedule.
- Avoid personal conflict during meetings.
- Do not be sarcastic towards other people's ideas.
- Don't engage in disruptive side conversations.
- Take personal responsibility for the outcome of the meeting.
- Encourage those people with less confidence.
- Work for win-win situations.
- Include/inform people who will be impacted by team decisions.

The group can arrive at a short list of items from a brainstorming session. The prioritized list may be displayed prominently in the meeting room to remind each member of the commitment necessary for success.

Technique Number 2. Take a Problem-Solving Approach Involving Team Members

Meeting with the group, the leader should devote the meeting to solving its problem. A problem-solving approach is ideal.

First, the group should define its problem. Examples may be: "We are unproductive," or "No one cares about our project," or "Members are not pulling their weight," or "We are all being too territorial."

Next, the group should brainstorm for all possible causes. From the long list, major causes need to be extracted through an elimination process.

Knowing the major causes of the problem will help the group with the next phase, which is to determine solutions. Again, brainstorming can be used. The best solutions can be extracted from the list through discussion and negotiation.

Finally, an action plan is drawn up to implement the best solutions. It is important that all members buy into the solutions. An example of an action plan is shown in *Table 3-1*.

Technique Number 3. Provide Constructive Feedback to the Group

Giving the group regular feedback will allow them to become more conscious about their effective use of the process.

When should this be done? Possibly the best time is at the end of the meeting; the business of the meeting is behind the group and they can apply their minds to how they arrived at their meeting results.

How should feedback be given? The leader should adopt the 10 golden rules of effective feedback:

Table 3-1. Team Building Action Plan.

WHAT	**WHO**	**WHEN**
All agree to be on time. $1 fine for late comers.	All	Immediate
Complete first draft design.	Mike	Set date
Agree to listen to each other.	All	Immediate
Adopt "round robin" to give everyone a chance to speak.	All	Immediate

1. **Do it with Care.** To be useful, feedback requires the giver to feel concern for and to care for the person receiving feedback—to want to help, not hurt the other person.
2. **Give Your Full Attention**. It is important to pay attention to what you are doing as you give feedback. This helps you to engage in a two-way exchange with some depth of communication.
3. **Get an Invitation.** Feedback is most effective when the receiver has invited the comments. This provides a platform for openness and some guidelines; it also gives the receiver an opportunity to identify and explore particular areas of concern.
4. **Deal Directly with Issues.** Good feedback is specific and deals clearly with particular incidents and behavior. Foot-dragging or making vague statements is of little value. The most useful help is direct, open, and concrete.
5. **Effective feedback.** This feedback requires more than a statement of facts. Feelings also need to be expressed so that the receiver can judge the full impact of his or her behavior.
6. **Do Not Clutter the Feedback with Personal Judgements.** Often it is helpful not to give feedback composed of judgements or evaluations. If you wish to offer judgements, then state clearly that these are matters of subjective evaluation, and then describe the situation as you see it and let the person concerned make the evaluation.
7. **Do it at an Appropriate Time.** The most useful feedback is given when the receiver is receptive to it and is sufficiently close to the particular event being discussed for it to be fresh in his or her mind. Storing comments can lead to a build-up of recriminations and reduce the effectiveness of feedback when it is finally given.
8. **Make Sure that the Ideas are Actionable.** The most useful feedback centers around behavior that can be changed by the receiver. Feedback concerning matters outside the control of the receiver is less useful. It is

often helpful to suggest alternative ways of behaving that allow the receiver to think about new ways of tackling old problems.

9. **Check and Clarify the Feedback.** If possible, feedback should be checked out with other people to explore whether one person's perceptions are shared by others. This is especially useful in a training group and can also be promoted in a work team. Different viewpoints can be collected and assimilated, points of difference and similarity clarified, and a more objective picture developed.

10. **Involve the Recipient(s).** Ask the recipient to identify solutions. This will get their input and ensure commitment to change.

Clearly, the development of effective teams can present a major time-saving impact both in product design and in manufacturing process. Drawing design and manufacturing together can significantly reduce product lead time.

The concept of design for manufacturability (DFM) is representative of a new awareness of the importance of design as the first step in manufacturing.

DFM expert and noted author Henry W. Stoll addressed this issue in January 1988 in *Manufacturing Engineering* magazine. In it he wrote:

"The DFM approach embodies certain underlying imperatives that help maintain communication between all components of the manufacturing system and permit flexibility to adapt and to modify the design during each stage of the product's realization. Chief among these is the team approach or *simultaneous engineering*, in which all relevant components of the manufacturing system including outside suppliers are made active participants in the design effort from the start. The team approach helps ensure that total product knowledge is as complete as possible at the time each design decision is made. Other imperatives include a general attitude that resists making irreversible design decisions before they absolutely must be made and a commitment to continuous optimization of product and process.

"The objectives of the design for manufacture approach are to identify product concepts that are inherently easy to manufacture, to focus on component design for ease of manufacture and assembly, and to integrate manufacturing process design and product design to ensure the best matching of needs and requirements."[1]

---

[1] Stoll, Henry W., "Design for Manufacture," *Manufacturing Engineering,* January 1988.

QUESTIONNAIRE

Answer the following questions ranking your answers from 1 to 5.
1 - very poor,
2 - poor,
3 - average,
4 - good, and
5 - very good.

- Are your engineering groups divided by function?
  1 - Yes,
  3 - Yes, but with dotted lines to Simultaneous Engineering Project Leader,
  5 - No, all report to the same person.

- Do your design and manufacturing engineers work together or separately?
  1 - Separately,
  2 - Mostly separate,
  3 - Somewhat together,
  4 - Together often,
  5 - Totally integrated.

- Do your manufacturing and design staff have access to the same computer database?
  1 - No,
  3 - Partial information shared,
  5 - Total information.

- Are designs capable of being transferred electronically to all interested parties, including vendors?
  1 - No,
  3 - Partially,
  5 - Yes.

- Is your design process sequential, or is it simultaneous?
  1 - Sequential,
  3 - Partially sequential, partially simultaneous,
  5 - Totally simultaneous.

- Does your multi-functional team have a clear mandate?
  - 1 - Not defined,
  - 2 - Vague,
  - 3 - General,
  - 4 - Fairly clear,
  - 5 - Crystal clear.

- What is the level of management support?
  - 1 - No support,
  - 2 - Little support,
  - 3 - Reasonable support,
  - 4 - Good support,
  - 5 - Unequivocal.

- What is the extent of the team's authority?
  - 1 - Has no power,
  - 2 - Little power,
  - 3 - Fair power,
  - 4 - Reasonable power.

- What is the rank of the project "Champion"?
  - 1 - Shop floor,
  - 2 - Supervision,
  - 3 - Manager,
  - 4 - Director,
  - 5 - Vice President.

- How close are people physically?
  - 1 - Not in the same state,
  - 2 - Not in the same city,
  - 3 - Not on the same property,
  - 4 - Not in the same office,
  - 5 - In the same office area.

- What is the extent of the team's training?
  - 1 - None,
  - 2 - Minimum,
  - 3 - Reasonable,
  - 4 - Good,
  - 5 - Extensive.

- Are members given an opportunity to get to know each other?
  1 = No,
  3 = Socially,
  5 = Specific methodology (like the Myers-Briggs Type Indicator™).

- Are team building activities undertaken?
  1 = No,
  2 = Informally,
  3 = Somewhat,
  4 = Reasonably well,
  5 = Do so professionally as needed.

TOTAL SCORES

Interpretation:

In relation to the elements of Simultaneous Engineering,
- A score of 13 to 23 indicates that you need dramatic changes.
- A score of 24 to 34 indicates that you are in need of improvement.
- A score of 35 to 44 indicates that you are in reasonable shape.
- A score of 45 to 55 indicates that you are in good shape.
- A score in excess of 55 indicates that you are doing a great job!

chapter **4**

Implementing Time To Market Teams

Because no two organizations are the same, each will set up TTM groups in different ways. It is important that they *customize* the process to fit their own specific needs and circumstances. However, there are many steps that are fairly described as generic to many organizations.

After reviewing the 12 steps below, decide which are appropriate and in what order they should occur in your organization.

Step Number 1. Get Top Management Involvement and Support

It is not sufficient to get only verbal support from senior management. They must be actively involved in the project as well. Senior management sets direction, influences values, and dispenses rewards. Their actions send clear signals to others about what is important.

The continued involvement of senior management helps convince skeptics that the Time To Market strategy is for real. While changes will be made as circumstances require, the focus on speed will continue.

To encourage the use of TTM strategies, senior management should invest some of their time in familiarizing themselves with the subject. This can be done by:

- reading articles and books on the subject,
- attending workshops and conferences, and

- visiting with other organizations that have adopted similar strategies.

This knowledge, when shared, will help to build enthusiasm and promote a determination to make the process work.

Complete top management support for the TTM strategy can be achieved if it is expressed in the company's mission statement.

Step Number 2. Appoint a Project Coordinator

It is best if one person has ultimate responsibility for coordinating a TTM project.

Since the choice of a coordinator can be difficult, it is useful to know some key characteristics of people who succeed at the task. The important attributes are found among those who:

- have "clout" by virtue of their status in the organization,
- are good team players,
- have a great track record,
- have excellent written and verbal communication skills,
- have worked their way up in the organization,
- have the ability to influence people,
- are well organized,
- have worked in a variety of areas, including the shop floor, and
- have successfully completed other projects on time and within budget.

The project coordinator can make or break the project. Following some simple rules of project management will help enormously. The most important rules for a project manager to follow are explored on the following pages:

Don't Do the Work Yourself. Some people are good at doing. Others are good at organizing. A project manager focuses on the latter. If he or she has to do everyone's task instead of having team members do the work, then the manager:

- has picked the wrong people. They don't have the skill, or
- doesn't know how to motivate through the delegating process,
- or both.

Plan the Project Meticulously. Keep on Top of Matters Constantly. The project manager should make certain that everybody knows where they are in the project, what they are to do, and when tasks have to be completed. The how-to-do-it can generally be delegated.

Focus on Key Issues. It is easy to get sidetracked by ill-defined projects on to issues that rapidly become nebulous. Clear goals allow you to put aside frivolous issues and focus on what is really important to the project. Remember the Pareto, or 80/20 principle; 20% of your activities will give you 80% of the results. Do these first. Do them best.

Communicate, Communicate, Communicate. Communications is a bottom-less pit. A team leader can never do enough. Be aware that you never will satisfy everyone. Usually, you will be accused of poor communications despite your best efforts.

Keep people informed. Don't hide information—share it. The more "sensitive" it is, the more value people put on receiving it. Such disclosures motivate people. They accept some "ownership" over the project. Keeping information a secret will serve only to alienate you from people whose support is needed.

Keep in mind that communications is a two-way street. The other side of communication is receiving and listening to it. A good project manager listens to people. The manager hears what they are saying and is attuned to what they are not saying. The manager watches for nonverbal cues. Body language, for instance, often tells you more about what people feel or believe than the words they utter.

Spread the Accolades Around. A good project manager gets rewards. Consistent good results almost axiomatically lead to promotions, more authority/responsibility, even bonuses. But the key to getting results is to get them through people. To get the most out of team members, it is important to ensure that each gets a piece of the action. Recognition for team members can include:
- a letter of appreciation and commendation to the member, with a copy sent to that person's boss,
- inclusion of the contributor among the team members making the final presentation to management .

Know Your Parameters. Before setting out for the goals, be certain to accurately and realistically define the scope of the project. The four most commonly addressed areas are:
- *Project* - does it cover one; a few; one line; or all items such as canned goods rather than a single item (such as baked beans)?
- *Area* - Are you talking about just one location; the city of Toronto; its province, Ontario; the national scene; or are you tackling international arenas?
- *Organization* - Who are you trying to deal with: specific people; a department; a level of government; a union; distributors; the media?
- *Resources* - How much of the budget do you have available? Who in the organization is available to help you, and for how long?
- When these parameters are known, document them and have people with ultimate accountability sign off on them.

Be Clear About Your Goals. Setting clear goals for a project helps to keep everyone's energies focused. A goal is a statement of results to be achieved. Goals describe:
- the conditions to be met if the goal is achieved,
- the time frame during which the goal is to be reached, and
- the resources the organization is willing to commit to achieve the desired result.

59

To be effective goals should be:
- specific,
- measurable,
- realistic,
- challenging,
- achievable, and
- desirable.

An example of a good goal is: "To complete the design of the XY widget so it is ready for manufacture by June 14, 1991 with a budget of $275,000." Such a goal should be set by the group to ensure all members buy in.

Be Clear About Who Has Authority, Who is Responsible, and Who is Accountable. Project managers and team members need to know the real differences inherent in the terms *authority*, *responsibility*, and *accountability*.

Authority is the power to make final decisions that others must follow.

Responsibility is the obligation to perform tasks effectively, and results from a formal role in the organization.

Accountability means being answerable for the satisfactory completion of a specific task (see *Figure 4-1*).

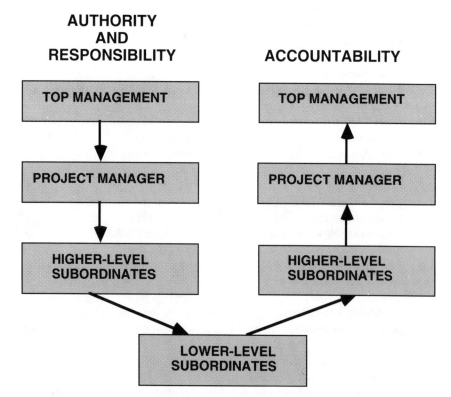

Figure 4-1. The Role of Authority, Responsibility and Accountability.

Conceptually, authority and responsibility go together as they move down the organization. However, accountability goes upward only. In practice, this may not always be so. The theory is impacted by people's perceptions and intentions. Successful people tend to optimize each situation.

Being appointed project manager, however, does not guarantee success. Once you have been given formal authority you have to:

- Assume authority,
- Exercise authority, and
- Be backed up by authority.

The greater the formal authority, the easier it will be to get things done.

Step Number 3. Set Up a Team

Attracting the right people for the job should not be taken lightly. A rotten apple in any bag poisons the others. Determining who to involve in the team can be difficult. The choice should be made after consulting the managers of the areas from which you need to draw people. Key criteria for getting the right people include:

- do they have the skill?
- do they have the interest?
- does their work load permit you to use them?

You should know each person's record of success on similar assignments. In addition, you should have a feel for how well the person works with others, in what situations the person operates best, and the person's ability to work under pressure.

You should also consider an employee's interest in and motivation for the task as well as their abilities.

You need to know the professional interests and goals of potential members. If you lack this information, speak with each of them to determine their interests and the goals they believe are reasonable for the department. Even if you don't immediately use the information, the employees will have contributed to the delegation process and be more willing to go along with it.

Consider also which employees have the time to take on the task, and how well each is handling the work.

While it may not always be possible, it is useful to include people who balance the teams in terms of style. For example, include a number of task-oriented people whose high energy allows them to gather information and do the number-crunching so essential to success. Other members should be more process-oriented. Such people are more concerned with group morale, aware of the need for avoiding friction, and intuitively understand how conflict can be managed.

Identifying the particular skills that a person brings to a team can be done by using simple psychological tests, such as the Myers-Briggs Type Indicator™. Indicator scores of each person can be shared as part of a team-building exercise. This way, people begin to appreciate the value of other team members instead of being suspicious, upset, or angered because they approach problems in such a different manner.

61

The composition of the team will vary depending upon factors such as:
- the strategic importance of the project,
- confidentiality requirements,
- complexity, and
- degree of innovation required.

In most manufacturing operations, a well-balanced team will come from:
- engineering design,
- manufacturing engineering,
- the shop floor,
- supervision,
- purchasing,
- finance,
- vendors, and
- customers.

Having chosen the members, a meeting should be held to explain:
- the nature of the project,
- goals in terms of output, time, and budget,
- training, and
- answer any questions.

It is vital that support groups be included in the pilot team. Excluding engineering and maintenance people will have disastrous effects on the project. Each group will fight to protect its own turf instead of working toward a common goal.

Step Number 4. Plan the Project

This may be the most critical step of the entire process. Few teams bother to map out where they are going. Fewer still detail the steps that they will take to get there.

There are a variety of tools that can make planning effective. A simple project can be planned using a Gantt chart (see *Figure 4-2* below).

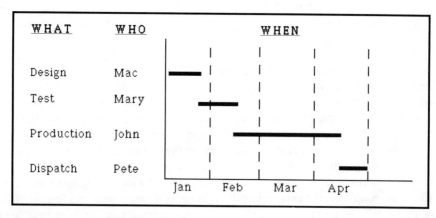

Figure 4-2. Gantt Chart Example.

For more sophisticated projects, a Project Evaluation and Review Technique (P.E.R.T.) chart is a better way to go (see *Figure 4-3*).

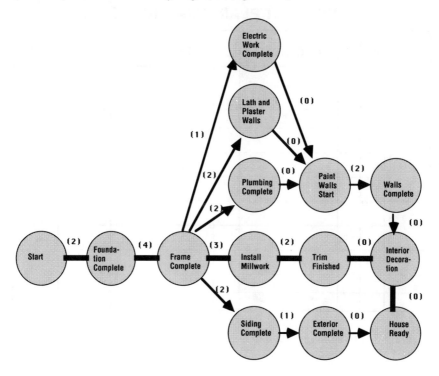

Figure 4-3. P.E.R.T. Diagram.

Both P.E.R.T. and Gantt charts can be done manually. Highly complex projects are more easily done on a computer.

Members of the team should be involved in planning to ensure that they buy into the timing of the project. A lack of timing commitment leads to delay, particularly if the project includes a critical path component.

Another useful technique is to involve members in mapping the major steps of the project and identifying the resources required for each step. One way to do this is through a process cause and effect diagram (see *Figure 4-4*).

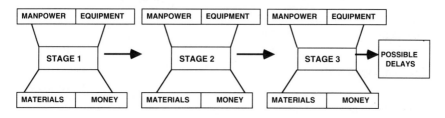

Figure 4-4. Cause and Effect Diagram.

The possible causes for delays are identified and plans developed to deal with them (see *Figure 4-5*).

PROJECT PLANNING PROCESS

HELP	#	P	OBSTACLE	C	SOLUTION	WHEN	WHO

Figure 4-5. Developing a Plan to Deal with Delays.

Table 4-1.
Action Plan to Take Care of Manpower Shortage in Stage Three.

WHAT	WHO	WHEN	INFORM
Place Ad in Newspaper	John	May 1	
Draft Ad for Newspaper	Mary	April 15	Mike
Develop Short List	Chuck & Greg	May 30	
Interview & Pick Two Candidates	Chuck & Greg	June 15	Pete H. Resources.
Hire Temporary Staff	John	July 1	Pete H. Resources.
Provide Orientation	Cindy	July 1-2	

Step Number 5. Train the Team

All members of the pilot group need training. This should include instruction in:

- the strategic importance of Time To Market strategies;
- how teams should work,
- decision-making,
- members' responsibility,
- how to manage differences,
- project planning,
- running team meetings,
- how to influence people outside the team, and
- value engineering.

As part of the training, members should also develop a contract of mutual expectations (see *Figure 4-6*).

- Everyone has equal importance,
- everyone participates,
- stupid questions do not exist,
- everyone listens to and is prepared to be influenced by the ideas of others;
- disruptive behavior is avoided,
- timely attendance is essential,
- timely assignment completion is vital,
- personal conflict during meetings is prohibited,
- sarcasm directed at others is not tolerated,
- disruptive side conversation is prohibited,
- members take personal responsibility for the outcome of the meeting;
- less confident team members are encouraged to participate;
- win-win situations are the objective for all meetings; and
- team decisions affecting others are always made known to those affected.

Figure 4-6. Typical Code of Conduct of a Multi-Functional Team.

The team should decide how to enforce disciplines critical to its success.

Step Number 6. Undertake the Design

Daniel Whitney[1]. from Charles Stark Draper Laboratory Inc., in Cambridge, MA, sees five key functions of the design team. These are:

- **Decide on the Character of the Product.** The team should develop a clear statement about what the product or service should be. They can decide then what methods are appropriate to design and/or manufacture it.

---

[1] Whitney, Daniel E. "Manufacturing by Design," *Harvard Business Review*, July-August 1988. p. 83-91.

- **Do a Function Analysis.** The team should begin by asking some basic questions such as, "How useful is the product and each of its components? Does each serve a purpose? Are they a value-added feature for the customer? How would the customer react if we eliminated them? Are there easier or better ways of providing a similar benefit? Can they be designed smaller or quicker? Do they need to be used at all? Is there a better way?"

  This approach typically looks at parts one at a time, simplifies or combines them, or adds features to them.

  Value-engineering techniques help to reduce manufacturing costs through a rational choice of materials and methods for making parts. For example, can a part be made from plastics instead of metal? Should the holes be punched or drilled?

- **Design an Assembly Process.** This step requires that a suitable step-by-step sequence for parts is determined. It ensures that each part is compatible with the assembly process, identifying subassemblies, quality-control tolerances, and procedures.

  To produce lot sizes of one, some manufacturers have created generic parts or subassemblies for any combination or variation of the basic parts to go together physically and functionally.

  As an example, Delco-Japan designed six basic parts of a new product, each available in three varieties. This allowed them to produce $3^6 = 729$ different models.

  It is also important to reduce reliance on single-use jigs when demands may change almost hourly. It is impossible to achieve a batch size of one if a separate jig is used for each product. Delco's engineers solved the problem by designing parts with common jigging features, so that one jig could hold all varieties. Another approach was to make parts that snap on or hold themselves together so that non closing jigs can be used.

- **Carry Out a Design For Manufacturability and Usability Study.** This research will help determine if the benefits derived in the function analysis can be made without affecting the product's functioning. It looks at the product as a whole, rather than a collection of parts.

- **Design the Factory Systems.** The last step will involve workers in setting up the manufacturing strategy. It will ensure minimal inventory handling and storage, and compatibility with vendors' methods and capabilities.

Step Number 7. Do Periodic Post-Mortems

To work effectively and quickly, the team needs to pull in the same direction. Often, members are so busy trying to get the task done they forget about the time wasted over personality conflicts or lack of full participation.

Every three or four months, take half of a day to review team performance. There are many ways to do this, but how it is done is less important than doing it. Regular reviews lead to renewed energy and commitment and a satisfying speeding up of the process.

66

Step Number 8. Do a Final Post-Mortem

At the end of the project, the team should reflect on what they have done. They should ask themselves:

- what went well?
- what mistakes did we make?
- how effective was the training?
- could the training be improved?
- what would we do differently next time?
- what did we learn from the project?
- what advice do we have for the team members of the next project?
- what benefits accrued?

These issues should be documented and reported to senior management. The findings should be available to people involved in future projects. A simplified evaluation sheet is shown in the *Figure 4-7*.

Step Number 9. The Pilot Team Should Report Back to Senior Management

All issues reviewed in the post-mortem should be reported to management. This is best done in the form of a management presentation at which all members of the team are present with as many as possible participating. This presentation serves the following purposes:

- bringing management up to date, and
- providing shared experience, both positive and negative, for decision makers and the team members;
- ensuring that team members are recognized for their efforts;
- providing an opportunity for management to learn more about the benefits of simultaneous engineering and multi-functional teams, so that their efforts to foster such initiatives increase.

A "typical" agenda for a final presentation might be similar to that shown in the next paragraph.

- Welcome attendees.
- Introduce the team.
- Describe (briefly) the project.
- Describe how the task was completed. Explain the process and the steps taken.
- Describe the benefits. Don't be modest.
- Thank those who helped you.
- Thank your audience for their attendance. Indicate that you know you can count on their support.

Step Number 10. Write Up a Case Study

For many organizations, using a simultaneous engineering approach for product design is new. The first time will be a learning experience. Some lessons will

PROJECT _____

PROJECT MANAGER _____

TEAM MEMBERS   _____   _____

               _____   _____

GOALS _____

ACHIEVEMENTS—TANGIBLE _____

ACHIEVEMENTS—INTANGIBLE _____

COMPLETION TIME _____ %

COMPLETION BUDGET _____ %

THE THINGS WE DID WELL WERE:

_____

_____

_____

THE THINGS WE DID POORLY WERE:

_____

_____

_____

LESSONS LEARNED:

1. _____

2. _____

3. _____

THINGS TO CHANGE NEXT TIME:

1. _____

2. _____

3. _____

Figure 4-7. Project Evaluation.

be positive. Quality of the design, time to design, changes, etc., should all show an improvement over the traditional, linear approach. But, there will surely have been some problems, too.

Making mistakes is a part of doing business. Repeating mistakes is not. Everything should be done to learn from the experience so that future teams can work better and quicker. Their efforts will be facilitated if they:
- get seasoned team members as part of their team, and
- anticipate and avoid problems.

A documented case study will help future design teams. It will describe:
- the team mandate,
- what they did well,
- what they did poorly,

- why they failed to reach some (or all) of their goals, and
- what they learned from the experience.

The case study will draw much of its information from the post-mortem (Step 8).

Step Number 11. Celebrate

There is a time for work and a time for play. Now is the time for play. It's time to celebrate. After months of hard work and stress, members need to feel good about themselves. They need to feel a sense of pride in what they achieved. Celebrations can be done in many ways depending on the magnitude of the project and the culture of the organization. Most typically would take the form of:

- a meal or banquet,
- verbal or written thanks from a senior officer of the company,
- a party,
- a financial bonus,
- promotions, or
- some combination of these.

Step Number 12. Do it all Over Again

The lessons learned from the first program will provide valuable insight into the future course of action and management of the process. The experience allows management to use the new concepts more aggressively. For example, if the organization started off with one multi-functional team, it may be possible to begin two more after the post-mortem.

The process would continue to expand until ALL new products use similar time-reducing techniques.

chapter 5

Computers In Design and Manufacturing

COMPUTER-INTEGRATED MANUFACTURING

Computer-Integrated Manufacturing (CIM) might be regarded as the "ultimate" system that links design, manufacturing, and coordination efforts through an integrated computer network. This network is capable of working, in some cases, most effectively with a minimum of human intervention.

The SME Blue Book entitled *CIM-Computer-Integrated Manufacturing: A Working Definition* notes: "*Manufacturing* in Computer-Integrated Manufacturing refers to the total manufacturing enterprise. It does not refer only to the manufacturing or the production function within that enterprise. It defines CIM as:

Integration of the total manufacturing enterprise for the use of integrated systems in data communications, coupled with new managerial philosophies that improve organizational and personnel efficiency."[1]

In a Time To Market sense, CIM is effective as the company that has implemented CIM successfully by getting the right information to the right people or devices in the correct places at the right times to make the right decisions.

---

[1] Warren L. Shrensker, ed., *CIM: Computer-Integrated Manufacturing: A Working Definition*, SME Blue Book Series, Dearborn, MI, Society of Manufacturing Engineers, 1990, p. 2.

The Blue Book goes on to report:

"Some companies at trade shows will claim to be selling CIM—but they are really selling elements that can go into a CIM system. One cannot purchase CIM, because Computer-Integrated Manufacturing is such a broad spectrum of technologies that at best can be thought of as a goal, a strategy, and a philosophy dependent upon a technology and management approach used within a corporation that manufactures products that are sold to customers."

A true CIM system provides computer assistance to all business functions. It provides inter/intra-functional integration within a manufacturing enterprise, whether it supports a job shop, batch production shop, mass production, continuous flow, or process type of manufacturing environment.[2]

The Blue Book discusses six systems that should be integrated into CIM (*Figure 5-1*). These include:

- pre-sale, business planning, and support;
- product/process design;
- manufacturing process planning;
- manufacturing process control;
- shop floor monitoring system; and
- process automation.

We will in this chapter discuss two major parts of CIM: Computer-Aided Design (CAD) and Computer-Aided Manufacturing (CAM). Flexible Manufacturing, Group Technology, and Computer-Assisted Process Planning will be discussed in *Chapter 7*.

The reader will notice that other areas of *Figure 5-1* are discussed throughout this book.

The concept of CIM is best depicted by the CIM Enterprise Wheel which was developed by the Computer and Automated Systems Association of the Society of Manufacturing Engineers (CASA/SME). This wheel (*Figure 5-2*) represents a structure needed to achieve CIM. When the wheel was developed, CASA/SME decided that there needed to be five fundamental dimensions to the wheel. They are:

1. General business management,
2. Product and process definition,
3. Manufacturing planning and control,
4. Factory automation, and
5. Information resource management.

General business management's family of applications (the outer ring of the wheel) proves a wide range of automated processes. These may include cost accounting, marketing, sales order entry, human relations decision support, program scheduling, cost-status report, labor collection, etc.

---

[1] Warren L. Shrensker, ed., *CIM: Computer-Integrated Manufacturing: A Working Definition*, SME Blue Book Series, Dearborn, MI, Society of Manufacturing Engineers, 1990, p. 3.

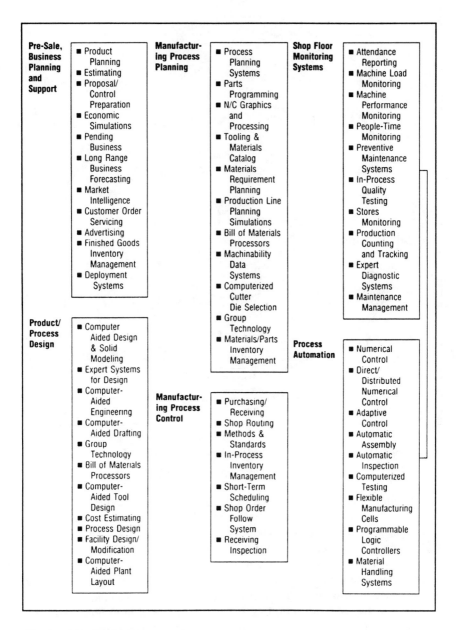

Figure 5-1. CIM Subsystems/Systems Which Should Be Integrated.

The product and process definition portion of the wheel may include CAD/ CAM, group technology, configuration management, modeling, simulation, Computer-aided process planning, etc.

The section of the wheel dealing with manufacturing planning and control consists of islands such as inventory control, shop loading, capacity planning, faster production, purchasing, etc.

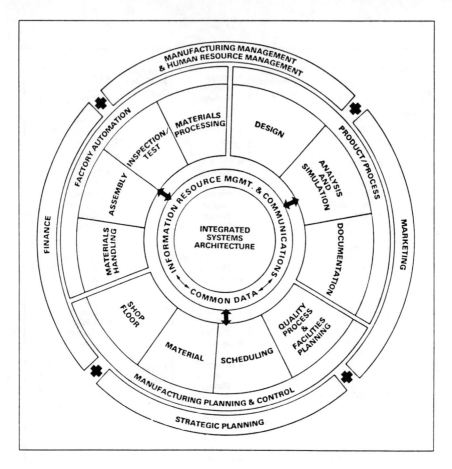

Figure 5-2. Computer-Integrated Manufacturing Enterprise.

(CASA/SME)—Copyright © 1985 SME, Second Edition, Revised November 5, 1985

The third family of CIM processes located in the inner circle of the wheel deals with factory automation. Industrial robots, numerical control, flexible machining systems, and process controllers are all a part of this area.

Information resource management makes up the hub of the wheel. At the heart of CIM, information resource management is the concept of data management. Manufacturing productivity is believed to be linked to the notion of shared or common data, especially data shared between engineering and manufacturing. It is an objective of CIM information resource management to break down the walls that have existed between those two organizations and render them into one organization through a common database.

The tangible aspect of CIM information resource management includes the tools of information. These tools may include not only the computers but also the disk storage devices, printers and plotters, tapes, communication devices, and operating systems. The intangible aspect of the CIM information resource management is the information itself.

This wheel is very useful in providing the conceptual framework for describing how applications relate to one another and how they can be integrated. There is, however, no absolute technique for determining which of the many manufacturing applications fit into which process family. Different CIM program managers will undoubtedly come up with their own logic and their own groupings of automated processes as well as how those processes or groupings relate to one another.

COMPUTER-AIDED DESIGN/COMPUTER-AIDED MANUFACTURING (CAD/CAM)

There are many who would argue that CIM is the grandchild of CAD/CAM. Computer-aided design and Computer-aided manufacturing were two of the original applications of computers in the manufacturing environment. Initially, these applications consisted of simple line drawings and very fundamental numerical control of machine tools.

The SME Blue Book, *The Role of CAD/CAM in CIM,* presents a brief history of CAD/CAM as follows:

"As CAD/CAM systems took shape in the late 1960s and early 1970s, fierce competition developed between manufacturers of "turnkey" systems or systems that contained everything bundled together. Loyalties to particular vendors often dictated the system to buy and companies became associated with that vendor. As time went on, many companies began buying different systems. As computers became cheaper, faster, and available in an increasing variety, software proliferated at an exponential rate.

"Today it is hard to find even a small manufacturer who is only concerned with one type of system. In companies with multiple plants, there are also multiple types of systems. The companies that did not contain primarily one type of system almost always find themselves concerned with transfer of data either to or from a dissimilar system. Advancing computer technology has provided new types of hardware and software, further clouding the issue. Confusion over which type of system is best for an application has reached a crescendo. Yet, in the nearly 30 years that CAD/CAM systems have been in use, the fundamental processes of manufacturing are still alive and well. While individual actions have changed, the underlying reasons for those actions remain the same. Companies that have changed systems as well as those who are a little bewildered in choosing an initial system today can find stability in numerically examining their needs. They're finding that there are common issues regardless of which system they have or are considering." [3]

Most jobs now demand at least some fluency in the new literacy of the work-a-day world: computer literacy. Once the arcane and private world of a scientific elite, literacy in computers is as expected of and by employers as is reading and writing literacy.

---

[3] Gary Conkol, ed., *The Role of CAD/CAM in CIM,* SME Blue Book Series, Dearborn, MI, Society of Manufacturing Engineers, 1990, p. 3.

Computers are showing up everywhere in the plant and in the office. While the intention is to facilitate tasks by doing work faster, this goal is not always achieved. There are two primary causes:

1. Failure to understand a process. If something does not work effectively as it is, it makes no sense to automate it.
2. Failure to train people to run the equipment at the optimum level. A lot of operators are left frustrated and angry because systems do not work the way they were supposed to. They find it difficult and time-consuming to deal with glitches.

COMPUTER AUTOMATION IN ORGANIZATIONS

A visit to almost any cross section of organizations discloses several truths.

- The sophistication of computers and their speed is increasing dramatically.
- The number of computers continues to increase.
- Computer use is not evenly spread. There are some pockets of high level use and little use in others.
- The functions of computers are changing. Early in-plant computers were used for monitoring. Now they are also used as control devices.
- Communications technology is becoming more widespread as the integration of different computer technologies increases in importance and the transfer of data between computers promotes an increasing level of integration of functions.
- Functional barriers are becoming less important as previously isolated operations become integrated. Design and manufacturing functions are much more interdependent, especially with growing levels of office and plant networking.

The need to know more, immediately, as organizations strive to be totally responsive to customer requests has caused major use (both successful and unsuccessful) of computer technologies in administrative functions.

- In the communications area, technologies such as fiber optics allow for more new features within existing products as well as for the introduction of new products which will become more commonplace. This trend will continue as computers become more user friendly. As an example, more software is bringing the graphic approach for computer commands and the mouse to MS-DOS © machines. In addition, current computer and telephone integration allows for instant voice, text, and data, and picture transmission.
- In the area of power, capacity grows from the use of more powerful microchips. The ability to store and retrieve information can become mind-boggling.
- The number of functions that computers perform is increasing. Computer graphics and desktop publishing are but two of a host of new applications which are now commonplace.

The technological race has created a dilemma for manufacturers of computer-based products. Because innovations occur around the clock, obsolescence is leading to shorter and shorter product life cycles. New feature software is extending life cycles and enabling manufacturers to provide value added features as a marketing tool. For example, Northern Telecom's switching system, the DMS-100, now offers users 1,400 features compared to the 300 originally offered.[4]

In addition, the mounting use of computers in the office has occasioned significant changes in the location and method of data collection. As mainframe computers decline in importance relative to PCs, more data are input at the source instead of sent to a central location for key punching and batch processing.

The ability to network and gather information from around the globe has led to increasingly effective management information systems. The result is the ability to make better and more time-critical decisions which can improve efficiencies and lead to faster response time.

COMPUTERS IN DESIGN

Until a decade ago most design engineers produced drawings of products and parts by manual methods. It was a demanding and painstaking task. When compared with today's Computer-Aided Design (CAD), early designers

- took longer to produce drawings;
- took even longer to introduce change;
- did not promote information exchanges with design people as a result of different locations and difficulties in transmitting information.

Modern CAD systems on the other hand have the potential to:

- speed design through faster input;
- allow for quick updates and change;
- improve the quality of drawings;
- allow many people to share information simultaneously;
- promote a team approach to the design so that manufacturability is increased.

Modern computerized tools make simultaneous engineering much easier. CAD systems have the ability to produce a three-dimensional model that is useful for end users, particularly manufacturing people (internal) or vendors (external). As equipment is standardized, the integration of ideas is becoming a reality. People on opposite sides of the world can review the latest versions of a design immediately (see *Figure 5-3*).

CAD is a computerized system for design. It comprises three integrated elements —hardware, software, and firmware.

The hardware consists of a central processor, a workstation which includes a keyboard, color monitor and "menus," and a plotter to produce the final hardcopy drawing.

The software is a basic computer operating system which includes features that can do mathematical calculations and graphical shapes such as lines, circles, arcs, mirror images, and 3-D models.

---

[4] David Robertson and Jeff Wareham, "Changing Technology and Work: Northern Telecom." *A CAW Technology Report*, October 1989.

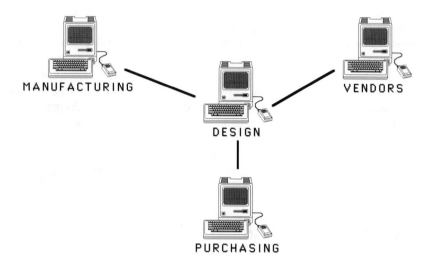

MANUFACTURING

VENDORS

DESIGN

PURCHASING

Figure 5-3. Simultaneous Engineering Using Computer-Aided Design Tools.

Firmware is the added-on memory boards which provide the system with increased power. This capacity stores a library of previous designs, including individual parts or components.

As the engineering and manufacturing industry is, by nature competitive, the design stage can contribute mightily to corporate success or failure. The two factors which would seem to provide this edge, as they have for the past 50 years, are speed and integrity in design and manufacture.

Designs must be manufactured. But design alternatives, revisions, versions, and iterations may be investigated and analyzed before a final production decision is reached. In this way the expenses of add-on production and experimentation are avoided.

Ultimately, however, a design is created so that a company can make a product and sell it at a profit.

Traditionally, the preferred method of design has always been through manually prepared plans, bills of material, and estimates. Even as we enter the 1990s, the majority of engineering drawings and take-offs are still done on manual drafting boards with T-squares and calculators. The traditional approach to engineering design has been the same for years; rough concept sketches of a new part or assembly are put together by either the engineering staff itself or in conjunction with a specialized product design group or model shop.

From these rough drafts, a physical mock-up of the product or part is produced so that the viability of the design can be further studied. In the case of a smaller company, this step is often completed outside the firm at an independent design or model shop. Only after this step are the artistic or functional merits of the design considered.

Unfortunately, the time lag between the steps can be considerable and even further extended if the initial design is found to be somehow flawed, a condition common to most designs. This initial procedure of rough concept design and ultimate confirmation can be the most time-consuming portion of any engineering team's timesheets. For every change in design, there is a time-consuming procedure for redesign; all activity stages are reset to the beginning, and the work starts again.

A great deal of effort is required in these initial design stages since this is the time to identify and correct flaws. Consideration must be given to many factors before actual production planning can begin. Product or part design most often must pass some or all of these tests:

1. Are government standards for the product or part met or exceeded?
2. Can the item or product be made within a specified budget?
3. Does the design conform to the industry's accepted standard?
4. In the case of retail or consumer products particularly, have all artistic and aesthetic factors been considered?
5. In an innovative or revolutionary design, is there a general and favorable acceptance of the finished product by employees, vendors, and customers?
6. Can the item or product be produced within a specified lead time as determined by market demand?

After the initial design has been approved, which can be a lengthy procedure in itself, the job of preparing working drawings and manufacturing plans commences. The traditional methods of manual drafting are the tools often used at this stage. While the drawings produced are effective in conveying a visual message to the rest of the manufacturing team, other necessary information must still be gathered manually. Bills of materials, manufacturing schedules, part or component attributes must be obtained using a manual method.

Any changes to the working drawings, and there are usually many of them, will necessitate changes all along the line. Materials may change, parts counts will vary, and so on. Lead times will obviously suffer any time a change in design is made, so that compensation in time must be made to account for these inevitable changes.

To repeat, since design time consumes much of the Time To Market, it is imperative that this period be as short as possible. There are a number of ways the time demanded for design can be cut. The most obvious is to automate the process using computers. People who have been designing manually for years claim that they can work as fast in producing the first mock-up as anyone using a computer. But few would claim that design changes can be done in the same time. Revisions of a single element of a drawing can be done in minutes on a CAD system, but will often take hours if done manually because of the need to redo the entire drawing. Of course there may be the temptation in a manual process to either ignore the change or produce minor changes, but this can have serious consequences down the road for manufacturing if optimized drawings are not used.

Some people are still not convinced about the advantages of CAD. So let us examine the pros and cons of each method.

Manual Design Methods

It is estimated that of all potential CAD users, only about one-third use computers to assist their design activities. There are a number of reasons for this and all are often seen as advantages for continuance of manual design.

- The manual system has been around for many years. It works, so why change?
- Most design engineers have been trained to work manually, so it is easy to find people to undertake manual design functions.
- People naturally resist change. So why make life difficult for them by forcing them to adapt to new technologies?
- The cost of continuing with existing methods is undoubtedly less expensive than investing in hardware, software, training, and consulting.
- Horror stories about Computer-Aided Design abound. So why switch to something that may not work?

Everything that has advantages, has a bad side too. Among the most commonly experienced and admitted disadvantages are that:

- manual design has been around for a great many years. It has hardly changed. And that surely must indicate something is wrong.
- It is slow.

Designs are now so complex that it is difficult to correctly produce them right the first time. So the need for change is all but inevitable. And it is design modification that is so extremely time-consuming since an entire drawing may need to be redone to accommodate a single change. Searching, sorting, and retrieving records are fairly simple. And changes are, too. For example: a shaft, the dimensions may need to change in any one of several parameters such as: length, outside diameter, inside diameter, length step, or surface finish. A common rationale against CAD adoption is exemplified in the case of an outside diameter needing to be changed. The rationale is that this can be done simply by updating the spreadsheet in the database, by tying in a number. This datum will automatically update the corresponding entities on the drawing.

Computer-Aided Design Methods

There are a number of advantages to CAD.

- CAD is often seen as a step which can lead an organization toward Computer-Integrated Manufacturing. But CAD does not lead directly to CIM. Nor does a successful CAD installation guarantee a successful CIM implementation. Drafting is a very minor activity when compared to all manufacturing activities. So it follows that CAD will be one component of CIM. But CAD is a good—even essential—starting point for a CIM program. It requires that people become comfortable with the use of micro, mini or mainframe computer hardware and software. CAD can also promote a uniform, portable electronic data storage system for design geometry.
- Filing and retrieval are easy. CAD software allows the designer to attach attributes, or non geographic properties to drawing entities and input them into a database. This base is easy to retrieve based on the drawing title, drawing creation date, designer name, or bills of material data.

- Repetitive tasks are easy. For example, if one is manually designing a part with a number of sockethead d-cap screws, each would have to be drawn using a circle and hex template. With a CAD system, the designer has access to an unlimited number of symbols in a library, each of which are readily accessible to insert into the drawing, once, twice, 50 or 100 times. The process becomes one of drawing assembly as opposed to individual creation. As the library of parts grows, the drafts-person never has to re-draw those parts.
- Changing the text is simple. With a manual system text has to be erased or pasted over.
- CAD systems can link, ultimately, with other elements of the manufacturing process. For example, a designer can influence production of a part by modifying it. The data can be sent to the CAM software which converts it into numerical control code. This data in turn can be sent to a milling machine which will cut and carve the part to new design specifications.

THE IMPACT OF CAD ON PEOPLE

CAD has changed people's working lives in a variety of ways. The positive changes include:
- use of more sophisticated tools;
- work may be more challenging;
- work may be more interesting;
- less monotony;
- more creativity.

As technology has advanced, new challenges have presented themselves and each has required more learning and experimentation, giving participants a feeling of self-fulfillment and growth.

There is a negative side too. Frustration occurs with the difficulty that operators have in meeting the expectations of managers. Too often, management members find themselves sold on the idea that CAD will revolutionize their design operations, not appreciating that it takes longer than overnight to get results. It takes time to exceed the speed of drawing manually. Operators may take several weeks to become adept with the technology and build a significant data bank to use. Until then, operators usually feel more and more stressed as they try to meet the unrealistic expectations of others.

Finally, all too often people are inadequately trained. This causes enormous frustration and delay. Hitting a wrong key and producing the wrong function is difficult to reverse without resorting to manual keyboard use. And having to find solutions in a manual also is frustrating because of the length and complexity of some manuals for first-time users.

DEFINING CAD/CAM

Computer-Aided Design (CAD), Computer-Aided Manufacturing (CAM), and their combination into CAD/CAM as well as Computer-Assisted Engineering (CAE) and Computer-Integrated Manufacturing (CIM) are all methods used by engineers and designers to enhance design and manufacturing capability. Each is described as follows:

1. **Computer-Aided Design (CAD)** sometimes called CADD (Computer-Aided Design and Drafting) refers to a computer's ability to provide a platform to actually design and draft a particular part or assembly. It replaces the traditional drafting table and T-square. Drawings created using CAD can be outputted to a plotter or printer to obtain a hard copy of the work. CAD can be the basis for building an entire Computer-integrated manufacturing system.

2. **Computer-Aided Manufacturing (CAM)** refers to a computer's ability to control the machine tools that perform the manufacturing process. Information is obtained usually from a CAD drawing and a code is generated in a form that the particular machine tool will understand. CAM existed before CAD in the form of numerical control (NC) programming. Historically, the NC programmer had control over geometric data used to create NC programs. The programmer received a blueprint or sketch from engineering—the original engineering database—then interpreted the drawing and (re)defined the geometry according to the requirements for machining the part, whether in two-dimensional data or three-dimensional data. Any engineering changes made to the original blueprint were painstakingly communicated to all who needed them.

3. **CAD/CAM** refers to a process continuum during which computers and information processing technology are applied to the design and manufacture of a product. In some highly sophisticated Computer Integrated Manufacturing (CIM) systems, where large amounts of time, effort, and dollars have sometimes been invested, this scenario is true. In most companies, however, CAD/CAM is not yet a continuum. Rather, islands of automation, such as a CAD system for design, are linked with other islands, such as a CAM system and numerical control machine tools. These islands are usually dependent on human operators. Human intervention bridges all the islands.

4. **Computer-Assisted Engineering (CAE)** refers to a computer's ability to generate information about a part or assembly (such as centers of gravity, moments of inertia, etc.) by analyzing the data regarding the part. In a true integrated system, this information is obtained from a CAD drawing of the part or assembly.

5. **Computer-Integrated Manufacturing (CIM)** is the integration of all the above components into a true computerized design system.

CAD Systems

Most CAD applications can be seen as an electronic drawing board, in much the same way as word processing is mechanical handwriting. While the drawing function is automated, with the associated time savings, CAD has greatest value when used to speed editing of drawings. Editing is now proven to be useful even in sophisticated operations such as the design of printed circuit boards.

CAD Costs are Dropping while Sophistication Grows

The technology of CAD/CAM changes daily. The power usefulness and costs of systems bear little resemblance to those of yesterday.

Consider costs. Major marketers of systems in earlier days charged upward of a half a million dollars for proprietary hardware and software. With the proliferation of more and increasingly powerful PCs, an exploding market helped bring about significant economies which, in turn, cut purchase prices to one-tenth that of earlier systems. Now, an effective system can be bought for less than $10,000.

For companies with smaller budgets, the workstation platforms offer power and performance that five years ago were possible only with multi-million dollar mainframes.

Current workstations allow larger and more sophisticated applications, such as finite element analysis, truly a futuristic tool. They permit "what-if" estimation of the effects of such esoteric factors as metal fatigue, electrostatic conflict, and even such unlikely considerations as inadvertent remote site stress creation.

CAD Speeds Change

CAD designers and drafters usually can complete final drawings well ahead of their manual counterparts since they have the ability to "take specific features of a design and copy them to other areas of the design, a function which eliminates repetitive drawing.

"Sections of the design can be moved around, and the screen and images can be rotated to present different angles and perspectives. The system can change the scale of a part of the design or the whole design, it can focus in and enlarge parts of the design to show assembly procedures, with there-is-no-question clarity.

For instance, it can perform fit and tolerance checks in design. In addition, once a drawing has been completed, it can be stored in a design library or database which is readily accessible in subsequent design efforts."[5]

CHOOSING A CAD SYSTEM

Implementation of an automated system gives a unique opportunity to review operations from a fresh perspective based on the capabilities that the new system will provide. Information flows will change, and new data will be available. Some tasks or functions may be merged or eliminated, and new requirements may need to be addressed. Lines of reporting and communication will change with organizational structure revised accordingly.

---

[5] David Robertson and Jeff Wareham, "Changing Technology and Work: Northern Telecom," *A CAW Technology Report,* October 1989.

If the reason for implementing CAD is simply to replace drawing boards with computers, because everyone else is doing the same, or just to increase drafting productivity, almost any CAD system will do. Even low-end CAD programs will improve drawing quality and increase productivity. As a starting point for a CIM program, however, not just any CAD system will do.

When choosing a CAD system with CIM in mind, choose a proven one. Although the products of some start-up CAD vendors seem superior to mainstream CAD products, do not gamble on the success of a "WonderCAD" package. The success of a given CAD product is not just a function of its wondrous features or lack thereof, but also of marketing savvy, financing, timing, and plain old luck. Early success does not guarantee continued success, but a proven market leader is more likely to survive than is a startup. The point, of course, is that a CIM system cannot be built on a foundation that includes an outdated CAD system.

Ideally, the CAD system's drawing file structure is documented and accessible, that is, drawing files can be edited with other programs. CAD vendors who began in the minicomputer and mainframe CAD arena are more likely to allow this type of access than are vendors who began with micros. Some of these vendors even provide non graphic drawing file editors as basic software components.

The CAD system should include programming facilities: a CAD programming language, a host language interface, or both. A CAD programming language should be a general purpose programming language augmented by CAD-specific functions. A simple macro facility is of questionable value. CAD programming facilities are used typically to implement parametric design, but that is not the reason for including them in this list of features. The reason is that programs written in CAD programming language can be used in data management tasks, if the language includes a reasonable number of file handling functions.

Ideally, the CAD programming language should include a basic data management system as well as file handling functions, including database search and retrieval functions. A number of CAD packages also offer database management system interfaces. In most cases, the interface is specific to a particular DBMS program, and the appropriate data management functions are included in the CAD programming language.

Warren Vandal, a CAD/CAM consultant at CADworks in Toronto, gives a number of warnings to would-be converters to CAD/CAM. First, he says, get senior management backing. Start-up of CAD/CAM applications is more than the introduction of new technology. The applications can change the competitive advantage of a company. In reality, they are agents for strategic change. Management needs to establish how competitors are utilizing these new technologies. They need also to look beyond their industry to see what others are doing to harness this technology. When they see how CAD/CAM can reduce design time by 50% or more, their support for the best hardware and/or software and training combination will grow.

Once the importance of CAD/CAM is established as essential technology,

84

users need to become informed before committing dollars to a system. Get as much information as possible. Read books and magazines. Attend trade fairs. Visit other companies that have been down the same road. Find out what they did well, and more importantly what went wrong. And if they had to do it all again, what would they do differently?

Having made the decision to "go," find a dealer to work with. The decision should be based on at least these factors: How long has the dealer been in business? Have they done installations similar to yours? Do they represent one software house, or a number? What has been their experience in your industry? What training facilities do they have? What is the nature of after-sales service?

Training , perhaps, is the key component. Software effectiveness and value is optimized by the quality of training for its use. People with inadequate training find that they cannot speed design because they really cannot use the software.

Next, Vandal says, set realistic goals. CAD/CAM applications are not instant solutions. Typically it takes three to six months before there are any significant benefits.

Before using CAM on the shop floor, a study of existing practices and systems is crucial. Putting an overlay of CAM on poor methods brings limited benefit. Removing inefficiencies and bottlenecks before automating processes, produces much larger gains.

Also, implementation should be phased in. Doing it too quickly can cause major disruptions. As people learn the system and realize the benefits, they will be more likely to support additional applications, and get them done faster and better as experience grows.

THE USE OF COMPUTERS IN MANUFACTURING

Industry's mounting use of computers is seldom successful if it reflects a drive to replace people: rather, it should be a move to reduce the number of mundane mind-numbing repetitive jobs through automation. Computers have the greatest value when they are integrated into a network of common software languages. In this way, they can move information from one system to another to promote communications and common understanding. An integrated system promotes a schedule that optimizes the use of all resources; human, materials, and finances.

Ideally, computers used in the design and manufacturing process should work together. A single network is created by:

- centralizing design and manufacturing computer systems in a common location;
- linking together dissimilar systems to exchange data;
- providing direct sharing of common data for all steps in the manufacturing process; and
- to make it most effective, providing easy user access to the data banks for users.

Computerized equipment in manufacturing facilities can be viewed in two categories. The first is the *robot* which cannot only be controlled by a computer but is, itself, programmable equipment. The early 1950s saw the proliferation of single-function machines as attempts were made to replace people with equipment that could work reliably around the clock. The automotive industry was a leader in this area, installing robots to do some menial jobs. Typical tasks included spray painting and spot welding.

With time, robots became more effective as one part of a flexible system.

The second category is *programmable equipment*, a term which refers to a broad range of machines that use digital logic and programmable electronic devices to direct functional performance in many ways. Examples include:

- computerized numerical control (CNC) machines can make metal molds, parts, or fixtures of various sizes and shapes.
- tape controlled drills can deliver an infinite variety of predetermined holes.
- automatic part insertion machines now can place a range of different parts into a variety of objects such as circuit boards. Some of these machines can also perform sequence insertion, which eliminates the need to sequence components into types.
- materials handling systems, and
- maintenance.

With quality now a key variable in differentiating suppliers, the importance of testing and inspection by operators is vital. However, the process is tedious and time-consuming for many. To cope with the problem, some organizations resort to smaller samples, but this leaves them open to the pass-through of substandard products or parts that may reach the client. To address this concern, more use is made of automated test and inspection, which can do a 100% test with almost no delay in the process. On metal can lines, for example, instead of testing for pinholes, or leaks, with a water test or visual scan, laser technology is far more accurate and significantly faster as testers simply reject any items through which the laser has penetrated.

Automated inspection checks the integrity of each part of the process before any additional value-added activity is performed. Automated testing, on the other hand, assesses the functional integrity of the whole system, including its components.

GETTING A PAYBACK

The benefits of CAD/CAM clearly seem obvious. So why have new installations and applications not swept through the manufacturing world? And why have organizations that made some attempt at utilizing such systems, since abandoned them? The reason, most experts agree, is poor primary planning coupled with ad hoc implementation. Inevitably, the result is higher than expected start-up costs and poor-results system use.

To avoid these problems, Carol Beatty and John Gordon of Queen's University, School of Business at Kingston, Ontario, suggest the following remedies:

1. **Define productivity broadly**. When firms define productivity as broadly as possible, they include payback calculations that embrace yield, scrap and material-cost savings, improvements in quality control and reductions

in errors, rework, repairs, and rejects. Aside from savings in indirect labor, computer systems can reduce production lead times and improve flexibility in making product changes. By considering these items, firms can better justify the time required to select the right system and thus the money required to train operating personnel.

2. **Upgrade the efficiency** of manufacturing processes before using computers.

3. **Revise management-reward systems** so that costs and benefits are on a company-wide basis. For example, if the total cost of the computer system must be recovered by the drafting section alone, the manager will resist computerization. By contrast, section and department managers will champion rather than resist computers if budget calculations reflect their functional involvement and benefit.

4. **Change reporting relationships** to encourage cooperation between design/engineering and manufacturing. Top management needs to prevent any "we-they" conflict among users of the computer functions. Step one, of course, is to ensure compatibility in hardware and software across the organization.

5. **Budget sufficient time and money for training.** Productivity gains are directly proportional to this kind of investment. Allow five months for personnel to equal their previous manual system proficiency.

6. **Anticipate a net increase in engineering-department payroll.** Most purchasers of computer systems learn quickly that it pays to hire a systems manager to take care of the hardware and software. Although computer-assisted design and manufacturing can even double productivity, the demand for slight variations or improvements to designs expands in direct proportion to the system's capacity to generate them, a condition that is usually much to be desired.

7. **Counteract uncertainty and resistance** among management and operating personnel with information and involvement. Communicate often with operators. Seek their input in equipment selection, modification, programming, and customizing. Reinforce the efforts of middle management by appointing a senior manager to act as "godfather" and to lend additional expertise, credibility, and political skills to project implementation.

8. **Plan ahead**. The most successful computer implementations involve the appointment of a project manager and/or steering committee well in advance of equipment selection and installation. The individual or team can use the time to consult with all personnel about their needs and how the implemen-

tation should proceed. In this way, personnel share ownership in the project's design and become committed to its successful implementation.

CASE STUDY

Sewell Plastics

Innovative product development and vigorous customer service helped make Sewell Plastics, Inc., the largest manufacturer of rigid plastic containers in the United States. The company designs and produces a complete line of plastic containers with manufacturing activities in 23 production facilities in 16 states as well as Canada. Sewell Plastics currently supplies 35% of the U.S. market for beverage containers, and the company is making inroads into containers for the food industry.

In the early 1980s, Sewell Plastics realized the demand for new plastic containers was growing rapidly, as the lower cost, lighter weight, and durability of plastics were found to be ideal replacements for traditional glass. The growth in demand brought problems, however. Packagers were asking for more innovative containers to help them differentiate their products from competitive offerings on crowded store shelves. The design and drafting department at Sewell found it increasingly difficult to keep up.

Without a CAD system, every container had to be painstakingly designed and dimensioned by hand. Volumetric calculations were done manually, often resulting in rough approximations of how much product each bottle or jar would hold. To find the precise volume of irregularly shaped containers, it was necessary to carve full-size wooden models, submerse them in water, and accurately measure the amount of water displaced. Using this method, an experienced designer might have to spend several weeks working with the prototype shop to incrementally re-shape a container model, measure displacement every time the model changed until the desired capacity was attained, and only then could final drawings be prepared and released to the mold maker.

To serve its growing list of customers and generate a greater number of unique container designs, Sewell Plastics determined that a CAD/CAM system was necessary. The benefits of a solids modeling approach, especially on-demand, as well as mass properties calculations and good visualization capabilities, were important to the company, so Sewell Plastics paid particular attention to finding a system easy to use and with the ability to quickly and accurately compute container capacities. In addition to designing plastic containers, Sewell Plastics also anticipated using the system for possible reconfiguration of manufacturing plant layouts, determining plant engineering priorities, creating specialized machinery designs, and designing machining molds for prototypes.

One of the reasons Sewell Plastics chose a solids-based CAD/CAM system rather than a conventional 3-D wireframe system came from the characteristics of solid models. A solid model is a computer-coded, three-dimensional representation of reality, providing a complete, unambiguous model from which it is possible to determine mass properties, physical characteristics, thermal properties, stress, and more. Since the solid model is a simulation of reality (electronic prototype), Sewell Plastics' engineers wanted to be able to design a container, analyze it as if it were real, and make modifications prescribed by the results of the analysis. Thus, solid models would let them reduce or, in some cases eliminate, expensive and time-consuming physical prototypes.

In general, solid modeling systems have been criticized for slowness. However, by storing solid models in dynamic memory, Sewell Plastics' CAE/CAD/CAM system responds to commands immediately, thus eliminating this perceived objection.

Sewell Plastics' system can store solid model geometry much more compactly and efficiently than other CAD/CAM systems because it has been optimized for solids. When a container design is complete, both the data and the construction "process," which has been charted by the CSG tree, are saved. By saving the process, anyone who later accesses the design can understand how the object was designed and so gain a time savings.

System color shading capability makes it possible to paint and realistically shade solid models, giving Sewell Plastics' marketing department realistic, photographic-like designs to review with clients, and so avoid expensive, less-attractive, and sometimes inaccurate technical drawings that might have been produced manually.

Because a solid model defines an object completely, mass properties are determined instantaneously and accurately. Curve lengths, surface areas, weights, volumes, centers of gravity, moments of inertia, and radii of gyration are among calculations always available. Mass properties are important in the plastic container business because accurate statements of container capacities are just as important as size and shape calculations.

For complex shapes, Sewell Plastics enhances solid models using sculptured surfaces. The CAE/CAD/CAM system provides integral surface modeling technology for modeling the intricate sculptured surfaces of plastic containers. After creating a solid model, the system generates information for precisely machining the container mold from the surface boundary. Surfaces are created and modified with many of the same tools used in solid modeling.

A high-performance CAE/CAD/CAM system for designing containers must also offer advanced capabilities for generating parametric contours. Parameters such as distance, length, angle, and radius, once defined, must be easy to modify without altering the underlying characteristics of the original contour. Designers at Sewell Plastics now often develop families of containers with small, medium, and large sizes, using such parametric procedures.

Further, Sewell Plastics' CAD/CAM system includes a powerful programming language which provides a complete tool kit for capturing empirical information and automating the container design process. For example, one program references solid models of newly designed containers and automatically designs the preforms used in the blow-molding process so that each can be evaluated.

Quick, accurate generation of drawings is a fundamental requirement of any effective CAD/CAM system. By integrating 3-D descriptions of models with advanced construction, dimensioning, and detailing features, coherent, unambiguous drawings can be produced easily and efficiently. Automatic hidden-line removal makes it easy to see and work with various views. Errors are eliminated, and users are freed of the constraints of describing complex 3-D geometry within a 2-D drawing.

Different departments at Sewell Plastics use information about a project in different ways, which means all data must be consistent, accessible, and shared freely and efficiently throughout the organization. Because information is not stored at a single physical location, the distributed database allows data to reside throughout various storage devices, no matter where installed, with no loss of integrity. Distributed databases are essential to support the concept of simultaneous engineering using today's high-performance engineering workstations, server nodes, and local area networks.

In addition to shortening product development cycles, the CAE/CAD/CAM system is an effective selling tool. Customers often visit the design center and sit with a product designer to take part in creating a new container using solids modeling. Client participation, which is usually most enthusiastic, helps ensure that there are no surprises downstream. This approach works so well that Sewell Plastics created a new CAE/CAD/CAM-equipped conceptual design studio to encourage customers to actively participate with designers from the earliest stages of container development to actual production scheduling.

Today, with over six years of experience in solids-based design, three full-time product designers, working on a network of Digital VAX stations, complete three times as many designs as the six designers and draftsmen earlier responsible for new product development at Sewell Plastics. Company-wide, the work force is 15% smaller than it was three years ago, but it produces 40% more bottles. Among other things, the bottles are 30% lighter than a decade ago, which makes them less expensive to manufacture. Proud of the substantial gains in productivity and manufacturability, Sewell Plastics invites new customers to watch and participate in the design process as ideas and rough sketches become reality through the power of solids modeling. A prospective customer can visit the Atlanta design in the afternoon, and within a period of a few days to three weeks, receive prototype containers. To do this, Sewell Plastics transfers both drawings and IGES-format data files to prototype mold making facilities equipped with CNC machining systems.

With the plastic container industry currently requiring an average of three to four months to deliver a prototype product, Sewell Plastics' turnaround time between concept and samples is an impressive example of the power of CAE/CAD/CAM at work in reducing the Time To Market.

The benefits of the system don't stop at product design. Sewell Plastics also uses it to plan facility and equipment layout at its manufacturing centers. Sewell

Plastics prefers to do their plant layouts in three dimensions due to the complex up-down conveyor systems and materials-handling systems used. Every machine needs to be checked for interferences, and the CAE/CAD/CAM system is perfect for this application. In addition, Sewell Plastics uses the system to design the complex, one-of-a-kind container manufacturing machinery used at their plants and has plans to machine molds for making prototype containers as well.

Sewell Plastics is proud of its return on investment since installing solid-modeling-based CAD/CAM. Payback came within one year on the $300,000 spent on hardware, software, and training. Best of all, this superb return on investment is credited to straight productivity gains. Most importantly, Sewell gets more done in less time and a lower unit cost.

Adapted from George L. Leblanc, "How Sewell Plastics Harnesses the Power of CAE/CAD/CAM," *SME Technical Paper* MS90-774.

CASE STUDY

Compact Industries

This firm long specialized in the manufacture of a single product line—non conductive wooden ladders for the public utility and telecommunications industry—with great success and profitability. For some 30 years they were generally regarded, as the sole supplier in Canada. Compact Industries' ladders were used almost exclusively by their customers, mainly because of habit and availability.

The design for Compact ladders had been done in the 1950s and because of the nature of the product no significant redesigning had ever been done. Likewise, the method of manufacturing had changed little. The frequency, size, and regularity of utility and government orders had not even nudged the company to look for ways to trim manufacturing costs. However, any outside observer would have said the company was "stodgy."

About 1985, the company awoke to a serious crisis. The market for its sole product was seriously sagging. Wooden ladders, although excellent insulators against electric shock, were very heavy. The introduction of lighter, more non conductive materials that were now suitable for ladder construction had become available. In fact, several competitors introduced new product lines that incorporated the new composite materials. It became clear that the company's future depended on producing a product line based on new materials. Because the competition had already announced new products, it was evident that the design and manufacture of a new product line would have to be fast.

A new engineering team member was hired to oversee the production of the new product line. It had already been decided that pultruded (extruded) fiberglass likely would be the best replacement material for the ladders. However, a final materials choice would depend on extensive testing to ensure product safety and integrity as well as manufacturability. The new engineering leader agreed that tests were needed to ensure that fiberglass would meet all specifications. However, he noted, if time constraints placed on the project were to be met, it just couldn't be done. A total retooling of the manufacturing area would be necessary to change weight parameters.

But the new engineer had an ace up his sleeve. Through personal experience, he knew that computerization could be the salvation of the project. His main goal was to test fiberglass shape designs without actually building them. He wanted to be able to test strengths, centers of gravity, and moments of inertia of specified shapes to determine each shape's properties and thus its inherent suitability for manufacture. If this could be achieved, the lead time for the design portion of the project would be reduced from four to six months to three to four weeks. Success would put the company at a significant competitive advantage. If the new ladders could be designed to suit existing shop tooling, lengthy retooling times and related costs could be avoided.

An experienced local CAD vendor was asked to:

1. Provide a computer system to facilitate the design and drafting of individual part sections and complete assemblies. The finished drawings had to be easily modified as many design changes were anticipated.
2. Provide a computer system allowing relatively simple shapes analysis and automatic evaluation of pertinent physical properties.
3. Make possible hard-copy drawing information as required.
4. Ensure that learn-to-use streams would be logical, acceptable, and easy for draftsmen and engineers.
5. Verify that training for all aspects of the computer system could be immediate.
6. Be sure that budget would not be exceeded.

With these factors in mind, the CAD vendor made recommendations. A single MS-DOS © based computer with color display was chosen for its versatility and compatibility. Because the finished drawings for manufacturing were not large, a small A-B size pen plotter with multi-color capability was chosen for drawing output. A simple dot-matrix printer was included for output of engineering reports. Because the actual drawings of the individual components were fairly small and straightforward, an easy to learn 2-D drafting and design software package was identified. The key to the CAD system was the ability to take the drawing information generated in the 2-D drafting software and transfer it to another software package for analysis.

The decision to proceed was made after the system was demonstrated, most effectively on a sample part drawing, by the CAD vendor. The computer equipment was installed later that week and CAD system training followed. Actual work on the system began within three weeks of its conception, an extremely fast implementation to be sure! The intended shapes for the ladder components were designed and drafted quickly and the required data was extracted. After the optimum shapes were decided upon, the fiberglass supplier was given the finished engineering drawings and costs were established. The lead time from commencing work on the CAD system to approving the new designs was reduced, as a result, to only four weeks.

Speed in design and manufacturing had been achieved most effectively. The company is now enjoying such success with the new product line that the old line of wooden ladders has been dropped from production. The keys to the conversion to Computer-Aided Design in this case were quick implementation and effective sourcing of only those components necessary to complete the intended tasks.

CASE STUDY

Patterson Industries Ltd.

This company had a long-lived reputation as a producer of high-quality boilers and pressure vessels for the international market. Most of the units sold were custom built to customer specifications. The owner of the company had identified several competitors currently using Computer-Aided Design to assist in design and manufacture. Because many of the parts used in boiler systems are similar, conversion to a CAD system seemed a naturally evolutionary step. Even though the owner had a background in computers, none of it was in Computer-Aided Design. In addition, none of his current design staff had any experience with CAD. Intelligently, the owner decided to collect as much information as possible about possible conversion to CAD. He did this by attending several trade shows featuring vendors who specialized in CAD systems.

Because the individual assembly drawings created by Patterson's design staff were of relatively low complexity, it was reasoned that one of the less expensive CAD software packages that ran on industry standard IBM compatible PCs would be most suitable.

In the fall of 1987, Patterson Industries acquired an IBM-AT compatible computer, with color monitor, mouse, pen plotter, and CAD software. Because the software was advertised as very easy to learn, no software training was requested. The only training taken was a brief orientation of the operation of the CAD system's individual components. The bulk of the software training was left up to the individual designers. In other words, they were to become self-taught. The other perceived benefit of this self-training method was that it would be much cheaper than outside training. Or so the owner thought. Several other CAD system components were also offered at "budget-prices" that would save money for the company initially, but they lacked some of the performance characteristics of the higher end components offered.

After several months, the designers and the owner were somewhat dismayed to find that the extra performance they expected was not realized. They found that they were producing drawings and designs more slowly using CAD than they were while they were using the old manual drafting method. Furthermore, they were disappointed in the speed performance of the computer system itself. The inexpensive unit they had purchased was just not up to the task of serious CAD work. The system was too slow to regenerate the screen every time a designer wanted to zoom on a portion of his work.

It was also found that many expected time-saving functions of the CAD software were not realized, simply because nobody knew how to use the program. To familiarize others in the design engineering staff, existing users of the software were required to try to train new staff. This further tied up precious design time.

After approximately a year, the owner decided to make an evaluation of his first CAD workstation. His evaluation in summary:

1. None of the designers were able to attain potential CAD speed. They could still work faster, manually. This was because of a combination of:
    a) Insufficient training on the CAD software. The complex nature of CAD software makes self-training extremely difficult.
    b) The IBM compatible hardware purchased was not suited to function as a CAD workstation.
    c) The maximum productivity for their design application was not realized with "easy-to-use" CAD software packages. Clearly, more sophisticated software packages incorporating parametrics were needed.
2. Though productivity was not as expected, Patterson customers were impressed by the quality and accuracy of finished drawings and designs.
3. Even after a year, there was still enthusiasm in the design group for working on the CAD system.
4. Although the first year could not be considered a success because of low productivity, it was a worthwhile learning experience. There were enough minor successes to consider upgrading the system to compensate for its weak areas.

QUESTIONNAIRE

Answer the following questions ranking your answers from 1 to 5.
1- represents very poor,
2 - poor,
3 - average,
4 - good, and
5 - very good.

Use of Computers in Design and Manufacturing

Before Implementation

- Have you conducted research that has convinced you of the advantage of Computer-based technology to your operation?
    1 - None,
    2 - A little,
    3 - Some,
    4 - Fair amount,
    5 - Extensive.

- Are your existing manual systems as effective/efficient as they could be?
  1 - No,
  2 - A little,
  3 - Somewhat,
  4 - Fairly effective,
  5 - Excellent.

- Have you reviewed the CAD/CAM systems of other organizations?
  1 - None,
  2 - Small amount,
  3 - Somewhat,
  4 - Fairly well,
  5 - Extensive.

- Do you have management support to acquire an effective CAD/CAM system needing extensive training/support?
  1 - None,
  2 - Luke warm,
  3 - Some,
  4 - Good,
  5 - Unequivocal.

- Does your management believe in the strategic and competitive advantage of CAD/CAM?
  1 - No,
  2 - A little,
  3 - Somewhat,
  4 - Fairly convinced,
  5 - Total belief.

After Implementation
- Do your designers use CAD tools?
  1 - Never,
  2 - Infrequently,
  3 - Sometimes,
  4 - Most times,
  5 - Always.

- Is the database of your CAD system shared throughout your organization?
  1 - Never,
  2 - Infrequently,
  3 - Sometimes,
  4 - Most times,
  5 - Always.

- Are 100% of your designs available on a database and current?
  1 - None,
  2 - Few,
  3 - About half,
  4 - Most,
  5 - All.

- Can your CAD system modifications influence the manufacturing process through a shared database?
  1 - No,
  3 - Somewhat,
  5 - Total integration of both systems.

- Have you combined manually driven operations into computer-driven flexible manufacturing cells?
  1 - No,
  3 - Some,
  5 - All.

- Is your material handling automated?
  1 - No,
  2 - A little,
  3 - Somewhat,
  4 - Mostly,
  5 - Totally.

- Do you have software to integrate manufacturing cells into an integrated system?
  1 - No,
  3 - Somewhat,
  5 - Totally.

TOTAL SCORES

Interpretation:

In relation to the elements of Computers in Design and Manufacturing;

- 7 to 10 indicates that you are doing poorly,
- 11 to 17 indicates that you are weak,
- 18 to 25 indicates that you are O.K. but can improve,
- 26 to 31 indicates that you are in good shape with some opportunities for improvement, and
- 32 or higher indicates that you are doing a terrific job!

chapter **6**

World Class Time-Reducing Manufacturing Techniques

INTRODUCTION

In general, time-based manufacturing policies and practices differ from those of traditional manufacturers in three key ways: length of production runs, organization of process components, and complexity of scheduling procedures. For instance, traditional factories attempt to maximize production runs, while time-based manufacturers try to shorten their production runs as much as possible (see *Figure 6-1*).

The layout of a factory is vital to the realization of time-based competitive advantages. Traditional factories are usually organized by process technology centers. Parts move from one process technology center to the next. Each step consumes valuable time: parts sit, waiting to move; then move; then wait to be used in the next step. In a traditional manufacturing system, products usually gain value for only .05% to 2.5% of the time that they are in the factory.

Time-based factories are organized by product. To minimize handling and moving of parts, the manufacturing functions for a component or a product are as close together as possible. Parts flow quickly and efficiently through the factory.

Scheduling is also a source of delay and waste in most traditional factories. They use central scheduling that requires sophisticated materials resource planning and shop-floor control systems. Even though these systems are advanced, they still waste time; work orders usually flow to the factory floor on a monthly

TIME BASED	TRADITIONAL
Small batches profitable.	Profitable only in large runs.
Product and process designed simultaneouosly.	Product and process designed in linear manner.
Small inventory, fast turnover.	Large inventory, slow turnover.
Close, long term relationship with suppliers.	Acrimonious, short term, relationship with suppliers.
Engineering welcomes input from other players.	Engineers insular and unreceptive to ideas from "outsiders."
Multi-skilled staff willing to contribute as and where needed.	Single skilled people unwilling to be flexible.
Focus on collaborative approach and teamwork.	Emphasis on shifting blame and territorialism.
Continuous improvement part of daily work.	Major breakthroughs sought.
Production driven by "pull" system of customer order.	Production driven by "push" system based on forecasts.
Continuous training of people.	Minimal training of people.
Clear direction set and communicated by top management.	Little or clear direction from top management.
Collaboration between departments.	Territorialism and turf protection.

Figure 6-1. A Comparison Between Time-Based/Flexible Manufacturing and Long-Time/Inflexible Manufacturing.

or weekly basis. In the meantime, parts are idle. In time-based factories, local scheduling enables employees to make more production control decisions on the factory floor, without the time-consuming loop back to management for approval. Moreover, the combination of the product-oriented layout of the factory and local scheduling makes the total production process run more smoothly.

Toyota offers a dramatic example of the kinds of improvements that leading time-based competitors are making. Dissatisfied with the response time of a supplier, Toyota went to work. It took the supplier 15 days to produce a component after arrival of the raw materials at its factory. The first step was to cut lot sizes, reducing response time to six days. Next, Toyota streamlined the factory layout, reducing the number of inventory holding points. The response time fell to three days. Finally, Toyota eliminated all work-in-progress inventories at the supplier's plant. New response time: one day.

A cardinal mistake organizations make in their efforts to reduce costs, improve productivity or quality, is to introduce isolated "programs." Statistical Process Control (SPC), Value Engineering (VE), Just In Time (JIT) are a few examples.

Only some organizations reap the real rewards that these programs are touted to provide.

This chapter explains how SPC and JIT can add enormously to the speed in which manufacturing can respond to market needs. The chapter will also show how both these programs can be optimized with solid management practices that give real decision-making power to people at the lower levels of the organization (see *Figure 6-2*).

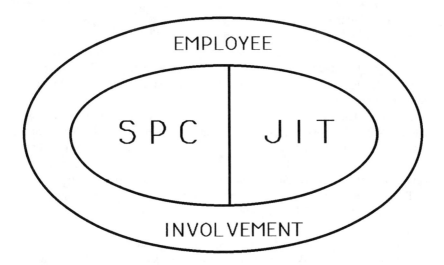

Figure 6-2. Making SPC and JIT Work With Employee Involvement.

JUST IN TIME

Introduction

The sole objective of manufacturing is to produce an acceptable product for a customer on time, at a profit. Responding quicker than any competitor at the lowest possible cost has, for the longest time, been done in a linear/batch system. That is to say, batches of product from each step in the process move together from one process to the next. From cutting, to painting, and then on to assembly. It is believed that production runs should be as long as possible. In this way, unit costs should fall as changeovers are reduced to a minimum.

In reality this seldom worked. Special customers get priority so when they place orders and want it "yesterday," the whole system comes to a standstill.

Batches are broken as time-consuming changeovers are made, resulting in significant cost increases. Work-in-process (WIP) and storage increases as parts are put aside.

Alternatively, important customer requests can be denied. They have to stand in line before being taken care of. And line-up times tend to be long. Traditional factories manufacture according to forecasting methods.

Forecasting, of course, is part science and part art. As such, it is seldom right. So, planning people need to look longer ahead. As forecasting errors occur, they become manifest in terms of higher levels of safety stocks and increased expediting of rush orders. As a result, lead times continue to grow, costs get driven upward, delays increase, and waste escalates.

Flexible Factories

The most effective way to get off the high-cost treadmill is to reduce the use of time throughout the system.

This reduces the need for lead times. A flexible, responsive factory will emerge. A flexible factory is based on much different principles than its traditional counterpart. Flexible factories thrive on short production runs. They keep costs down by reducing the complexity of setups and changeovers, thereby reducing both time and costs.

A flexible factory layout is different, too. Instead of organizing equipment in a line based on process, the factory is organized by grouping together all of the equipment that makes a single product. This is referred to as a *focused factory*. In such a system, material handling is reduced, allowing for little or no time delays between work stations or equipment (see *Figure 6-3*).

The third major difference between a traditional and a flexible manufacturing production system is the level at which decisions relating to planning and scheduling take place.

In the traditional model, production scheduling is centralized. However, in a flexible factory, the task is undertaken by employees in the focused factory. Their task is relatively simple since production runs are short —sometimes lot sizes are as small as one—and the plant layout is simple. Time is saved through quicker decision making, too. Employees do not have to wait for decisions from management or others in staff roles, many of which are delayed because of differing priorities.

How JIT Started

The earliest JIT implementation can be traced back to the days of Henry Ford. Ford's first plants were virtually integrated right from the mining of raw material to make steel, through to final production. Shiploads of materials would arrive each day sufficient only for the day's production.

The term *Just In Time* was coined by Mr. Kii Chiio Toyoda, the first president of Toyota. An executive in Toyota, Mr. Taiichi Ohno, perfected the system. His research started from the frustrations that Toyota experienced very soon after World War II, as a result of a grossly inefficient production system. Excess work,

Traditional Factory

Steps:
1. Incoming stock
2. Manufacturing process for product
3. Assembly
4. Finishing (paint, powder coating, etc.)
5. Shipment

Flexible Factory

Steps:
1. Incoming material
2. Manufacturing process (performed in a cell or system, product-oriented)
   a - cell
   b - assembly
   c - finishing
3. Shipment

Figure 6-3. Comparision of Traditional Versus Flexible Plant Layout.

waste, and uneven production were the order of the day.

Mr. Ohno found many of the answers he was looking for in a totally different environment. The American supermarket system offered ideas that he felt could be applied in a plant environment. He observed that the typical shopper would come into the supermarket with a list of items needed. The list would be based on the person's estimates based on family consumption, the size of refrigerator and closet storage capacity, and the amount of time until the next shopping trip.

The supermarket did a daily check of items sold, and ordered just enough replacement merchandise to replenish its stock.

This was different in Japan. Ohno recalled that the system was archaic. For example, if one was buying an item for home consumption, it would be delivered. But it would be impolite to buy just one of an item. So the buyer ordered a larger quantity. In the home, cupboards were constantly filled with excess foods, some of which could not be consumed because other items to mix it with were not available. Some foodstuffs would go bad before they were consumed. Others lay around, not consumed but taking up space.

Objectives of JIT

Many people consider JIT as the most effective method of production available. Because of the benefits achieved, some have described the system as "stockless production." Others define it as "production on demand." Whichever description is used, the business makes more money when costs are reduced.

And every business can reduce costs by reducing waste, since all have an excess amount of:

- inventory produced for inaccurate forecasts;
- scrap;
- rework of product not made right the first time;
- setup delays because of ineffective changeovers;
- machinery breakdown due to poor preventive maintenance;
- lost business caused by not meeting delivery schedule, and
- space where materials are stored waiting to be processed.

These sources of waste can account for up to 70% of manufacturing costs.

The Benefits of JIT

Few new initiatives in manufacturing organizations appear to have brought comparable bottom-line benefits as has JIT. The benefits are extolled by CEOs in-house as well as at conferences and in the media.

One of the most highly publicized turnarounds in the 1980s was made by Harley-Davidson, the last remaining major motorcycle producer in North America. While poor quality and high costs brought it to the brink of extinction, management and workers engineered a turnaround that has made the company the toast of those who believe in North America's ability to compete, as well as an ongoing cult of Harley devotees. Harley-Davidson's JIT program was labeled MAN, short for Materials As Needed. A drive to superb quality, inside its own plant and from suppliers, helped to reduce breakdown costs by 32% in 1982. Scrap rates dropped by more than half and rework by an astonishing 80%. With such improvements in quality, it was not surprising that warranty costs per unit fell by 46%.

A trend toward a pull system of material flow and daily parts deliveries from an increasing number of suppliers helped to increase the inventory and work in process turns from six to 17 in the following two years. Slow setup times have been slashed by 75%, allowing for increased flexibility. The average time taken to produce a bike was cut from three days to a half day.

Black and Decker, an organization known for quality tools, has long been a proponent of advanced manufacturing techniques. In a pilot plant, the application of JIT techniques brought about a 300% improvement in plant throughput. At the same time, lead times for customer orders to be fulfilled dropped by more than 50% while inventory turns were booted 10 fold.

While the Just In Time philosophy of waste elimination proves helpful in virtually all types of manufacturing (and service) environments, some types of manufacturing offer more opportunity than others.

Table 6-1 shows the estimated improvements for different types of manufacturing.

Coopers and Lybrand's Chicago Managing Partner, Dale Zampel, has found that process industries such as paper mills, chemical manufacturers, and food producers seem to have less ability to reduce setup times or improve process flow

Table 6-1. Estimated Percent Improvement for Different Industries as a Result of JIT Implementation.*

Reductions	Automotive Supplier	Printer	Fashion Goods	Mechanical Equipment	Electric Components	Range
Manufacturing						
lead time	89	86	92	83	85	83-92
Inventory						
Raw	35	70	70	73	50	35-73
WIP	89	82	85	70	85	70-89
Finished goods	61	71	70	0	100	0-100
Changeover time	75	75	91	75	94	75-94
Labor						
Direct	19	50		5	0	0-50
Indirect	60	50	29	21	38	21-60
Exempt	?	?	22	?	?	?-22
Space	53	N/A	39	?	80(est)	39-80
Cost of quality	50	63	61	33	26	26-63
Purchased Material						
(Net)	?	7	11	6	N/A	6-11
Additional						
capacity	N/A	36	42	N/A	0	0-42

* *JIT Themes and Modules,* Tool and Manufacturing Engineers Handbook, Fourth Edition, Volume 5, Society of Manufacturing Engineers, Dearborn, MI, 1986 p. 15-2.

since each part of the process is closely connected with the next. Repetitive and discrete manufacturing operations, such as metal stamping or machining, have far larger opportunities for improvement by virtue of their functional layout and more frequent and elaborate setup procedures.

However, process industries can show large benefits from better material planning and procurement since they typically consume large amounts of raw materials. In a single-source relationship with suppliers, they have the ability to negotiate significant cost, quality, and delivery advantages.

But Zampel points out that there can also be significant differences within an industry, so one should be wary of assuming gains depending upon the type of manufacturing process alone. Other factors such as operator skills and motivation, plant layout, and management-union relationships will influence the size and speed of benefits.

JIT is Based on Simple Principles
JIT is a manufacturing system, not a program. It is an integral part of the total management and manufacturing process. As such, it is dependent on a few key principles.
- **JIT is an ongoing process.** JIT never stops. No company has reached the end—perfection or zero waste. There is always room for improvement. The road is a long one, so long in fact that many companies get sidetracked.

In so doing, their journey of continuous improvement is slower and more arduous than it needs to be.

- **JIT is based on a people philosophy.** It works on the assumption that people, not machines, are the most under-utilized resource in factories. It assumes that people have ideas and energies far beyond what most organizations use. The system encourages people to get involved and take ownership of their segment of the process. A key to helping people contribute effectively is training. People might want to do the best job possible, but they will fall short if they don't have the tools or skills to do it.

- **Problems must be dealt with.** Organizations have all kinds of problems. The expression "Thank God it's Friday" came from the belief that work is unpleasant since we never seem to resolve so many of our problems. When we do so, our approach is to use "band-aid" solutions. We fail to get to the bottom (real cause) of the problem and eliminate it once and for all. We also make the mistake of solving trivial issues first. However, avoiding key issues leaves the major problems unresolved.

  Problem solving can often be compared to driving a boat in hazardous waters—hazardous because of rocks that could damage the boat. Some rocks can be seen and, therefore, easily dealt with. But many—in fact the majority—are below the surface and need to be dealt with, too. Any process based on continuous improvement requires that known and hidden problems both be dealt with.

- **The system should be kept as simple as possible.** Complex systems are rarely used. They scare most people. And a system that is not used can't be implemented. Every system needs to be simplified as much as possible to encourage universal use. Simplicity leads to major time savings, particularly in the areas of training. Simplicity also saves time because it reduces mistakes.

- **A systems approach is important.** JIT can be seen as a whole, but it is more effective when it is viewed as a system made up of a number of component parts. Compare it to a car. If we left the battery out, the car could travel downhill with some occupants having to push-start it. And if we took the wheels off, we could run the engine, but the vehicle wouldn't move. So, all the components are important. It is true that some are more important than others. Each part can operate more effectively depending on its quality. For example, a new radial tire will operate better than an old, bald one. So it is with JIT. The more effectively we execute each component part of the system, the greater the impact on the whole. The JIT system comprises many parts (*Figure 6-4*). Each component will be examined in some detail.

Synchronous Production (or Uniform Plant Loading)

In spite of its title, synchronous production (or uniform plant loading) is a simple concept. It requires that you build what you sell, on a daily basis. With most organizations, a variety of products are offered and sold, requiring manufac-

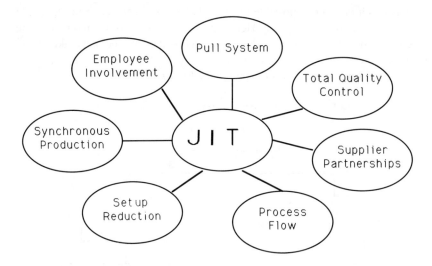

Figure 6-4. Component Parts of a JIT System.

tured batch sizes to be small. The idea of supplying from manufacturing and not from stock is revolutionary for most manufacturers since they are not geared to provide a product quickly unless it is already on the shelf.

Synchronous production requires that manufacturing cycle times equate with, but do not exceed, customer demand. In such a situation, the rate of production is not tied to machine rates, productive capacity, or sales forecasts.

In an ideal situation, a synchronized production system is driven by sales orders (pull system) that cause production to flow from one operation to the next in the production sequence. Some people have compared the flow to a drum beat that sees material flow at a consistent, even pace.

Achieving a synchronized process can lead to real time and cost savings. Lead times are reduced by as much as 90% as backlogs, caused by large batch production, disappear. Costs can be cut, as indirect labor costs fall as a result of reduced management and transportation of excess inventory between operations. Indirect labor is more effectively used as personnel are moved between work stations to ensure that production rates are achieved. People who are not needed in one part of the plant might be moved to another that needs additional resources to cope with throughput. Naturally, this is only practical if workers are cross-trained and motivated to handle different tasks with equal ability. In unionized situations, this is more challenging. For example, job classification systems may prevent an operator from doing preventive maintenance if the classification does not provide for this type of work.

The Pull System

The pull system of production responds to customer orders immediately after an order has been received. It is different from a push process which tries to move as much product as possible through the system, whether or not there are confirmed orders for the product. Hence, a pull system can bring about dramatic reduction in inventory since everything produced will be immediately taken-up in the marketplace.

A simple example illustrates the point (see *Figure 6-5*).[1]

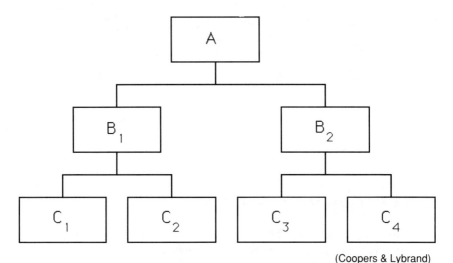

(Coopers & Lybrand)

Figure 6-5. Comparision of Pull Versus Push Manufacturing Process.

Assume that we are producing "widget wonderful," made of a number of component parts. Let us assume that a problem arises with the production of part B_1. The process is not meeting specs, so the operator has shut the machine down.

As other operators are some distance away and not in touch with the operator, they continue to produce parts C_1, C_2, C_3, and C_4.

Again, assuming that the problems relating to part B_1 cannot be overcome, the operators might switch to producing something else. Time and effort will be spent expediting other components. Also, surplus production of parts C_1, C_2, C_3, and C_4 must be moved to storage or a WIP holding area.

When production problems are eventually overcome, priorities will change again. Time and effort will be needed to reschedule each workstation to compensate for the imbalances and timing problems that have arisen.

If the same problem occurred in a plant working on a JIT system, the scenario would be quite different. We again assume that a problem halts production of part B_1. Since B_1 is not available, production of the preceding operation (A) will stop. When this happens, the demand for B_2, C_1, C_2, C_3, and C_4 will cease as there

---

[1] From Coopers & Lybrand as quoted in <u>JIT Themes and Modules</u>, *Tool and Manufacturing Engineers Handbook*, Fourth Edition. Volume 5. Society of Manufacturing Engineers, Dearborn, MI, 1988, p. 15-9.

is no Kanban to draw them through the system, so production will stop. As their production is affected and as they jointly share responsibility for the production, operators at the various workstations will converge to the problem point and assist in resolving the problem. When the problem is fixed, there is no need to realign priorities. No surplus WIP has to be dealt with.

Pull systems tend to operate in one of two modes, known as an overlapped system, or a linked system (*Figure 6-6*).

(a)

OVERLAPPED PULL SYSTEM

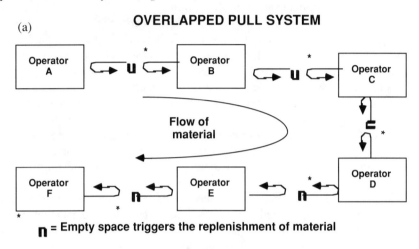

n = Empty space triggers the replenishment of material

(b)

LINKED FORM SYSTEM

(Pneumatic tube)

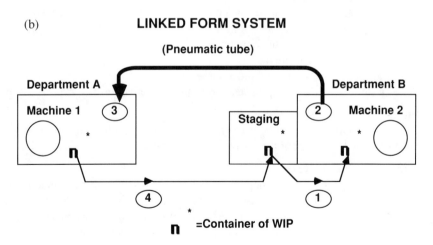

n =Container of WIP

1. Operator of Machine Two withdraws materials from Staging.
2. Operator of Machine Two issues Kanban.
3. Operator of Machine One replenishes container of WIP.
4. Container of WIP is moved to Staging.

Figure 6-6. Production System in a JIT Environment Is Usually by the Pull System, Which Can Be of the (a) Overlapped or (b) Linked Form.

The overlapped pull system uses an empty space as its "pull signal." This empty space can take the form of an empty bin which requires more parts, or a designated spot on the floor in which a certain number of units are placed. No production occurs until a signal is received to replenish an item or parts.

The overlapped system is most commonly used when workstations are in close proximity. Visual inspection triggers the decision to replenish.

Setup and Die-Changeover Time Reduction

The setup and die change refers to the time lost between the production of the last item until the production of a new item of acceptable quality is made. The time includes teardown, rebuilding of the new process, and inspection of the first pieces.

A major reason for extended setup times lies in perception and tradition. It is extremely difficult to make major improvements when people continuously look backward rather than forward. If a changeover has taken up to eight hours for the previous five years, it is hard to think in terms of 30 minutes or less now. Our perception is heavily influenced by past experience. The problem can be compared to driving a car. You can't do it by looking through the rear view mirror all the time. You have to look ahead!

In an environment geared to more demanding consumers, we no longer have the luxury of offering limited choices. We need to cater to the expanding choices of the consumer, so producing what they want is crucial. Anything we can do to produce lot sizes of one will help in this quest.

A team approach will do the job best

To make major reductions in changeover time, a team should be formed to:
- study existing practices;
- devise methods of improvement;
- implement improvements;
- train operators in the new procedures.

The key steps which will help the team reach its objectives are:

Number 1.   Pick an area for a pilot site

Identify an area where there is a significant opportunity for improvement and a willingness on the part of the people to be innovative.

Number 2.   Form a team

Recruit members from the shop, supervisors, middle management, maintenance, and engineering. This cross-section of people will ensure that each area of the shop that needs to contribute to change, "buys into" the process. Members should be chosen for their positive attitude and influence among their peers. The management person should be someone who has sufficient "clout" to influence changes quickly. The team should meet often.

Number 3.   Study the existing process

Document current methods. This can be done in any number of ways. A video tape can be useful for people to observe their own inefficiencies. A flow

110

diagram can be constructed detailing each step. Also, the time that it takes to carry out each step should be recorded. This is best done if a digital clock is activated in the video recorder.

Experience has shown that the times will be reduced measurably when people are conscious of being recorded on camera, simply because they do not want to be seen as inept.

Number 4. Categorize the activities

An analysis of the time taken to conduct each activity should be made, and then graphed. A pie chart or Pareto will highlight the area of greatest opportunity (*Figure 6-7*).

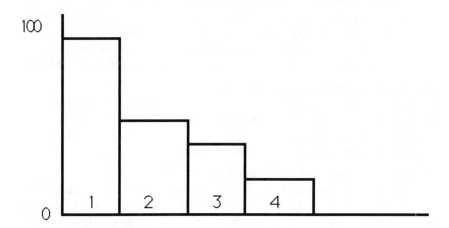

Key: 1. Adjustment and trial processing the molds and jigs.
      2. Preparation of materials, jigs, tools, molds, and fittings.
      3. Centering and fixing the measurement.
      4. Taking down and replacing molds and jigs.

Figure 6-7. Pareto Diagram of Time Exchange Die.

The analysis of activities should also include a division of the activities that can be done outside of the actual downtime and those that need to be done during the downtime period. The reason is obvious. Anything that can be done to prepare for the changeover while the machine is still running will save time. Examples include:

- preparation and assembly of molds, jigs, and tools beforehand;
- cleaning and storage of molds, jigs and tools after the machine is running.

Number 5. Find creative ways for improvement

If the group challenges all activities in a brainstorming session, they will come up with many ideas that will be time-reducing. Some will be obvious and some ingenious. Typical improvements include:

- Replacing nuts and bolts with changing devices.

- Changing devices reduce the steps taken to make a changeover and shorten the time, too.
- Reducing or eliminating adjustments.
- Anything that can promote self-squaring by the machine or fixture will save time. An analysis of machine settings will identify a few positions that cover all possibilities. These possibilities can be covered using mechanical devices, or stops, such as slots, notches, or pins.
- Color-coordinating tools and bolts. All items that are used at the same time can be color coordinated. This will help reduce mistakes and will help speed the process.
- Preheating the next die. In some shops, the remaining heat of the retaining boiler preheats the next die. Both time and money are saved.
- Using supplementary jigs. Time can be saved when installing a die into a bolster, or cutting tools directly to a clutch. In preparation for a change-up, the dies can be placed on a supplementary jig and then installed promptly when needed. This same technique can be applied to centering a drill bit.

Number 6. Document the new system

When the main changes have been tried and installed, the new procedures should be documented. This documentation should be short, to the point, and easy to follow. It should include diagrams and pictures where possible, as most operators learn more quickly by seeing than by reading.

Number 7. Train people in the new process

Time should be taken to train remaining operators in the new process. There may be some resistance to changes, so patience will be needed. On the other hand, the trainer should listen too, as new ideas might surface. These should be built into the system and the documentation revised.

Number 8. Continuously improve the process

Initial studies and changes will probably lead to time reductions in excess of 50%. But this is not the end of the road. As circumstances change, new ideas must be incorporated in the process and further improvements derived.

Integration of Suppliers

The trend toward subcontracting components to specialists seems to be a strong one. The automotive industry is a prime example. The major automotive producers are producing fewer and fewer parts, preferring to be assemblers, distributors, and marketers of vehicles. And this trend is not only feasible, but desirable, as work is given to specialists who can do it quicker, better, and cheaper.

The Traditional Approach

Subcontracting elements of one's manufacturing process does not always work effectively. Until fairly recently, the relationship with outside suppliers was adversarial. Mutual benefits were dissipated as inordinate amounts of time and energy were consumed in finding fault with one another. The adversarial relationship (which still persists in many organizations) is based on:

- having many competing sources of supply;
- playing one supplier against the other;
- buying decisions based primarily on price;
- competitive bids;
- inspection of incoming products to ensure adequate quality, and
- rating various suppliers on the basis of selective performance criteria and awarding a share of purchases based on that rating.

The Team Approach

Organizations that are in highly competitive situations need to develop a strategic advantage from relationships with suppliers. This can only be done when the supplier is considered to be an integral part of operations and is treated as an equal partner.

A reluctance to link too closely with one supplier is based on two misconceptions:

First, single sourcing can spell disaster if the source of supply stops. The stoppage could be permanent as in the case of bankruptcy, or temporary as in the case of an Act of God or labor dispute.

Second, the supplier can leak confidential information to competitors.

There are few documented cases of any of these potential disadvantages actually becoming a reality. In the first place, few companies actually single-source their production. They may give the bulk of their business to one supplier, but also give about 10% to a backup supplier "just in case." Secondly, the possibility of industrial espionage is no greater than having people from one organization leave and disclose details to competitors. Moreover, the closer the relationship with a supplier, the greater the incentive to treat the relationship as "special" and in total confidence.

Picking Members of the Team

Finding the right organizations to work with is not easy. And in some cases, it will be difficult to sever relationships that go back for some time. Yet the process of moving from multiple to few relationships is important. It is best done if suppliers are judged on objective criteria such as:

- **Price, delivery and quality variables**. It is important to check the supplier's records rather than rely on their verbal responses. For example, do they track defect rates? How have they changed over time? Who keeps the figures? Is there a chance that these numbers are altered?
- **Reputation.** It is important to check the supplier's reputation for fairness, integrity, professionalism, and attitude toward working closely with others. Do they have a strong customer bias?
- **History**. How long has this company been in business? Over the years, have they increased their level of sophistication?
- **Financial stability**. While initial contacts will probably not get you access to balance sheets, particularly if the company is privately owned, it is

possible to increase one's confidence that the supplier will not go out of business through bank checks, Dun & Bradstreet reports, and the like. For larger organizations, their stability can be checked through financial reports in publications such as Barron's, Business Week, Forbes, and other business publications.

- **Geographic location**. The closer suppliers are to you, the easier it is to work with them. Daily deliveries, face-to-face meetings, training sessions, are all facilitated.
- **Experience with JIT concepts**. Is the potential supplier involved in other JIT relationships? How have they worked? Is the organization using JIT principles in its own operation?
- **Use of electronic data interchange**. Do the suppliers have the capability to transfer information to you electronically? Are they willing to do so? Do they have the ability to network with your CAD hardware/software? Do they have plans to expand these facilities?
- **Material handling**. Does the supplier have specialized containers which can help reduce costs of transportation and material handling?
- **Efficiency**. Does the supplier run an effective production facility? Is a preventive maintenance program in place?
- **Capacity**. To what extent is the capacity of the supplier's facilities used? If significant increased business resulted from the partnership, how would they cope?

Because this information is often technical, it is best gathered by a team of people representing purchasing, engineering, and manufacturing. The data can be collated on a summary sheet (*Figure 6-8*) which will facilitate the decision-making process.

The decision-making matrix can be modified to incorporate more criteria. It can also use a weighting system to increase the value of certain criteria relative to others. For example, if being geographically close was the most important, the rating of the item might be on a one -10 scale. On the other hand, if having the capacity to share data electronically was relatively unimportant, this rating scale might vary between one and five.

The team approach to supplier relationships is characterized by a number of component parts (*Figure 6-9*).

Let us examine each in more detail.

Continuous Improvement Teams

No operation is perfect. Opportunities abound in every operation. Quality can be improved and measured in defects per million. Cycle times can be reduced and measured in minutes. Costs can be reduced and measured in terms of dollars per unit. Improvements must be discussed so that competitiveness of both parties is improved.

The size of improvements will be greater if a team approach is used. A variety of people from differing backgrounds can look at each project from a unique perspective. Having key members of the team from the purchasing company in

Suppliers	Criterion 1 Score	Criterion 2 Score	Criterion 3 Score	Criterion 4 Score	Total Score

Figure 6-8. Decision Making Matrix For Alternative Suppliers.

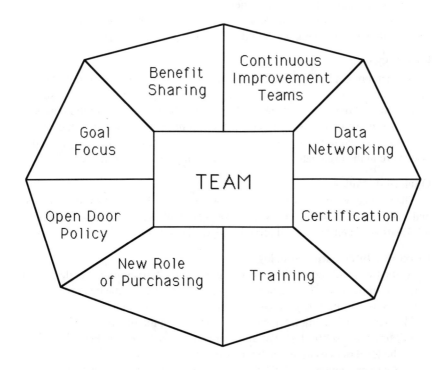

Figure 6-9. Component Parts of the Supplier Relationship in a Team Environment.

the supplier organization can be invaluable because these team members can see problems for what they are, and not have their viewpoint tainted by territorialism or narrow political perspectives.

The team will benefit significantly by inviting someone from either organization who has the reputation of a maverick. Such a person tends not to be bound by conventional wisdom. Off-the-wall ideas can often be built upon to produce solutions that are ground-breaking.

To coordinate the activities of teams that are working on individual projects, it is sometimes useful to establish a steering committee staffed equally between the two organizations to facilitate and monitor improvements from individual projects.

Depending on the level of training of the people on the teams, it might be necessary for the steering committee to provide members with training in such skills as project management, teamwork, running effective meetings, cost/benefit analysis, decision making, and problem solving.

Goal Focus

While improvement for the sake of improvement is praiseworthy, it is more effective when targets are set. While management should have some influence in setting goals, final numbers should be set by the team whose task it is to achieve the numbers. This will promote ownership of the target.

The task force team should be ambitious in its goal, but should temper enthusiasm with realism. The goal should always be specific and measurable.

Benefit Sharing

As each project is completed and benefits begin to accrue, it is important that they be shared to make both organizations more competitive. The supplier organization should not be reluctant to pass on the advantages to the purchaser, since by doing so they are building trust and confidence. Moreover, the changes are usually not confined to one product or process. They can generally be applied elsewhere in the organization, so that additional profits can be made.

Open Door Policy

The trust between purchaser and suppliers manifests itself in a spirit of openness and cooperation. Both parties increase their willingness to share proprietary information. Their books and records are available to each other at any time.

Electronic Information Sharing

As the two plants continue to operate in tandem, their ability to get things done quickly is important. The reliance on paper flowing between the two organizations decreases as information gets passed back and forth electronically.

The type of information typically shared between the two parties includes:

- Production schedules. The supplier can gear up or down depending upon the level of activity in the buyer's plant.
- Sales projections. While forecasts are seldom precise, they do give the supplier some basis for medium-term planning of people, materials, and equipment.

- Process control. As key process variables are automated, it is possible for the buyer to monitor the process. This data increases confidence in the quality of the product and reduces the necessity for incoming inspection.
- Design details. Suppliers are no less important than the manufacturing facility. As such, they should be able to see a design evolve and have input into the manufacturability of the part or product. Moreover, they have the ability to design the manufacturing process while the item is produced, thereby reducing the time that it will take to deliver acceptable quality parts.

Certification

Certification refers to the formalization of the relationship between buyer and supplier which recognizes that:
- the responsibility to enforce zero defects is with the supplier;
- incoming inspection is done away with; and
- the relationship will continue for at least three to five years.

Training

Helping a supplier use Just In Time concepts has benefits for all parties, so ensuring that the transition is as smooth as possible can benefit both parties. While this requires careful planning, it also depends on an extensive amount of training.

Both planning and training can be provided by an independent consultant, or by the purchasing company. If the latter approach is taken, it brings with it the commitment to mutual help and the further development of relationships between the people of both organizations.

New Role for Purchasing

Many roles are being redefined in a world-class manufacturing environment. Managers are called upon to lead. Supervisors are becoming coaches. Quality inspectors are joining shop teams to act as resource trainers and coaches. The same is happening to purchasing professionals. As relationships between organizations change from an adversarial to a collaborative one, the time spent on working with vendors will increase.

If an organization is developed to the point where it comprises a number of focused factories, the mechanical task of placing orders with suppliers can be left to shop floor people. The more challenging tasks of certification, problem solving, and cost reduction activities will consume more time (see *Figure 6-10*).

The Timing

Asking suppliers to make major changes within their organization is unlikely to work unless your own organization has gone down the road before. One has little credibility when asking people to do things that are quite foreign to them, you must be able to demonstrate your ability to do likewise. Organizations that begin their Just In Time initiative with a vendor certification process usually fail to make much headway.

BEFORE *	AFTER

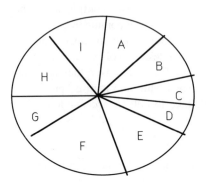 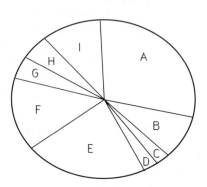

Key

	BEFORE			AFTER
A	Vendor Meetings	10%	A Vendor Meetings	30%
B	Plant Meetings	5%	B Plant Meetings	10%
C	Quotations	5%	C Quotations	2%
D	Supervision	2%	D Supervision	2%
E	Vendor Visits	10%	E Vendor Visits	20%
F	Paperwork	30%	F Paperwork	15%
G	Professional Reading	5%	G Professional Reading	5%
H	Expediting	20%	H Expediting	5%
I	Other	13%	I Other	11%

Based on figures from Coopers & Lybrand.

Figure 6-10. Typical Time Breakdown of Time Usage for Purchasing Professionals Before and After JIT Introduction.

CASE STUDY

NORTHERN TELECOM'S CERTIFICATION FOR EXCELLENCE

As a major player in the global market for telecommunications equipment, Northern Telecom Limited has looked for new ways to enhance its relationship with suppliers for mutual benefit. John A. Roth, Executive Vice President of Product Line Management, puts it this way:

High-quality, reliable products, delivered on time and within budget, are crucially important in satisfying the full needs and expectations of Northern Telecom customers. In today's highly competitive telecommunications market-place, it's essential that we work in close cooperation with our suppliers to ensure maximum quality, efficiency, and reliability at every part in the process from source of supply through design and manufacturing questions, product installation and field maintenance.

The formalization of the relationship is a certification program, whose theme is "Reaching for Perfection." This slogan reflects the ongoing commitment to

118

excellence through continuous improvement.

Northern has two primary objectives from the certification process:

1. foster Just In Time relationship with suppliers, and
2. reduce any activities that do not add value to Northern and supplier organizations.

PRODUCTS OR SERVICES

Both objectives will help Northern in its quest for perfection: zero defects, 100% on time delivery, and exceptional service.

In promoting its program to suppliers, Northern Telecom points to the benefits that they will derive from participation. These include:

- an opportunity to get a greater share of Northern Telecom's growing business,
- recognition for superior performance,
- regular and timely information on sales forecasts, and
- measurement and feedback on performance.

From its perspective, Northern's benefits will be significant, too. These include:

- the facilitation of process improvement through better-quality incoming parts and products.
- better utilization of resources.
- a better database for planning and decision-making.
- increased material throughput.
- lower purchasing costs.
- greater customer satisfaction.

HOW SUPPLIERS ARE CERTIFIED

Northern Telecom has developed a systematic, step-by-step process of certification (see *Figure 6-11*). The process is based on the following steps:

Number 1.   Become an Approved Supplier

Northern Telecom's corporate engineers test the quality of products or components. If they are satisfied, the supplier is put on the Approved Vendor List.

Number 2.   Divisions may Sponsor Suppliers

Since the certification process is a collaborative effort between Northern Telecom's headquarters and suppliers, any subsection of the organization will carry out the certification process in terms of its own needs, guided by the corporation's documented policies and procedures.

Number 3.   Supplier Commits to the Program

A team composed of corporate and divisional staff will work with management of the supplier to develop a plan which will lead to certification. This plan will cover such things as documentation of the process, measurement, sampling inspection, and provision for regular audits.

Number 4.   Accurate Specifications are Documented

The sponsoring division will document the product or part specifications to make sure that these are clear and unambiguous.

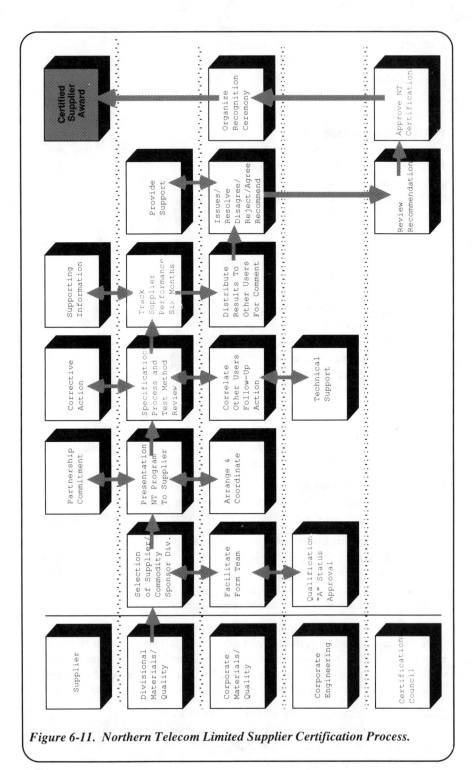

Figure 6-11. Northern Telecom Limited Supplier Certification Process.

120

Number 5. The Inspection Test Correlation

The sponsoring division will do a detailed comparison of inspection and test methods comparing Northern Telecom's criteria with those of the vendor. It will work with the supplier to develop procedures that ensure that inspection and test results correlate.

Number 6. Process Controls

Suppliers are required to have documentation showing that their processes are in control. They are also expected to continuously improve their process to reduce part-to-part variation. The suppliers are required to notify Northern Telecom of process or design changes prior to their implementation.

Number 7. Performance is Regularly Evaluated

Each division maintains accurate records of the performance of suppliers in terms of their quality, delivery, and service. This data is fed back to the supplier who is also informed when the performance reaches an acceptable level sufficient to warrant certification.

Number 8. High Standards of Performance are Expected

Suppliers are measured regularly on the three key performance criteria— quality, delivery, and service. Quality is measured against Northern Telecom's Procurement Specifications for a maximum period of six consecutive months. In the final three months, a minimum of 99% of lots must be acceptable, but the objective remains the achievement of a defect rate of less than 100 defects per million.

A similar approach is taken to delivery. However, the standard for acceptance is that at least 98% of lots must have been shipped within four days early to zero days late. The objective remains 100% on-time delivery.

The service rating is also done over the same period. Each supplier is ranked, on a scale of one to 10. While they must achieve a 75% overall rating, the objective is to achieve 100%.

THE CERTIFICATION AWARD

At a time when a supplier meets the Certification Standards of a division, these details are sent to the corporate contracts manager. He/she in turn circulates these recommendations to other divisions for comment. If the feedback is still positive, Certification can proceed. If not, a suitable plan for correction of outstanding problems is drawn up.

The formal certification is made by Northern Telecom's Certification Council. This is done at a ceremony at which the vendor is presented with a plaque which embodies the logo "Reaching for Perfection."

Of course certification is not the end of the road. Standards are expected to improve. And if standards actually drop and it appears that the supplier cannot, or will not, take steps to rectify the situation, then the certification status will be withdrawn.

The information contained in this study is based on a booklet "Northern Telecom:Guide to Supplier Certification."

CASE STUDY

HENREDON POSITIONING ITSELF TO IMPROVE CUSTOMER RESPONSE TIME

Background

Henredon Furniture, founded in 1945, is a manufacturer of high-end case goods and upholstered furniture. Henredon's customer is typically in the top two percent of the wage earners in the country. For years, Henredon has been the leader in style and quality. In the past, customers were willing to wait four to six months to receive their product. Today's customers are not willing to wait that long. For the last 10 years the competition has chipped at market share. A decision had to be made by Henredon management to devise a manufacturing strategy that would allow Henredon to provide goods to customers in a more timely manner yet maintain the quality and style that made this company famous. Dealers have often told Henredon that if they could just get the product to the customer more quickly they would be overwhelmed with orders.

Planning the Changes

In 1989, Henredon management made a commitment to improve customer response times. An aggressive quality improvement effort began along with a concurrent setup-reduction program and a pilot plant to test cellular manufacturing capabilities. The quality improvement program currently consists of 40 teams working together to solve specific problems encountered both on the shop floor and in other areas, if appropriate. The setup reduction effort is underway in all of the Henredon plants. All three of these efforts are having an impact on increased responsiveness to customer demands. The focus of this case study is directed toward the reasoning behind, objectives of, and preliminary results of the cellular manufacturing portion of Henredon's manufacturing excellence program.

The cellular manufacturing program got under way in June 1989. The motivation behind this effort was to pilot these techniques on a product that would have an immediate impact on "shippable" orders.

The first major step was the decision of "where to begin." Management picked the dining room chair department for the following reasons: 1) considering Henredon's "ship complete" policy, chairs were a predominant reason for holding up shipments; 2) chairs were a manageable portion of production; 3) the process for chairs is representative of most parts, and 4) efforts could begin in the upholstery/pack/rub (UPR) area as well as the machine/sanding area.

The objective of the program was to test the JIT principles and practices in the furniture industry. The goal was to deliver a quality product to customers at a price that is perceived as a good value for their dollar delivered to the customer when they want it, not when it is convenient for Henredon to produce.

Getting Started in the Chair Work Area

To get the program started, a team was formed and given the objective of designing and implementing the first machining work center. Second, a study began in the UPR area with the objective of reducing throughput time while creating a smoother flow. Third, a setup-reduction program was started by forming teams to study machines which were critical to the manufacturing operation. On the next page, *Figure 6-12* shows the cell implementation plan.

As part of Phase One, a JIT machining/sanding work center was created. The center included six different machines that were dedicated to running chair rail parts only. This center was manned by experienced machining and sanding operators. Six months later, this center was expanded to include 11 machines that would allow the center to run a variety of other chair parts (Phase Two). Full-time operators were chosen, half of whom had no previous machine room background.

In Phase Three, more machines were added to the work center. The inclusion of more equipment (primarily sanding) allowed introducing additional types of parts to the work center, thereby enabling complete manufacturing of the part from beginning to end.

The actions of the chair work center can be summarized as follows: They:

- Developed a work program listing responsibilities, names, and dates, then followed and tracked the plan.
- Trained the operators chosen for the work center.
- Created a new compensation program to accommodate the work center goals. The compensation package allows Henredon to provide additional pay when an operator obtains additional machining/ sanding/setup skills.
- Established "rules" for the work center (even though different than the rest of the plant).

The results that emerged were gratifying. They included:

- Cross-training has allowed the operators to become certified on approximately 90% of the machines.
- All operators have received promotions and pay increases due to acquiring additional skills.
- The close proximity of machines and personnel has created a synergistic environment with group problem-solving, quality at the source, and improved morale.
- Lead time has been reduced from approximately four days to two hours, a 94% improvement.
- The scheduling system has been updated to reflect the work center as a separate department to allow better planning/execution.
- Four operators and one assistant supervisor operate the 11 machines, as opposed to one operator per machine previously running the same operations.

Upholstery, Pack , Rub (UPR)

The objectives of the chair review were to analyze the current process and determine the best opportunities to create a more demand-driven environment.

The most obvious drawback in the previous method was that each department, upholstery, pack, and rub, had separate goals and measurements. So even though

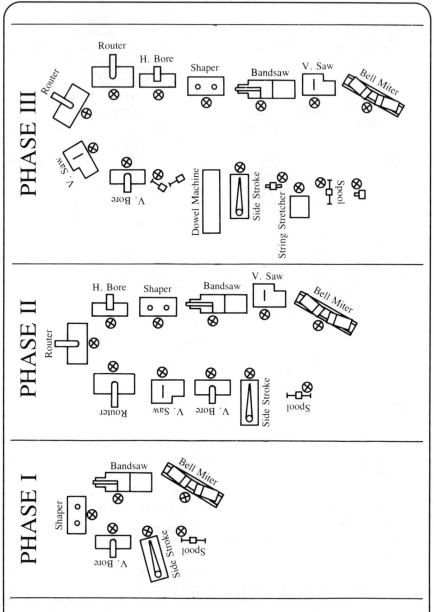

Figure 6-12. Cell Implementation Plan for Henredon.

each department met its daily production quotas, actual orders were not getting shipped.

The first action taken was to bring the three departments together both physically and as a reporting unit. Next, a sequential schedule of shippable orders was prepared so all three areas could rub, upholster, and pack only those chairs that are going to be shipped.

The benefits achieved were both tangible and intangible. They include:

- order sequencing reduced lead times from 20 days to less than three days (85% reduction).
- WIP inventories were reduced from 3,500 seats to 400 (85% reduction).
- the backlog of orders was reduced from 14,000 to 6,000 (57% reduction).
- finished chairs were reduced from 21,000 to 9,500 (55% reduction).
- operators have begun to assist in areas that were once "not their problem" to help balance the work load.

To date, the efforts in the UPR area have had excellent and—more importantly—immediate results. A good measure of how well the department is functioning is to track the number of calls received from customer service on a daily basis. Before the rearrangement, the packing department usually received 10 to 15 calls per day inquiring as to when the chairs would be ready for shipment. Now it is a rare occurrence to receive a call from customer service unless it is a change order. One complaint that has come up in meetings from customer service is that the UPR area is now too fast! Previously, they could place orders and then cancel them three to four weeks later, knowing that the chair would not be ready for shipment.

Actually, it now takes longer to process the paperwork (average of five days) than it does to rub, upholster and pack a chair (average of three days).

Setup Reduction Program

The goal of the setup-reduction program was to identify and reduce the time spent in changing from one part to another on critical machines in the machining department. This allows Henredon to reduce batch cutting sizes and improve responsiveness to customer demand.

The game plan for improvement was to:

- pick the machines which are critical to the ability to manage changeover: Bell miter, Tenoner, Shaper, Molder.
- train all team members,
- videotape setups on each machine,
- break out "internal" and "external" times in the setup process,
- brainstorm solutions to reduce setups, and
- implement solutions.

In this area, the benefits include enhancements on the machines (laser alignment lights, new hand adjustment cranks, new heads, new tools for machines, tool locators at the machine) which in turn have reduced setup times on all equipment.

The Future

Even though Henredon has been involved with the program for over a year, in truth, this is just the beginning. Many improvements have been made as well as some mistakes. There is too much opportunity and too much potential to risk jumping into a project like this and doing it wrong. Henredon has shown that a machine work center is a more responsive way to produce chair components, and that by setting common goals and objectives, impressive gains can be made.

But to truly reap the benefits of the manufacturing excellence program, it will be imperative that all the pieces be put together. Currently, efforts are under way to create a dining room chair "focused factory." This facility will be manufacturing chairs from beginning to end utilizing cellular manufacturing techniques. Eventually the facility will be able to produce the more popular chairs every one or two months, and the lower-selling chairs two to three times a year instead of just once. This capability will allow Henredon to provide a high-quality product to customers in a much shorter time period than in the past.

Case Study based on information provided by Daniel R. Bradley, Henredon Furniture.

QUALITY

Toward A Definition of Quality

The concept of quality has changed over time, as has its definition. In the immediate post war period, the quality of a product was seen mainly in terms of its "fitness for use" or "goodness." The reader will no doubt see the problem with such a description. Beauty is in the eye of the beholder, and different beholders may see beauty differently. Take the quality of an automobile starting system for example. Some people might expect a car to start on the first kick to be acceptable. Others, with a similar desire may, in addition, expect the car to start on the first engine turn. So the first consumer may be happy with most cars as his/her definition is considerably looser than the second, whose definition is more specific.

A second and more recent approach to quality is that it must conform to specification. Again this definition can lead to problems in cases where specifications are inadequate, arbitrarily conceived, too large, too small, etc.

Within the definition of conformance to specification, we can approach quality from the point of view of quality of design, quality of conformance to design, and quality of performance. Quality of design has most serious implications for time. Quality of design is high on the list of causes for time delay. The quality of design refers to the specific expectations of the designer or engineer. It is typically described in terms of the maximum tolerable variation which can exist in the final product. It is referred to as the tolerance or tolerance specification.

Let us take the example of two parts A and B, both manufactured for a nominal (aimed for) size of .55 in. (13.97 mm). Part A is designed with a tolerance of +/- .003 in. (0.076 mm). Part B, on the other hand, is designed with a tolerance of .005 in. (0.127 mm). Part A can be considered a superior quality design.

Quality of conformance to design also will impact time. The closer the actual manufactured tolerances are to the ideal, the better the quality.

A third classification of quality can be on the basis of quality of performance. As consumers, this description is most meaningful to us. We judge the success of our automobile, TVs and other consumer products in this way. Archibald Jamieson of the Niagara College of Applied Arts and Technology describes it this way: "Quality of performance is basically the ability of the product to perform its technical function in a satisfactory manner at an economically acceptable price. We expect a lawn mower to be able to cut grass and be maneuverable; we expect an electric shaver to give a close shave and to do it in a relatively short time; we expect paint to retain its color and texture and to adhere to a surface for a long period of time; and we expect all these things at a competitive market price." [2]

Finally, organizations more recently are spending more time looking at a definition of quality that goes beyond meeting customers expectations or specifications each time. As competition improves quality, it becomes increasingly difficult to differentiate products in the marketplace. A select few manufacturers are looking to exceed customers expectations by offering more than anyone else. Take Toyota's new Lexus LS400, for example. This vehicle sells in the mid-$30,000 price range and is going head to head with Mercedes, Audi, and BMW cars. Producing an equivalent car would not be sufficient to win a reputation for luxury, so 1,400 engineers and 2,300 technicians built 450 prototypes and registered 300 new patents as part of their determination to meet the mandate to build the best car in the world. Categories in which the consumers' expectations were to be exceeded included "speed, safety, comfort, elegance, dignity, and beauty." For example, wind tunnel tests and constant modifications reduced drag to 0.29, lower than any competitor in the luxury car market.[3] "All moving parts are balanced to tolerances four times greater than normal production standards, thereby sharply reducing engine vibration."

No matter how you look at quality, any task that is not done right the first time will result in time delays to the market. Additional time is consumed in activities such as:

- greater inspection of incoming raw materials,
- time spent on separating good from bad parts,
- inspection during the process,
- problem solving,
- rework time,
- pacifying irate customers, and
- following up customer complaints.

Higher Quality Actually Reduces Costs

Higher quality means doing things right the first time. It also means keeping an eye open for improvements for the future. It sometimes means spending even more time at the initiation of a new product introduction—making sure that

---

[2] Archibald Jamieson. "Introduction to Quality Control." Reston Publishing Company Inc., Reston, Virginia, 1982.
[3] *Financial Post*, "Special Report on Automobiles. " Toronto, September 24, 1990. p. 32.

things get done right later. Fewer problems that have to be corrected mean significantly less wasted time and reduced capital requirements. When all losses are considered, higher quality usually costs less than poor quality.

It is believed that, the cost of meeting the needs of customers is about 20% of sales. The major portion—about 85% —rightly called consequential—are incurred because we manage quality in a poor manner.

There are situations where better quality does cost more. An example may include fine jewelry. However, in this example, quality describes a grade of product or a number of features rather than the absence of defects. This is an important distinction. Failing to make this distinction may lead us to go after perfection in the name of quality improvement, and manufacturing products that far exceed specifications. This may produce a feeling of confidence and well being, but it will also lead to increased costs which may not be recovered from the customer.

Traditional Quality Management

Organizations plagued with high rework, scrap, returns, lost business or a combination of such problems, tend to share a similar approach to quality management. Typically they:

- **Focus on the Output.** Every manufacturing process is the result of inputs and outputs. The inputs—people, equipment, methods, materials, and the environment—combine to produce a product. Instead of trying to arrive at the ideal combination of inputs, most organizations focus on the completed part or product by inspecting the problem out. Discovering defects or errors after the job has been done is most typical. Inspection keeps most problems away from customers, but it does little to keep costs down or improve the processes that created the defects or errors in the first place.

- **Responsibility with Quality Staff.** In traditionally run factories, responsibility for finding problems lies with the quality professional. When problems occur, the Quality Department is the first to be blamed. Needless to say, this approach is ludicrous. How can the inspector fix the problem? Or prevent it? Inspecting it out only takes time; it doesn't get to the source of the problem. The only way of fixing the problem is to make the inspector responsible. They would then inspect their own processes and use their considerable knowledge to prevent problems.

- **Skills Concentrated with Quality Control Staff.** Most organizations with QC departments provide quality-related training to the QC staff, but not to the operators. So awareness of quality improvement techniques does not get to those best able to use them.

- **No Operator Input.** In most traditionally managed organizations, operators are seen as mere extensions of their machines. Each is regarded as a pair of arms and legs that need to be kept as busy as possible. It is difficult for managers in this environment to appreciate that people also come to work with their heads which contain brains that cannot be left at home. So for the same hourly rate, surely it makes most sense to optimize the use of people's knowledge and experience.

- **Acceptable Quality Level (AQL) Philosophy.** Companies that manage quality in a traditional manner expect and accept a certain defect rate. This is unacceptable in the marketplace because anyone buying from a parts supplier with an AQL philosophy would need: inspections to find the defects; rework stations to repair defective parts; time to scrap defective parts; clerical people to make claims on suppliers; and shipping people to return defective parts.

Total Quality Control (TQC)

TQC refers to an organization-wide program aimed at:
- identifying the real customers of each area,
- identifying key indices or measurements of what constitutes acceptable performance;
- monitoring levels of performance,
- continuous problem solving to improve customer satisfaction;
- fixing problems within and between departments through collaborative approaches; and
- encouraging change and innovation, and involvement of people in decisions that affect their working life.

As one aspect of a TQC approach, an increasing number of organizations now use statistical process control (SPC) techniques to measure individual processes.

Statistical Process Control (SPC)

SPC is both a technology and a management process. As a technology, it can be defined as the use of data to promote a better understanding of a process to bring the process under control.

Each of the three words making up the title SPC is important and need to be examined in some detail. The first is statistical.

We all use **statistics** in our daily lives, although the mere mention of the word frightens most people. For example, we use numbers to do comparison shopping. We use statistics to see if we are doing better or worse, going faster or slower, etc.

Endless statistics are worthless unless they are arranged in a format which allows for easy interpretation. It is said that a picture says a thousand words. So it is with a graph. The SPC system requires that each operator maintain, either manually or mechanically, a graph of the process so that they can monitor changes or **variations**. In so doing, the operator is taught to recognize changes in the process and to take action to prevent problems before they occur.

Variations occur in the **process** because of the complex interplay of the inputs (see *Figure 6-13*).

Inputs are always changing. For example, **people** change. The same operator performs differently as the day progresses, or after a break. People perform differently because of physical differences, attitudes, and training. **Materials** change too. Incoming raw materials from different suppliers vary. Incoming

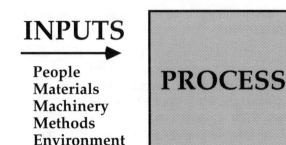

INPUTS
→

People
Materials
Machinery
Methods
Environment

PROCESS

OUTPUT
→

Finished
Part
or Product

Figure 6-13. The Process of Making a Product.

parts from different operators or shifts vary. And **machines** vary because they are newer, or older, or from different vendors. Some vary because they have been maintained better. **Methods** vary too. In so many organizations, operators develop their own "witchcraft," or secret methods. And it is astonishing how reluctant they are to pass on these techniques to new operators. It is also astonishing that even if a process is operating perfectly on one shift, that the next shift operators will readjust all the knobs and dials in accordance with their own systems.

And to complicate methods further, the end product can be influenced by the **environment**. Temperature, humidity, and light, for instance, are typical environmental factors influencing the processing of a product.

So when one puts all the inputs together, and they are all constantly changing, it is understandable why one gets a great amount of fluctuation in the process.

Experience tells us that up to 85% of problems are under the control of management. The operators might know the cause of the problem, but cannot change it because they do not have the authority to do so. These are the common causes.

Typical **common causes** of variation are:
- the capability of the machine;
- variations of incoming raw materials;
- overall gage accuracy;
- lack of operator training;
- variation in parts from prior operations, and
- environmental fluctuations such as temperature and humidity changes.

On the other hand, 15% of all variation is directly under the control of the operator.

Typical causes that are under the control of the operator are:
- broken tools,
- improper setup,
- operator errors,
- materials too hard or soft, and
- defective gaging.

These are known as **special causes**.

130

By making notations on a graph whenever something unusual happens, knowledge about the process increases. Recurring variances need to be eliminated first.

Operators need to do as much as they can to eliminate special causes. Having done so they must call on management to reduce the remaining causes, most of which will probably cost money.

The last key word is **control**. Through preventive action and continuous elimination of sources of variation, a team of people who are jointly responsible for a process can turn an unstable process (see *Figure 6-14*) into a process which has a predictable outcome (see *Figure 6-15*).

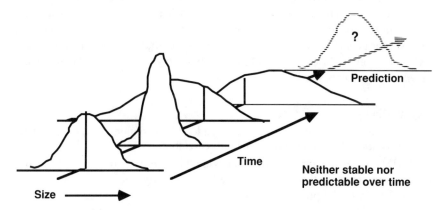

Figure 6-14. Frequency Distribution of a Process Out of Control.

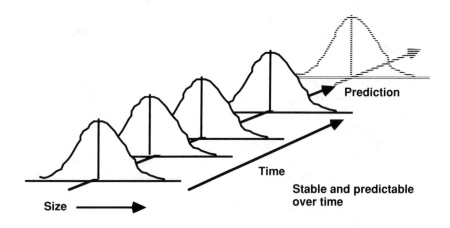

Figure 6-15. Frequency Distribution of a Process in Control.

Process Capability

Process capability refers to the ability or inability of a process to meet some specific expectations. These expectations, or specifications, can be internal—

such as engineering tolerances—or they can be external, as is the case with customer specifications.

Organizations that supply a part or a product to a variety of customers, all of whom have varying specifications, tend to set their own tolerances at a level which represents the most challenging specification required. If the process is geared to this tight tolerance, it will meet the needs of all customers by varying amounts.

The tolerances within which the process must operate should be noted on the graph to remind the operator of limitations within which they must operate. But these limitations are **different** from the statistical limits within which the process varies naturally. This helps to avoid confusion that occurs when parts that are statistically out of control are still given the green light to be shipped. In this way, the operator gets to understand that these parts are not "bad" but are simply the result of special causes of variation, which in any case should be removed. *Figure 6-16* presents some typical examples.

Explanation

The frequency distribution shows considerable variation over time. The process is not stable, and the outcome unpredictable.

On Day One, the process was behaving beautifully. It was well within specification, meeting the customer's needs consistently.

On Day Two, the process changed. Variation increased. The cause of the variation could be attributed to any number of reasons. And the situation, while still in control statistically and within specification, needs to be monitored very closely because any further variation is likely to produce out-of-control parts. The operator might be encouraged to sample more frequently to ensure that even small changes are picked up. If there is a known way of lightening the process, to allow some leeway between the statistical limit and the specifications, this should be done.

On Day Three, we find that the process has drifted and is sitting on the lower specification limit. This is good and bad. It could be good in the sense that we might be using cheaper incoming raw materials, thus saving money. On the other hand, we are exposing ourselves to the possibility of producing out of spec parts, if the process drifts further to the left.

On Day Four, we find ourselves in trouble. A small percentage of our production is not meeting specifications. Our cost of production will soar as we will have to follow a number of options.

- increase inspection and sorting to identify unacceptable parts. Our labor costs will likely go up.
- rework certain parts,
- scrap some parts,
- make additional parts to cover a shortfall in production,
- waste time explaining to the client why we might have short shipped their order,
- delay production of another batch to remake good parts, and

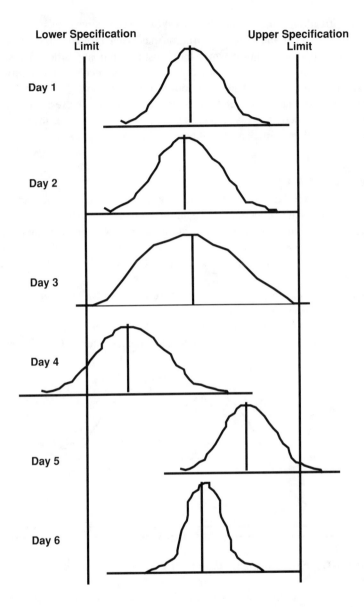

Figure 6-16. Frequency Distribution with Relation to Specification Limits Over Time.

- Reorder raw materials to replace bad parts.

On Day Five, we again did not meet specifications, this time producing items above the upper spec limit. Many of the same costs will be incurred as in Day Four.

Finally, on Day Six, find a process whose variation is well within the customers' specification limits. Depending upon the circumstances, this can be good or bad. It is good if the reduced variation has been brought about through the reduction of common causes, which have cost the company little. Our marketing people will be overjoyed since they can take this evidence of high quality into the marketplace and command a higher dollar for the product.

On the other hand, the better performance might be the result of high costs such as better incoming raw materials. If this were the case, then our cost of production will have increased well beyond the point of greatest economic viability.

The Tools of SPC

SPC requires those closest to the process to collect data for analysis and feedback. The data collection can be automated, or done manually. Most experts agree that the manual collection of data is the best way to start data collection, since operators tend to have more confidence in statistics that they have charted. When confidence builds in the system, it becomes feasible to automate the process.

The format of displaying data can vary, too. The two most often used tools are frequency distributions and control charts.

A frequency distribution displays data collected over a period on a bar graph. It displays how many occurrences took place in each interval (see *Figure 6-17*).

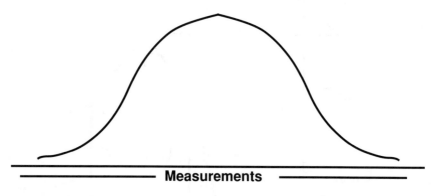

Measurements

Figure 6-17. Frequency Distribution of a Range of Outcomes.

When their distribution is shaped like a bell, as shown in *Figure 6-17*, we consider the data "normal." Data is also "normal" if the right side of the graph equals the left, or if data is distributed equally around the point of central tendency.

The frequency distribution also is very useful for **predictive** purposes (see *Figure 6-18*).

Dividing the data distribution into three segments on each side of the midpoint (mean)—known as standard deviations—one can predict that 99.7% of all data points will fall within the range between -3 and +3. Similarly, one can

134

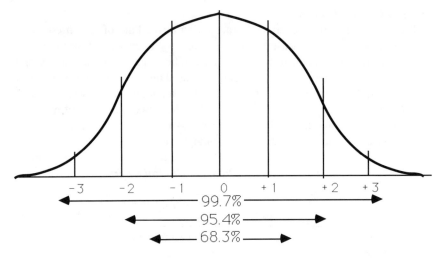

Figure 6-18. Frequency Distribution.

predict that almost half (49.87%) of all points will fall on either side of the mean, and roughly two-thirds of all points between the standard deviations on either side of the mean.

Knowing the information on the frequency distribution, one can predict the outcome of a process so long as it is stable.

Control Charts

While frequency distributions are excellent analytical tools, they do represent historical data. Typically, they show how a process has behaved over a period of 30 days. As such, they are less valuable as a tool that operators can use to prevent problems before they get out of hand.

A more useful tool is a control chart (*Figure 6-19*) which displays data over time.

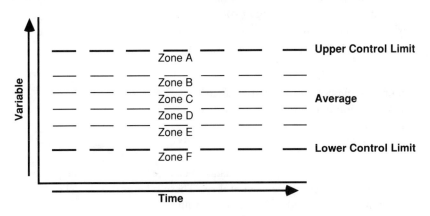

Figure 6-19. Control Chart.

Types of Control Charts

The form of a control chart varies according to the kind of data it contains. Some data are based on measurements such as the dimensions of unit parts (in mm), or yields of a chemical process (in g). These are known as "undiscrete values" or "continuous data." Other data are based on tallies, such as number of defective articles or the number of defects. They are known as "discrete values" or "enumerated data." Control charts based on these two categories of data will differ. *Table 6-2* shows the kind of control chart to be used in each case, depending on whether it is based on indiscreet or discrete values.

Table 6-2. Types of Data and Control Charts.

Types of Data	Control Chart Used
Examples: volume (cc)	measurements (1/100 mm)
product weight (g)	$\bar{X}$ & R
power consumption (kwh)	
Discrete Examples: number of defectives fraction defective second-class product rate	 pn p
Indiscrete Examples: number of pin holes in pieces of plated sheet metal, differing in area: number of foreign particles in pharma- ceutical compounds, differing in volumes (when the range in which the defects are possible, such as length, area, volume, is not fixed)	 u
number of pin holes in a specified area; number of foreign particles in a specified volume (when the length, area, volume, is fixed)	 c

As the operator collects and plots the data, no changes are made to the process unless one of a few "rules" have been broken. These rules are:
- a point has fallen outside of the control limits;
- there is a run of seven points either up or down;

- there are seven points on either side of the center line;
- there are two consecutive points in zone A or zone F; and
- there is more than 90% or less than 40% of points in zones C and D combined.

In such an event, the operator knows that the process is not "normal." Something is wrong. The next steps are to:
- check the data, to make sure that there are no arithmetic errors;
- check that the system for collecting the data hasn't changed;
- make sure that the data represents one process stream;
- find the cause of the problem and fix it; and
- call for help when the cause of the problem is out of control.

It is important that problems be dealt with quickly when they occur. That is the beauty of a measurement system controlled and operated by shop floor people. It is equally important to continuously improve the process by the removal, first of special causes of variation, and later of more difficult, sometimes costly, common causes.

What these causes are can sometimes be identified through the interpretation of patterns on the graph.

The six most typical patterns indicating abnormal conditions are illustrated in *Figure 6-20* to *Figure 6-25*.

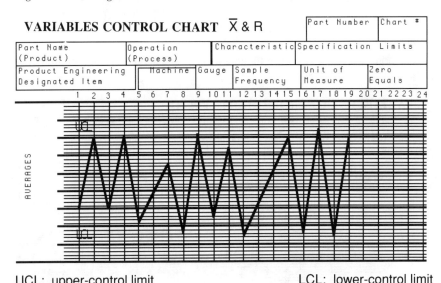

UCL: upper-control limit   LCL: lower-control limit

Figure 6-20. Unexpected variation.

The pattern in *Figure 6-20* occurs when two-thirds of the plotted points do not fall within one-third of the point of central tendency. Causes of this pattern, which will need to be eliminated, could include over-adjusting of the process by the operator. Other possibilities could be an overall increase in common cause variations such as a large number of untrained operators, unfamiliarity with the specs, or different methods of operation.

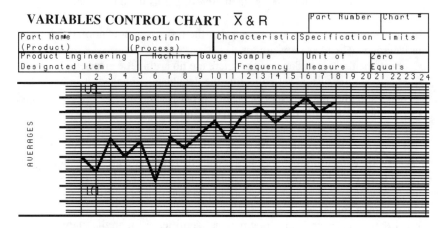

Figure 6-21. Runs.

The type of pattern in *Figure 6-21* occurs when about 50% of all plotted points don't fall on either side of the center line. It also occurs when there are 7 successive points, or 10 of 11 points on the same side, or 12 of 14 points on the same side.

The potential causes of a run include a change in setup, a change in material, or faulty gaging.

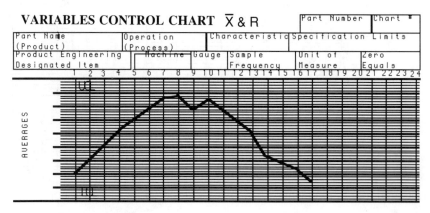

Figure 6-22. Trends.

The pattern shown in *Figure 6-22* occurs when there is continuous increase or decrease in a set of points.

The rule of thumb for a trend is seven or more consecutive points increasing or decreasing.

138

The potential causes on an $\overline{X}$ chart include tool wear and general deterioration of the process.

If a *trend* occurs on the R chart, it could be due to operator fatigue or deterioration in the process.

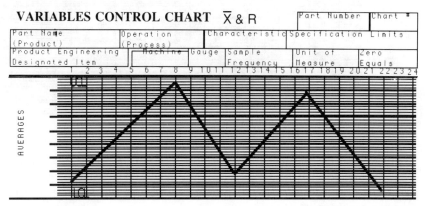

Figure 6-23. Cycles.

The pattern shown in *Figure 6-23* occurs when there are up and down movements of the data points in repeated patterns.

The potential causes of *Cycles* include changes in the environment, or changes in operators from shift to shift.

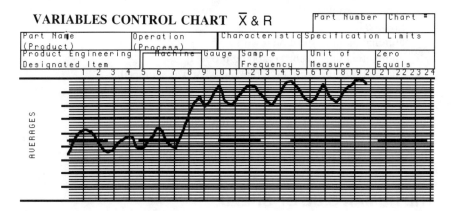

Figure 6-24. Shift in Process Level.

The pattern in *Figure 6-24* occurs when the process finds a new point of central tendency.

The potential causes of a shift include a dropped or changed measuring instrument, changes in material, different tooling, or a change in the speed of the machine.

139

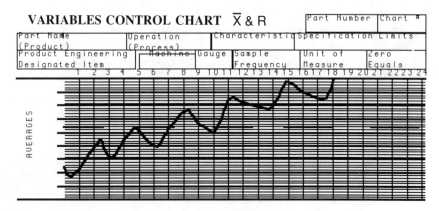

VARIABLES CONTROL CHART X̄ & R

Part Number	Chart #

Part Name (Product)	Operation (Process)	Characteristic	Specification Limits
Product Engineering Designated Item	Machine Gauge	Sample Frequency	Unit of Measure	Zero Equals

Figure 6-25. Process Drift.

Process drift, as illustrated in *Figure 6-25,* occurs when there is a gradual increase or decrease in the data points. These points do not have to be consecutive. The primary causes of this pattern include gradual loosening of a tool fixture or tool wear.

Reducing Time Wastage

A fully implemented SPC process will produce part-to-part uniformity and reduce variation. Producing the product right the first time, will save time. Time also will be saved by:

- cutting out inspection at the end of the line,
- eliminating inspection of incoming product,
- avoiding problems that could be solved more effectively if operators were involved,
- eliminating time spent on rework,
- eliminating time spent scrapping product,
- eliminating time spent on remaking what was scrapped,
- avoiding time spent on needless conflict caused by blaming everyone else for problems, and
- reducing time spent dealing with irate customers.

Charts do not solve problems, people do. But charts do give clues to alert teams as to the causes of variation so that the variation can be eliminated to save time and prevent waste.

THE HUMAN SIDE OF SPEED: EMPLOYEE INVOLVEMENT

Changing systems using JIT principals and measuring them using SPC techniques have limited impact on time unless somebody makes something happen. The human side of organizations provides the energy that changes ideas into reality, and programs into profits.

Getting people to work effectively in customer-focused activities continues to frustrate most managers. Yet success is closer now than it has been for some time. Now organizations that are leaner and flatter are built on the foundation of semi-autonomous work groups, and they are significantly outperforming auto-cratic, hierarchical, departmentalized organizations.

Maturing People with Technology

The process of continuous improvement to reduce time, improve quality, and cut costs often requires the introduction of new technologies. Technology for technology's sake has rarely given the benefits expected; most often this is because of problems associated with resistance by workers.

Some new technologies can make work more interesting and challenging. This can tie workers closer to the assembly line, causing them to feel that they have less control and less freedom.

To reduce the negative impact of new technologies such as robots, computer-numerical-controlled machine tools, lasers, or automatic guided vehicles, people need to be involved. They should participate in the selection of equipment and setups. Since this happens quite infrequently, time delays are caused by a lack of worker cooperation, and by further modifications required to accommodate the input of workers.

The involvement of workers in matters that they have control over and knowl-edge about has changed significantly over the years.

A Historical Perspective

The beginning of a new wave of team-based management principals began in the early 1980s which ushered in a wave of fascination with anything Japanese. The tidal wave of Japanese businessmen with cameras and notebooks that flooded North America in search of new ideas began to reverse itself as local business people saw their traditional competitive advantages dwindle. Naturally, Ameri-can and Canadian business people gave vent to their curiosity; they wanted to find out why, and so they began investigative visits to Japan.

What they found was an intensely cooperative effort by government, private enterprise, and labor. Each saw common good stemming from collaborative effort. Within organizations, this translated into:

- lifetime employment for full-time (male) employees;
- an exceptional work ethic involving promotions (and therefore rewards) based on seniority; and
- a variety of systems to tap into the ideas of people to continuously improve quality and productivity.

Extent of Employee Involvement in the U.S.

An important study was made by the U.S. General Accounting Office of various forms of employee involvement.[4] The survey focused on Fortune 500 Industrial and Fortune 500 Service companies. It covered 476 of these firms,

---

[4] Summarized in a report by the *Journal For Quality and Participation*, published by the Association for Quality and Participation, Cincinnati, Ohio, 1989, p. 49.

representing a response rate of 51%.

The survey found that between 25% and 70% of the companies had one or more forms of employee input (see *Table 6-3*).

Table 6-3. Employee Involvement Programs.

Program types	Corporations with some employee participation	Corporations which think the programs are successful[†]
Survey feedback	68%	69%
Job enrichment	60	51
QCCs	61	67
EI groups	70	69
QWL committees	30	48
Mini-enterprise units	35	56
SMWTs	28	53

[†] *consolidated responses of successful/very successful*

Other findings included:
- most programs were considered successful,
- survey feedback and Employee Involvement groups appeared to be most successful, followed by Quality Circles,
- most programs had been in existence for about four years,
- most programs were expanding (see *Table 6-4)*, and
- quality of working life committees showed the least growth, while surveys showed the most possible growth.

It should be noted that there is a relationship between the use of various forms of employee involvement, their perceived success, and the possibility of continued implementation. But sadly, the programs that have the highest levels of participation are methodologies that have the least ability to change the organization or share power with the lowest level of employees in the organization.

Table 6-4. Survey Results of Employee Involvement Programs.

Program types	Median number of years programs have been in use	Corporations whose use of the programs has increased during the past two years[‡]	Corporations that will implement or continue using programs during the next two years[‡]
Survey feedback	5 years	42%	65%
Job enrichment	4	37	48
QCCs	4	47	42
EI groups	4	54	62
QWL committees	4	25	20
Mini-enterprise units	2	48	19
SMWTs	2	50	23

[‡] *consolidated responses of increased/greatly increased and probably/definitely*

Furthermore, those organization structures which might have significant impact on organizational performance, such as self-managed work teams, quality of working life committees or self-contained work units, involve the smallest number of employees, and are not likely to be used more in the immediate future.

Quality Control Circles (QCC) and Employee Involvement Teams

The most popular "new" managerial process, borrowed from—or brought back to—North America was a team concept that came to be called Quality Control Circles.

Many of these programs dropped the name Quality Control Circles, referring to them simply as Employee Involvement. The process was similar, with the exception that membership of Quality Control Circles was voluntary, whereas most Employee Involvement Teams are mandated.

The process was used initially by Lockheed Aircraft Corporation at its plant in

Sunnyvale, California, and spread quickly across the country as thousands of organizations tried what they perceived as a "miracle cure."

How Quality Control Circles Worked

A QCC is a group of workers who meet voluntarily within a department, and identify, investigate, and analyze problems. Having done so, the team proposes solutions to managers for improvement (see *Figure 6-26).*

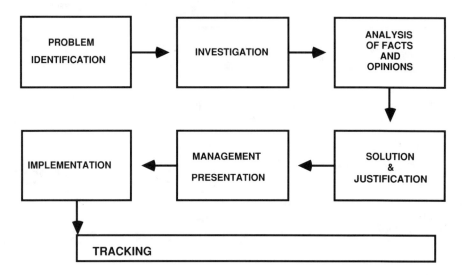

Figure 6-26. Problem Solving Process of Quality Control Circles.

The teams and supervisors are usually given training in problem solving, taught how to run meetings, and shown how to make presentations. This is done with the help of an outside consultant or an in-house facilitator.

Very often, organizations establish a steering committee to plan the implementation of QCCs and to track results. Most often, the committee consists of a cross-section of staff from different departments, and major efforts are made to include union participation. In this way, it was hoped that everybody will buy-in to the process and support the circles.

The committee typically establishes policies and procedures for the circles. Most common among these are:
- all leaders and members are to be trained;
- Circle membership is voluntary;
- meetings to resolve problems take place during business hours. If this is not possible, overtime rates will be paid to members meeting on their own time;
- meeting time will not continue beyond one hour per week; and
- final approval for any changes remains within the jurisdiction of management.

- the Circle must confine its discussions to matters directly affecting its members, and must not deal with items covered under any collective agreements or with personality issues.

Most organizations experience short-term gains from QCCs, or Employee Involvement Teams, as they later became known. The process gives people a feeling of self-worth, as well as the sense that the organization wants to change. They are made to feel that they have a meaningful role to play in the future. In most cases, the process fails to live up to its billing. Circles often make dramatic improvements in quality, reduce costs significantly, and cut cycle times consistently. So, why is it that most Quality Circle programs die a quiet death? There are no simple answers. The most commonly quoted "why-did-nothing-happen" survey responses give the following reasons discussed on this page and the next:

Top Management is Not Committed

Most QCC programs start with the blessing of top management. But Circle members seldom see senior people waving the flag or showing much follow-up support. What they see instead is:
- a real difficulty getting senior managers to attend presentations after the euphoria of the first few presentations had worn off;
- reluctance from management to implement proposals that involved any sizeable capital expenditure.

Organizations that sustained QCC programs, and turned it into a management process, are those where senior managers get involved. It is like the breakfast story. The chicken (which provides the eggs) is committed, but the pig (which provides the bacon) is involved! Involvement meant using the tools, attending workshops, acting as trainers, attending presentations, responding to ideas, and going to conferences prepared to commit resources.

The Process Starts and Finishes at the Shop Floor Level

In most organizations, top management, and often middle management, rarely use the skills which they expect those in the trenches to use. Ultimately, the QCC program is described as one that said "someone at the top tells someone in the middle to do something to someone at the bottom." It amounts to a "cast-in-stone" double-standard setting. The credibility of senior managers comes into question when they don't use the tools that are so useful for teams, to solve their own problems and make more effective decisions.

Organizations in which management used the tools—because they greatly believed in the process and learned the tools—benefit significantly. There is little question that the impact of senior management decisions can have a material influence on time, quality, and costs when compared to the decisions of the people on the shop floor.

The Programs Never Become Integrated Into the Management Processes

QCCs rarely become part of the day-to-day management process. Instead, they remain programs—in isolation, with no bearing on day-to-day operation.

A "program" can be defined as a series of events that have a beginning and an end. Many organizations referred to their "QCC program," not because they had an expectation that things would come to an end at some point, but because the QCC activity was so different, and removed, from day-to-day activities. Working as a team, solving problems, making decisions by consensus, training, having meetings for shop floor people, are all activities that are not typical of the activities of most organizations. So anything that isn't typical is a "program." Anything that fits into the day-to-day activities, on the other hand, would count as a process.

Bureaucracy Stopped QCCs from Working Effectively

Since most of the problem solving tools used by people are used only for one hour per week, participants fail to see any connection between using the tools inside and outside of the program.

Inside the program, problem solving is typically slow. Simple problems often take six or more months to solve. While solutions are usually obvious to Circle members from the beginning, teams are "forced" to follow prescribed steps and reach a conclusion using a variety of tools. While this might serve the purpose of learning about the tools, members often feel frustrated at the effort it takes to solve problems. The associated frustrations of working in a formalized team setting outweigh the benefits that solutions might bring.

The Law of "Ownership" is with Line People

"Ownership" did not rest with Circles. In looking at the implementation of most QCC programs, one finds it spearheaded by a coordinator/facilitator. This person is typically given a mandate by the steering committee or senior management to start the process, train the people, attend and monitor meetings, and act as a go-between among departments, or between the team and management.

The facilitator typically gains a rapid ride on the fast track. This person's exposure throughout the organization is extensive. And the facilitator gets the most "brownie points" for success. Little wonder, therefore, that line managers look to the facilitator rather than themselves to solve the problems related to QCCs.

Middle Managers Are Threatened by the Loss of Control

Working one's way up the corporate ladder doesn't happen overnight for most people. Ability counts in many organizations. So does seniority. It should come as no surprise then how hard it is for middle managers to relinquish power to shop floor people. Also, middle managers are supposed to have all the answers. For them, having to listen to the ideas from shop floor people that might be different from their own was a bitter pill to swallow—too bitter in fact for most middle managers. Typical behavior included giving mixed messages, such as saying in public that you support the process, but undermining it through daily work actions. These negative behaviors include criticizing the amount of time spent in meetings, and pressuring supervisors to make up productivity losses on days when meetings are held.

146

A Better Way to Involve People

The fact that most formalized Employee Involvement programs die does not signal a failure of the program or that people do not want to be involved. It merely reflects that the program doesn't meet the needs of the organization. Any management program needs to change continuously to adapt to or cope with new circumstances.

The next logical step in the evolution of organizations to a more democratic form is the use of task forces to solve problems.

Task forces are similar to Quality Control Circles in that they tackle projects systematically in a team format. They are different in many respects, too. Among the major differences are that they:

- focus on tangible, bottom-line problems, such as the reduction of cycle time, design time, scrap, or rework hours. On the other hand, QCCs often solved "soft" problems such as poor communications, lack of trust, and lack of cooperation—areas difficult to quantify.
- use people from different areas. QCCs confined their membership to departmental people only.
- focus on key issues only. QCCs sometimes got sidetracked into solving trivial problems, because the most important problems were outside of their direct control.
- have designated members. People are conscripted to join the team as opposed to volunteering.
- their membership is composed largely of professional and managerial people. QCCs, on the other hand, included primarily shop floor people in most cases.
- they exist only until their project is completed. QCCs continued to tackle problems one after another, even though there may have been some turnover in their membership.

One of the most effective task forces is a team setup to bring a product to the market quickly. This is described in Chapter 2.

Membership of the Team

Choosing the right people for the team will dramatically influence its effectiveness. People who don't have the skills, power, or time will make no contribution to the attainment of goals and will drain members' enthusiasm. Dr. Joseph M. Juran[5], a leading figure in quality improvement, suggests that you should consider the following:

1. which departments should be represented on the team?
2. what level in the organization hierarchy needs to be included?
3. which people at that level are appropriate?

He feels that a variety of departments are typically needed. These should include:

---

[5] Joseph M. Juran, *Juran On Quality*, Workbook at MICA Conference, Toronto, March 19, 1990.

- the "ailing" area, where the symptoms are manifest;
- the "remedial" department, which has power, knowledge, and resources to bring about solutions; and
- the "diagnostic" department, which can provide data collection and analysis expertise.

When picking an appropriate level in the organization from which to draw members, one can be guided by the nature of the task. Problems of a more technical nature are well-served by technical people in the lower echelons of the structure. Issues of a more global, strategic importance need to attract managerial level people.

Finally, deciding which individuals to include on the team should be influenced by individual time schedules, skills, and levels of interest.

The Next Step—Participatory Management

The second to last step on the path to full-democratic management is the adoption and encouragement of every-level participation. In a work area that operates on this basis, the supervisor is still the focal point for decisions. However, whenever there is an issue that requires input from front-line people, because they have the expertise or are impacted, they are consulted. This consultation can be formal or informal. This process happens frequently and spontaneously and this distinguishes it from QCCs which function only on a formalized basis. While formalized departmental meetings do occur off the shop floor in a participatory work environment, most problems are resolved at work stations. One problem, of course, is that, unlike QCC programs, it is difficult to see this as a program.

Departments operating on this participatory model are characterized by open communications. People come to trust each other and feel free to discuss "touchy" issues without fear of reprisals. Decisions are based on consensus. While the negotiation to find the middle ground often takes longer, the resulting commitment to follow through usually leads to time saving.

The types of problems tackled by departments tend to be more significant at this stage of team development. As members are fed all important operating data, they are positioned to act on the data and resolve key operating problems.

Self-Managing Work Teams: A New Form of Work Democracy

Self-directed work teams, self-managing work teams, semi-autonomous work teams, sociotechnical design, are but a few of the names used to describe a management process that aims to integrate each person comfortably within the work system. Unlike Frederick Taylor's model that sought to break jobs down to discrete parts and have people perform these single tasks repetitively, the sociotechnical process aims to pass control of the whole system to those closest to it, allowing them the freedom to design the jobs. In so doing, it is expected that each person will have enough scope not to lose sight of the end result—the customer and the product or service.

While self-managing teams are now used by only a minuscule number of organizations, interest in them is growing rapidly. One of the first reported examples of a successful implementation was at General Foods' Gravy Train pet food plant in Topeka, Kansas, which started operations in the early 1970s.

The organization used many techniques still considered to be on the leading edge today. These included: a vigorous screening system for employees, continuous training, a compensation system based on knowledge and skills, and the involvement of members in traditional supervisory tasks such as hiring, discipline, firing, and scheduling.

Procter & Gamble also is known to have used self-directed work teams more than a decade ago. Much less is known about their experimentation, since the organization has traditionally been loath to share operating strategies with outsiders.

Since that time, organizations such as Corning Inc., TRW, General Motors, Cummins Engine, Shell, Northern Telecom, and Digital Equipment, to name a few, have begun using sociotechnical methods to improve operations.

Characteristics of Self-Managed Teams

While organizations differ on the details of how they implement self-managing teams, their structures tend to have the following characteristics:

- Team sizes tend to number between eight and 15 people.
- The team covers all aspects of a single product, service or customer case. As a consequence, they develop knowledge of the whole system and feel some ownership for more than a single task.
- The members are multiskilled. They are systematically taught each task so that they can cover for people who are away. They also benefit from not experiencing the boredom that is associated with having to perform single repetitive tasks.
- The reward system provides incentives for people to acquire additional skills which they can use to better the performance of their work team. Typically, tasks are defined and training modules are developed for each. Members train and test each other (often with an outside auditor). On completion of each module, base salaries are adjusted upwards or a bonus is given.
- In many organizations, gainsharing systems exist, so that increases in productivity are shared with team members.
- Supervisory duties are assumed by the members. Tasks such as training, recruiting, discipline, scheduling, firing, responsibility for health and safety, quality, and other performance indicators are divided among members.
- Managerial levels decrease. Since work is delegated to the lowest possible level in the organization, fewer tasks are left for management. So, as fewer are needed, overhead savings will be considerable. More important, the speed with which decisions are taken, and their effectiveness, improves measurably, since only those close to and knowledgeable about problems are involved.

Changing Role of Managers

With greater authority and responsibility passed down the line, there is no question that managers—first level and middle—will become an endangered

149

species in the years ahead. In a globally competitive market, where overhead costs need to be cut to the bone, few organizations can afford or will have the need for anyone that is not adding value to the product or service. A time study of the activities of most managers would show that a good portion of their time—probably more than half—is spent on administrative activities, such as attending meetings, filling in reports, playing telephone tag, and the like.

So where does this leave middle managers? Clearly in a changed position. Their options are to:

- leave the organization,
- become a coach/resource person to one or a number of teams where they may involve themselves in training, problem solving, and accessing resources or
- move into a more senior management role where they can deal with strategic and conceptual issues.

Changing Organization Structures

A flatter organization will be more responsive to needs in the marketplace. But, flattening the organization needs to be done systematically and with a purpose in mind. Most successful changes to organizations have been aided by a model, which helps an organization to decide where it is, and more importantly, establishes a vision of what it would like to be in the future.

CASE STUDY

WORLD-CLASS MANUFACTURING IN ACTION: NORTHERN TELECOM'S SWITCHING DIVISION IN CALGARY, ALBERTA

Background

Northern Telecom is actively pursuing its goal of leadership in global telecommunications services by the turn of the century. This is their "Vision 2000."

One of two plants in Calgary, Alberta, is their switching division, which reports to its much larger counterpart in Bramalea outside Toronto, Ontario.

People at Calgary Switching have always had an enviable reputation as a leader in the use of Total Quality Management, Just In Time manufacturing, and Employee Involvement. They have aimed to be the pioneer, the model, for others to follow. Their 550-person facility has remained nonunion since it first opened 15 years ago, because of the excellent labor/management cooperation and the ongoing attempts made to eliminate any distinction between workers and management.

Executives at the switching division have also encouraged individual development, creativity, and innovation, and accepted each employee as a full partner in the business. Marwan Shishakly, the plant manager, puts it this way, "We have always had positive employee relations. The challenge is to maintain leadership in labor/management cooperation. Maintaining that leadership means eliminating the distinction between labor and management altogether. All employees at Calgary Switching are becoming business managers."

Having the highest expectations of its people has permitted management to empower people on the shop floor to continuously improve their work. Change is the norm. The encouragement of ongoing challenge to all plant processes has made the technical and social environment a state-of-the-art model of participation.

The company has also encouraged simplification. Doing more with less has led to the elimination of duplication, reduced inventories, fewer parts, and easier design, all of which have contributed to reduced cycle times (see *Table 6-5*).

Table 6-5.
The Results of JIT, TQC & SMWT.

	01/88	04/88	01/89	% Change
Service (%)	100	92	100	—
Inventory total ($M)	9.2	5.6	5.4	-42
Cycle Time (days)				
Circuit pack	2.3	1.3	1.7	-27
Line card	1.0	0.6	0.4	-60
Equipment	6-1	5.6	4.6	-25

Self-Managing Work Team (SMWT)

A key element of the Calgary Switching Division's technical and social change is the undertaking of SMWT. The process of having teams and members take responsibility for defect-free, on-time, and cost-competitive products is paying dividends as people learn to use the tools of Total Quality Management, Just In Time, and Cost Management.

SMWTs have been an integral part of the management process for a little more than a year, but they didn't happen overnight. They took years to evolve. The fact that they are successful is because they evolved from many steps which were implemented in previous years (see *Figure 6-27*).

It is interesting to note that many of the teamwork, problem solving, and decision making tools learned and used by the operators in the Quality Circles between 1982 and 1986 became useful tools in the processes that followed.

To ensure the effectiveness of the SMWT approach, management has provided a significant amount of training. This has been conducted in three phases. Phase One has had as its primary objective the creation of awareness of and enthusiasm for the SMWT concept. In this implementation phase members learn about:

- the value and importance of self-managing teams;
- the changing role of their boss;
- the parameters in which they need to work;
- how their performance will be measured, and
- team building.

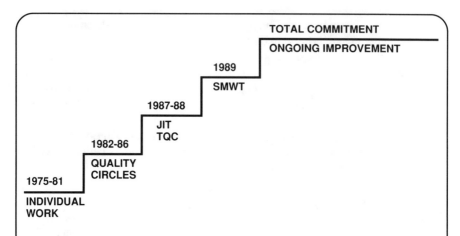

Figure 6-27. Self-Managing Work Teams Evolutionary Process.

Measurement is a key element of the total process. Calgary Switching's measurement system is comprehensive yet powerful. It focuses on five key performance categories—quality, cost, employee relations, safety/housekeeping, and customer service (see *Figure 6-28.)*

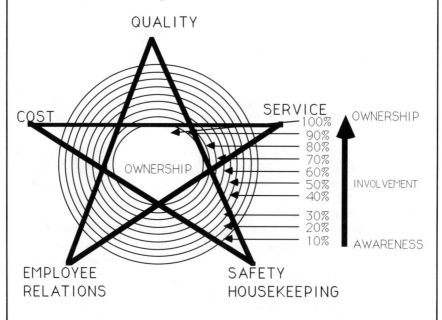

Figure 6-28. SMWT Star Measurement System.

Each of these categories is graded on a scale of zero to 100%, the latter suggesting that the ownership has passed totally from the manager to team members.

In Phase Two , Team Involvement, members' assumption of responsibility for performance becomes better defined. Members also learn how to coach one another so that people develop skills to handle each other's work. Also, instead of reporting problems to their boss, they are encouraged to take ownership to investigate and solve problems. Interestingly, they also become involved in regular peer reviews. A performance appraisal system has been developed, allowing all members to rate each other. The scores are then fed into a computer, the highest and lowest scores disregarded. Averages are then calculated. These are then fed back to individual members by managers. As groups mature, members are encouraged to give feedback directly to each other.

Phase Three is the point at which the team takes full ownership for all facets of their performance. They set their own goals, do their own budgeting and forecasting, and even deal with employee relations issues.

Just In Time

A $400,000 investment in training in 1989 launched the JIT/TQC initiative in earnest. This was accompanied by a new plant layout to improve product flow and upgrade facilities, costing in excess of $5 million. The traditional "push" system changed to a "pull" system, so that each team responded to the kanban, or signal, to replace what was used in the previous department.

Just In Time is seen not as a program at Northern's Switching plant in Calgary, but more as a journey. Instead of expecting major gains, each group focused on continuous improvement. The same principal applied to suppliers, although not all could be involved from the beginning. A few high-cost vendors were identified for certification, which promoted frequent, zero-defect deliveries direct to the line operation. Suppliers that could not adapt to the new model were often dropped for more responsive suppliers.

Total Quality Management

Quality has always been a Northern Telecom obsession. The goal is to attain perfection. To gain it, each team measures its own quality and meets daily to review performance. With increased focus on measurement of defects, the buck cannot be passed on. On the rare occasion that it is, each department, or final inspection, sends the product back to the team that caused the problem. In this way, there is direct awareness of how problems impact others.

The implementation of TQC did not take place without difficulty. As with the drop in individual productivity ratings, many workers felt a loss of individual identity and pride of personal workmanship. Many operators were reluctant to lose their individual quality rating and be measured as part of a team. Now they are bound to improve not only their own quality, but also that of everybody on the team. However, with time, a sense of pride and achievement in team quality has emerged.

Initially, teams did not want ownership of their quality because many defects were beyond their control. They saw engineering, maintenance, and suppliers of incoming materials as the chief culprits. However, they were encouraged to invite resource people from other groups to help them resolve such problems. It took time, but this ultimately created a more informal and more effective relationship within the plant.

Conclusion

The story of the success of the Calgary-based Switching Division of Northern Telecom illustrates the power of taking a long-term approach to improvement. It suggests that short-term programs—or "flavors of the month"—rarely help. However, when these programs are incorporated into the sociotechnical system of an organization and reinforced with significant management involvement and consistent, ongoing training, they really do improve the organization's ability to serve its customers better, quicker and at less cost. It gets to stay in business, at a profit.

QUESTIONNAIRE

Answer the following questions ranking your answers from 1 to 5.

1 - represents very poor,	4 - good and
2 - poor,	5 - very good.
3 - average,	

- Do you have a formalized JIT process?

1 - No,	4 - Have many aspects,
2 - A little,	5 - Totally.
3 - Somewhat,	

- Are your vendors certified on the basis of their ability to deliver quality parts, on time?

1 - Not at all,	4 - Mostly,
2 - A few,	5 - Totally.
3 - About half,	

- Do you have a push or a pull manufacturing system?

  1 - Exclusively push,
  3 - Combination,
  5 - Exclusively pull.

- Are incoming parts held in a storage area, or are they sent directly to the floor?

1 - All into storage,	4 - Mostly direct to floor,
2 - Mostly into storage,	5 - All direct to floor.
3 - Some into storage,	

- Are operators allowed to shut down the line if they know that poor quality parts are produced?

1 - Never,	4 - Most times,
2 - With permission,	5 - Always.
3 - Sometimes,	

- Do operators monitor key dimensions of their process on a
  statistical process control chart?
  - 1 - Never,
  - 2 - Infrequently,
  - 3 - Sometimes,
  - 4 - Most times,
  - 5 - Always.

- Are you capable of producing lot sizes of one without lost time?
  - 1 - No,
  - 3 - Sometimes,
  - 5 - Yes.

- Do you make regular changes to reduce changeover times?
  - 1 - Never,
  - 2 - Seldom,
  - 3 - Sometimes,
  - 4 - Quite often,
  - 5 - Regularly.

- Do you use a multi-disciplined team approach to find ways of
  reducing setup times?
  - 1- Never,
  - 3 - Sometimes,
  - 5 - Always.

- Do you document changes to ensure that they are standardized and
  used?
  - 1 - Never,
  - 2 - Seldom,
  - 3 - Sometimes,
  - 4 - Most Times,
  - 5 - Always.

- Is your plant designed to minimize material handling?
  - 1 - No,
  - 3 - Somewhat,
  - 5 - Totally.

- Are your shop floor people regularly consulted on process
  improvements?
  - 1 - Never,
  - 2 - Infrequently,
  - 3 - Sometimes,
  - 4 - Frequently,
  - 5 - Always.

•. Do parts arrive for assembly as needed?
  - 1 - Never,
  - 2 - Infrequently,
  - 3 - Sometimes,
  - 4 - Most times,
  - 5 - Always.

- Do you have a vendor certification program?
  - 1 - No,
  - 3 - Limited,
  - 5 - Total.

- What is your relationship with your suppliers ?
  - 1 - Hostile,
  - 2 - Somewhat adversarial,
  - 3 - Fair,
  - 4 - Good,
  - 5 - Excellent.

- What is the length of your contracts?
    - 1 - One year or less,
    - 2 - 1-2 year,
    - 3 - 2-3 years,
    - 4 - 3-4 years,
    - 5 - in excess of 5 years.
- Do your purchasing people spend time at the premises of existing and potential suppliers?
    - 1 - Less than 5% of time,
    - 2 - 6-10% of time,
    - 3 - 11-15% of time,
    - 4 - 16-20% of time,
    - 5 - 20% or more.
- . Do you share data electronically with your suppliers?
    - 1 - Never,
    - 2 - Limited,
    - 3 - Some,
    - 4 - Many,
    - 5 - All.
- Do you inspect products from your suppliers?
    - 1 - Check 100%,
    - 2 - Check most,
    - 3 - Check some,
    - 4 - Check few,
    - 5 - No incoming inspection.
- Do you have ongoing joint problem solving/cost reduction teams with your suppliers?
    - 1 - None,
    - 2 - Very limited,
    - 3 - Some,
    - 4 - With many key suppliers,
    - 5 - With all key suppliers.
- Do your operators monitor their own quality?
    - 1 - No,
    - 2 - Infrequently,
    - 3 - Sometimes,
    - 4 - Most times,
    - 5 - Always.
- Do you document your manufacturing processes?
    - 1 - None,
    - 2 - A few,
    - 3 - Some,
    - 4 - Most,
    - 5 - All.
- Do you audit to ensure that your processes are followed?
    - 1 - Never,
    - 2 - Infrequently,
    - 3 - Sometimes,
    - 4 - Frequently,
    - 5 - Always.

TOTAL SCORES

Interpretation

In relation to the element of World-Class Manufacturing:
- A score of 14 to 21 indicates that your quality process is very poor.
- A score of 22 to 35 indicates that your quality process is poor.
- A score of 36 to 49 indicates that you are doing a reasonable job.
- A score of 50 to 63 indicates that you are doing a fairly good job on quality
- A score in excess of 64 indicates that you are doing a superb job on your quality process.

chapter *7*

Additional Manufacturing Techniques To Speed Time To Market

This chapter will discuss a number of additional manufacturing techniques that will aid a company in bringing a product to market quicker. It will discuss Flexible Manufacturing, Computer-Aided Process Planning, Quick Die Change, quick part change in workholding systems, bar coding and automatic identification systems, and Group Technology. Many or all of these techniques may be considered part of Computer-Integrated Manufacturing (CIM).

FLEXIBLE MANUFACTURING

The technology of flexible manufacturing holds great promise for manufacturing. It has the potential to improve quality, reduce costs and inventory, and improve product turnaround. Flexible manufacturing might well be divided into two parts: Flexible Manufacturing Systems (FMS) and Flexible Manufacturing Cells (FMC).

Flexible Manufacturing Systems

A Flexible Manufacturing System consists of a group of computer-controlled machines that manage automated material handling, processing, and storage. Such systems can process a variety of different parts simultaneously.

To define a FMS is very difficult. People attempt to define a FMS from their own perspective. The *Tool and Manufacturing Engineers Handbook* provided some insight into this area when it noted:

157

"At a higher level, a FMS is a collection of Flexible Manufacturing Cells. It can also be a group of dedicated, single-purpose manufacturing machines, providing flexibility due to both the variable flow of material between stations and the different combinations of using various single-operation stations. In both cases, the end result is the ability to manufacture multiple parts for assemblies using the same collection of machines. A transfer line with variable usage and operation of the stations can function as a FMS. Therefore, *Flexible Manufacturing* describes any collection of machines or centers with a means to move material between them. The entire system is controlled by computers, which collectively can manufacture different parts and products from start to finish."

The handbook went on to explain "the unique feature of a FMS is the ability to manufacture more than one part, or in some cases, more than one family of parts in mid-volume output rates. Some systems require batching or piecing families, while other systems accept work pieces from various families of parts in random order."[1] In contrast to FMC, the FMS usually requires a larger capital investment. It also requires more sophisticated controls.

The meaning of the term *flexibility* in FMS can vary. It can encompass:

- Operating flexibility of equipment: the frequency and the time it takes to make tool adjustments and tool changes. For example, a lathe used to machine a part will have a tool that experiences wear. If not adjusted, the wear on the tool will cause the parts to go out of tolerance. With FMS, this adjustment is made automatically through the software. In a manual system, it would have to be done by the operator.

- Changeover flexibility: the ease in which machines can be changed over to produce different work pieces within specific part families. Take the example of an automotive family of differently sized brake drums. Produced on an automatic lathe, the machine would have a magazine of tools directed by the software and changed automatically depending upon the size of brake drum presented to the machine. The major benefit of changeover flexibility is that a drum can be produced economically on a per-car basis rather than in batch quantities. So, the work-in-process can be reduced, as would overheads.

- Process flexibility permits different workpiece types to be manufactured simultaneously. For example, different parts for different customers within the same part family, such as brake drums, could be produced at the same time.

- Reaction flexibility facilitates product mix change. Consider the brake drums again. If higher oil prices boost demand for smaller cars dramatically, manufacturers will need to convert production quickly to reflect the

---

[1] William Cubberly and Ramon Bakerjian, *Tool and Manufacturing Engineer's Handbook,* Desk Edition, 1989, Dearborn, MI, p. 4-1.

refocused market. If they fail to do so, they will have idle capacity and excess unwanted product.

- Routing flexibility reroutes parts if equipment breaks down. For example, assume a milling machine stops for any reason. FMS software automatically, and without human intervention, will redirect parts to another machine in the cell so that processing is uninterrupted.

- Volume flexibility is a machine's ability to run economically at differing output volumes. A FMS central computer controls the utilization of each machine in a cell. If a request to manufacture a part comes from sales, the computer can be interrogated to establish the idle capacity in the system among equipment capable of producing that part. This idle capacity is then compared to the necessary capacity to produce the parts. If there is sufficient capacity the order is accepted. If not, decisions are made to either increase capacity by adding equipment or to reject the order.

- Capacity flexibility is the capacity of a total system and its ability to expand. For example, it allows for management of manufacturing capacity so that decisions on capacity can be made well ahead of immediate need. In this way, costly overtime or order rejection can be avoided. This is made possible because the information generated by the computer-controlled system reports on day-to-day, month-to-month capacity requirements and utilizes computer software used by the Manufacturing Requirements Planning system.

FMS Technology

FMS technology can include computer-controlled machines with wide-part size capability and able to produce to required tolerances. Typical is a lathe capable of handling a wide range of lengths and diameters to a range of specifications.

FMS technology can also include Group Technology which is explained later in this chapter. The system has the ability to handle a group of different parts with similar characteristics such as a group of shafts with different lengths up to 24 in. (61 cm) and diameters up to 3 in. (7.6 cm).

FMS technology will likely include automated handling of materials between machines. This is often accomplished by using jigs or fixtures as parts carriers throughout the system. Jigs and fixtures used in this way are called "pallets." Pallets are moved from machine to machine on a conveyor system or on Automated Guided Vehicles.

There are five functions that a Flexible Manufacturing System should fulfill. It should allow:

1. random independent movement of work parts between workstations;
2. handling of a variety of work part configurations;
3. temporary storage for work in progress;
4. convenient access for loading and unloading work parts; and
5. supply the capability of direct computer control.

FMS works best for certain manufacturing volumes.

Data Requirements and Outputs

The five main data requirements for efficient FMS operation are:

- A part program file for each operating workstation. An example: a CNC program for each machining operation.
- A routing file for each work part. An example: route sheet information on each part.
- A part production file containing production control information. For example, the file contains the quantity to produce, inspection points, and production rates.
- A pallet reference file containing information on which pallets will accept which part numbers.
- A station tool control file containing the identification codes for each tool stored in the machine. This file also tracks tool life and replacement/resharpening needs.

Standard Outputs from FMS

Reports generated by a FMS system usually include a utilization report for each machine and for the complete FMS. A FMS should be capable of producing, on a daily or weekly basis, production reports showing quantities required and produced. A status report may be generated at any time by viewing the computer screen or printing hard copy. Also generally available is a tool report containing tool life, tool usage, and a comparison of the two for tool replacement decisions.

Benefits of FMS

Some of the benefits of FMS are:

- higher machine utilization than in a conventional batch production machine shop.
- reduced work-in-process because different parts are processed together using Group Technology.
- shorter manufacturing lead time because of reduced work-in-process volume.
- greater flexibility in production scheduling. Because of the flexibility of the system, parts do not have to be processed in batches.
- lower labor/part cost because of higher production rates and shorter setup times.

FLEXIBLE MANUFACTURING CELLS

A Flexible Manufacturing Cell is usually a group of related machines which are performing a process or step in a larger manufacturing process. A Flexible Manufacturing Cell may be a part of a Flexible Manufacturing System.

This cell may be segregated for a number of reasons. These include raw material needs, operator requirements, chemical requirements, noise, or manufacturing cycle times. The Flexible Manufacturing Cell is not restricted to one type of part or process. It can easily accommodate different parts and products. These products and parts are usually within families of similar dimensional characteristics and physical properties.

One of the distinctions between a FMS and a FMC is the lack of major material movement systems. These systems may include AGVs. FMC usually involves a roughly circular pattern of machines with a manual operator or robot in the center. This operator or robot moves from machine to machine. The machines in the cell are supportive of one another, as each is performing a basic, related activity. These activities include drilling, machining, finishing, or inspection.

FMC Advantages

It has been reported by some manufacturers that there is a major FMC benefit in the area of production control. Cells are capable of reducing work-in-process time as well as inventory.

By moving a number of processes into a single cell, tracking of different operations by production control may be eliminated. In this case, several production orders might be consolidated into one order.

An additional time-saving benefit rests in the fact that by producing parts in only one department, there is a large reduction in the movement of parts (usually by forklift). With FMC, equipment costs tend to be lower.

COMPUTER-AIDED PROCESS PLANNING (CAPP)

Process Planning is concerned with preparation of route sheets or process sheets which list the sequence of operations and work centers required to produce a product and its components. Route sheets or process sheets list the production steps needed to make the part, along with equipment, tooling, fixtures, and the standard time for each operation. CAPP systems help prepare these route or process sheets as a link between Design and Manufacturing. *Table 7-1* is an example.

The information used in *Table 7-1* utilizes an *Expert System*. Expert Systems are rule-based and aid basic decision making process as it relates to how to process a part. Basic decision choices include options for choices such as feeds and speeds for machining. For instance, if your apartment has an address, it requires a number. An Expert System would monitor the spelling of the names and the street numbers available. If the name is misspelled or the street number is not in its database, it is questioned or rejected.

The first advantage of CAPP is standardization of process plans. This means that there will be similar process plans for similar parts. Without CAPP, chaos could rule as each process planner's own ideas of how a part should move through the shop are input without regard to consistency. CAPP also provides faster planning of parts because the system needs fewer planners to do the same volume of work.

The third advantage is improved legibility and accuracy of process planning documents. No handwritten plans mean no sloppy writing/printing of codes and departments and more accurate routings.

A Common Database is Required for CAPP

Computer-Aided Process Planning accesses and shares a common database that contains a large volume of information. The Master Production Schedule

Table 7-1. Harvar Manufacturing Company Limited.

Part Number: 247A
Part Revision No.: C
Planner: Bob Carter

Part Name: Shower Head Defuser
Material: Brass Spec. 487
Date: 27 Aug, 1990

Op. No.	Description	Tools & Equipment	Run Time in S/U Hrs.	Hrs./ 100 Pcs.
10	Saw slug	Air saw	.5	0.14
20	Forge	3 man Maxi press	1.9	0.48
30	Blank - (trim)	Bliss 74 press	1.2	0.10
40	Pickle	HCL tank	-	0.01
50	Pierce (6) holes	Bliss 74 press	1.2	0.12
60	Rough ream & chamfer	Delta 17" drill	.3	0.62
70	Drill (3) holes	Avery drill press	.3	0.32
80	Machine stem & face	Number three W.& S.	.7	0.98
90	Machine O.D. & face	Number three W.& S.	.7	1.17
100	Stamp	Bliss number 20B press	1.2	0.10
110	Broach (6) holes & gage diameter	Bliss 74 press	1.2	0.27
120	Inspect (spot check)1/20 Vernier		-	0.70

balances production, and reduces needs for layoffs or wasted time. The Material Requirements Planning and Manufacturing Resource Planning system ensure that components are made on time with the most efficient use of company resources. The database will also include capacity plans. These are required to ensure that plant capacity is not exceeded causing unexpected overtime or increased supervision cost. If plant capacity is to be exceeded, it should be done with a plan in place so that costs can be justified. Computerized shop floor control data is required for machine/equipment work loading so that work is distributed and overtime is reduced. The database will also include engineering and manufacturing data. Engineering data indicates part configuration, material, cost, and gives a part breakdown for all assemblies. Manufacturing data shows machine part capacity, CNC parts programs, and inventory control data including stock conditions for component parts and assemblies. Purchasing data indicates whether a part is purchased or made in-house and includes costs and materials information. Finally, the database will include Group Technology systems data indicating the part coding so that similar parts can be processed together.

QUICK DIE CHANGE

It is well-understood that a key step toward Just In Time manufacturing is to cut setup times so that large work-in-process batches are reduced or eliminated. In the metalworking industry, Quick Die Change methods can achieve substantial setup time reductions. Case studies have shown that maintenance and teamwork are critical success factors in Quick Die Change. The documentation shows where die transition times of six to 10 *hours* have been reduced to five to 10 *minutes* on automated tandem lines through effective maintenance, teamwork, and training. The end result is that a greater number of jobs can be run and smaller batch sizes increase profitability.

Quick Die Change can increase stamping shop capacity without increasing shop size or purchasing new equipment. Increasing press up-time from 50% to 90% increases shop capacity by 80%. Because Quick Die Change requires the exact duplication of a standardized setup, and eliminates trial-and-error techniques, product quality is improved and scrap and rework are reduced or eliminated.

Even a conservative approach to Quick Die Change, such as adoption of improved clamping methods for the elimination of straps and adoption of a common tie-down height, can reduce setup time for a straight-side press from 40 minutes to under 20 minutes. Adoption of common load and shut-heights can reduce this figure to under 20 minutes, with the major factor being the threading of the stock. Once setup times have been reduced to under 20 minutes, cost studies should be done to determine if further retrofitting of existing equipment is required. Specialized equipment such as die subplates, hydraulic die clamps, in-bolster rollers, and specialized die carts are expensive, but may offer a good return on the investment.

Conversion to Quick Die Change provides an opportunity to improve die clamping methods and die handling, thus increasing safety of personnel and reducing die damage and maintenance costs. Increased up-time and productivity make short-production runs profitable and reduce inventory.

Careful planning and strategy are needed to implement Quick Die Change in an existing plant. The whole organization of a stamping facility must be involved. To be effective, Quick Die Change teams require the support of engineering, quality control, scheduling, material handling, maintenance, tool room, purchasing, and sales personnel.

Employee teamwork is the central theme of the quick die change in shops that are successful in substantial setup time reductions. In one shop for example, die-setting teams overcame problems by videotaping their setup procedures. They then reviewed the tapes and looked for other ways for improving performance. If these methods are to succeed, such teamwork must be encouraged.

Employee involvement is a proven method of improving work procedures and quality. Diesetters, die makers, maintenance employees, and operators should meet regularly in the plant for training and a discussion of methods of improving overall plant performance. Employee suggestion systems provide a valuable source of ideas for reducing setup times.

One element of reducing downtime is reducing delays. Waiting for materials, waiting for quality inspection and approval, and interruptions to the die change procedure can be shortened or eliminated by careful planning and scheduling.

One plant was able to reduce setup time from two hours 51 minutes to one hour 11 minutes by eliminating delays in material handling and interruptions, and training the diesetters to perform gage inspections and eliminate the quality approval delay.

A major modification of the dies and presses, attaching parallels on the die shoes and ledges on the parallels to provide a uniform clamping height, allowed the use of the same clamps on all dies, and easier handling of the dies. Milling a keyway down the length of the bolster, to match corresponding keyways in the parallels, permitted exact centering of the die. Common shut-height improvement, together with exact die relocation in the press, increased first-hit quality approval. These further improvements reduced the downtime to 34 minutes and later to 20 minutes.

As downtime is shortened and quality is improved, batch sizes can be reduced so that work-in-process and inventories are smaller. The advantages of reduced work-in-process include: less space required for production; lower operating costs due to less space to maintain; lower carrying costs due to smaller space requirements; quicker response to engineering changes; lower re-work costs; and lower loss and damage costs due to fewer work pieces on the shop floor.

After the adoption of Quick Die Change, additional reductions in downtime may be realized. Setup workers are well-trained, well-prepared, and well-organized, and standardized procedures and labor-saving devices are used. These factors contribute to more efficient and therefore faster die change procedures.[2]

Quick Part Change Work-holding Systems

The application of automation requires flexibility, precise workpiece positioning, and speedy changeover. This is especially true in the case of around-the-clock unattended automation.

Equipment and tool builders involved in automation application have made progress in evolving systems for quick part changing, but few standards have appeared for quick part change workholding systems, since parts are unique to most companies and industries. An exception is the electronics industry, because it has greater standardization of components.

There are a number of success stories. One case is from the metal working industry using one vendor's workholding products at E&E Special Products (Detroit), a division of E&E Engineering, Inc. The product is called a Rota-Shaft and is a powered hold-down clamp. The following is an excerpt from *Manufacturing Engineering*, February 1986, entitled "*Work-holding in Transition*" authored by William F. Nastali.

"Unlike many conventional clamps, this design's vertical motion is a result of the shaft rotating along a harmonically generated cam track, up to 165 degrees of rotation.

---

[2] David A. Smith, *Quick Die Change,* Dearborn, MI, Society of Manufacturing Engineers, 1991.

"Clamps are familiar throughout industry and even minor additions of automation can make a big difference in output, so E&E engineers developed a further use for the Roto-Shaft clamp. They turned it into an automatic parts handling device. By simply adding a vacuum cup or other gripping device to the end of the clamping detail of a 90-degree rotating Roto-Shaft, the device can pick up a part, rotate, then deposit it on the opposite side of the origination point—on a conveyor, for example.

"Through a little engineering ingenuity, a workholding device becomes a material handling device. A productivity paradox.

"The main question that must be answered when contemplating automated workholding is, "Who will be responsible for system design? Will it be "in-house" or a "turnkey" designed system?" In-house system design will insure more control over quality and delivery. It also means that your design group will gain the experience with workholding systems design and will be better able to modify it as products change. On the other hand, it will probably mean that the first few systems will cost more because of the inexperience of the design group and may be less reliable for the same reason.

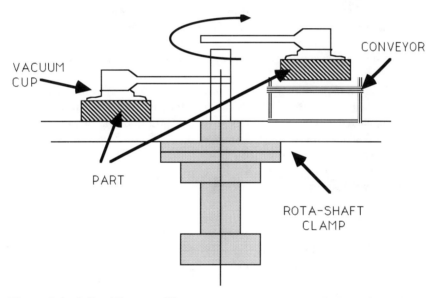

Figure 7-1. A Dual Purpose Clamp:
A work-holding clamp transformed into a material handling device.

"There are two main problems with workholding devices components. The first problem is reliability. Reliability is the mean time between failures and is a function of the design of the device and the quality of manufacturing the components and their assembly. Standard component reliability has been improving both for onshore and offshore manufacturing. Specialty components are a different story. The second main problem with workholding devices is a shortage of service and service parts. This problem can be minimized by dealing with companies with a good service reputation, who carry a good supply of service parts.

"In conclusion, the workholding industry has lagged behind other segments of the machine tool industry. So it will have a lot of catching up to do to ensure flexibility and speed in workpiece holding and handling."

Quick Setup and Small Lot Production

Kiyoshi Suzaki, author of *The New Manufacturing Challenge: Techniques for Continuous Improvement*, provided some interesting insight on Small Lot Production.

Clearly, there is a need to cut lead time for product delivery to customers. The most fundamental challenge, then, is to organize better, reduce setup time, and decrease production batch sizes. Also, inventory levels must be reduced in production and transportation systems. This will decrease the risk of carrying unneeded inventories.

- Take the example of a factory that produces both product A and product B. Because of the nuisance associated with setup, this factory runs the machine to produce five As followed by five Bs. But let's look at this from the customer's side. The customer who wants to buy product B has to wait for five As to be completed before they receive the product they want. Because of the long lead time (which is tied to the long setup time), this customer goes to a competitor to buy their product instead.

- How can the factory overcome this problem? One way is to accumulate a finished goods inventory of B so it can fill customer orders more quickly. But carrying excess inventories just adds a host of other dilemmas, such as space and organization problems, etc. Instead, why doesn't the factory try to figure out how to reduce the setup time by using its creativity? By producing goods in small lots, the factory can eliminate the wastes associated with overproduction and excess inventory.

There are many techniques that can be used to improve manufacturing operations. As history testifies, many great things have happened as a result of people using their creativity and inquisitiveness.

The same applies to the manufacturing environment. A need to improve and having the ability to imagine improved operations are prerequisite to understanding or to acquiring any techniques. To say it simply, there should be a need and even a personal desire before any techniques are brought in.

With this in mind, proceed to figure out how to reduce setup time and achieve small lot production. Follow these four steps:

1. Separate the work that must be done while the machine is stopped (internal setup) from work that can be done while the machine is in operation (external setup). Since the setup time is defined as the time from the production of the last good piece to the production of the next good piece, external setup work should not be mixed with internal setup work. Consider conducting a simple time study and videotaping the setup to separate

external work from internal work. This can generate a lot of ideas by the group of operators, engineers, maintenance crews, and quality assurance people.

2. Reduce internal setup by doing more work externally, such as preparing dies, transferring dies and fixtures, etc. Of course, practicing housekeeping and workplace organization is the basis for quick setup.

3. Reduce internal setup by eliminating adjustments and simplifying attachments and detachments. Since many adjustments take as much as half of the typical setup time, one of the keys to dramatically improving setup is to *eliminate* adjustments, not just reduce them. The same is true for developing simplified attachment and detachment methods. Question thoroughly and borrow ideas from others. In addition, consider adding a person to reduce the internal setup work (see *Figures* 7-2, 3, and 4).

4. Reduce the total time spent on both internal and external work. Practice the basic disciplines of housekeeping and workplace organization, simplify and standardize the setup procedures, and keep practicing so that skills are increased. *Figure* 7-5 is an example of parallel operations to save time.

Monitor the setup time as you go and share the progress (see the example setup performance chart in *Figure 7-6*). By understanding that there are a number of ways to improve setup times, by practicing the basic principles, and by brainstorming, tremendous gains will be made without incurring large expenditures. The elevated morale will become a major asset for the organization's continuous improvement efforts.[3]

Bar Coding and Automatic Identification Systems

Bar coding is one technology that continues to go through major evolutionary change. Right from its inception in the 1960s, it struggled to evolve as an industry standard. This technology has become the most popular method of data entry. "The Market for Bar Code Products: A Strategic Analysis," a study from Venture Development Corporation (Natick, MA), projects that U.S. shipments of bar code products, mainly input devices, printers, labels, and other consumables, software, system integration, and associated products, equalled $1.5 billion in 1988 and will increase by 18% per year to $2.6 billion in 1992 *(Figure 7-7)*.

The projection is based on traditional binary notation. Narrow elements are decoded as "0s," and wide elements are decoded as "1s." It is called Code 39 bar code symbology and is used by Department of Defense suppliers, automotive industry suppliers, and hundreds of other manufacturers that have adopted bar coding for identification purposes.

Bar coding application standards provide a common coding scheme and have been developed by the Department of Defense and the Automotive Industry Action Group of Southfield, MI. MIL-STD 1189A Code 39 symbology standard

---

[3] Kiyoshi Suzaki, *The New Manufacturing Challenge: Techniques for Continuous Improvement*, New York, The Free Press, 1987, p. 32-40.

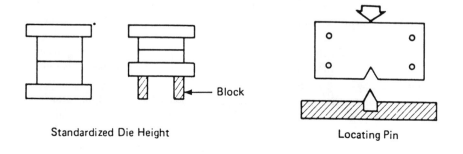

Standardized Die Height

← Block

Locating Pin

Figure 7-2. Two Examples of Ways to Eliminate Adjustment.

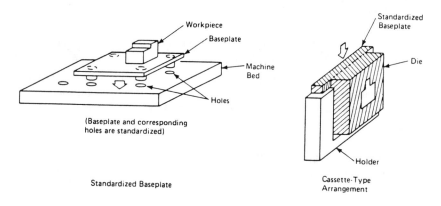

Standardized Baseplate

Cassette-Type
Arrangement

Figure 7-3. Use of Standardized Fixtures to Eliminate Adjustment.

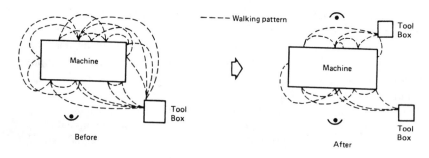

Figure 7-4. Example of Parallel Operations (Top View).

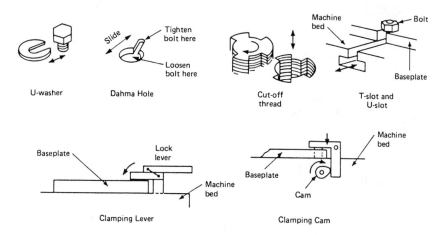

Figure 7-5. Improvements in Attachment and Detachment.

Date	Product From	To	Setup Time (min.)	Comments
5/10	A	B	20	
5/10	B	C	15	
5/11	C	D	40	die repair
5/12	D	A	10	

Figure 7-6. Setup Performance Chart.

and MIL-STD 129J application standard are part of the Logistics Applications of Automated Marking and Reading Symbols program that was instituted in 1982.

Another group that has been developing standards for bar coding is the Automotive Industry Action Group (AIAG) a nonprofit trade association whose members are North American automotive vehicle manufacturers and suppliers. They have published a number of standards including the following:

- AIAG-B-1, a symbology standard for Code 39;
- AIAG-B-2, a vehicle identification standard;
- AIAG-B-3, a shipping and parts identification standard;
- AIAG-B-4, an individual parts identification label standard;
- AIAG-B-5, a primary metals identification tag standard;
- AIAG-B-6, the data identifier dictionary standard.

How Bar Coding Works

A bar code scanner translates bar codes. When a bar code scanner's laser light beam is passed across a bar code symbol, a photodetector in the scanner converts

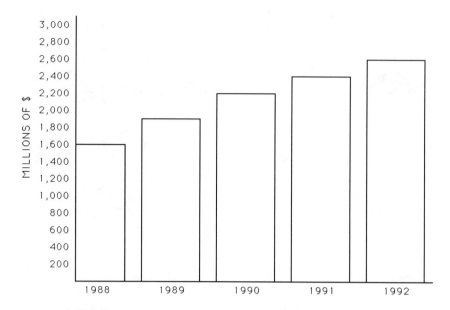

Figure 7-7. Projected Bar Code Shipments (USA).

the pattern of reflected light it receives into an analog signal. This signal is decoded by a microprocessor into characters that will be recognized and processed by a computer (*Figure 7-8*).

Bar code and other forms of automatic identification provides fast, accurate information. This is extremely important since manual data entry is the main source of data entry errors and manual input generally occurs after the fact.

This technology can help obtain product position in the process from the raw materials entry into the plant to its shipment to the customer. Bar code readers are integrated into the computerized materials management system and then into Computer-Integrated Manufacturing systems.

In many applications, the use of bar coding means replacing the computer keyboard as an input device with that of the bar code reader wands and scanners. This has been well-received by workers. It requires less manual dexterity because typing skills are not required. Also, it is easy to learn to operate the equipment. Company management has also been quick to see the benefits of fewer spelling errors. And this has also ensured that people with poor literacy levels do not make mistakes.

New Trends in Bar Coding

A number of trends are emerging. Equipment is becoming smaller, cheaper, lighter, and more powerful. This means that more people will have better access to more information. Technology is emerging that will allow encoding of very large amounts of information in a much smaller space. The automated identification systems are getting more sophisticated, thus allowing integration of all areas of manufacturing into the system. This all means that the user will have greater

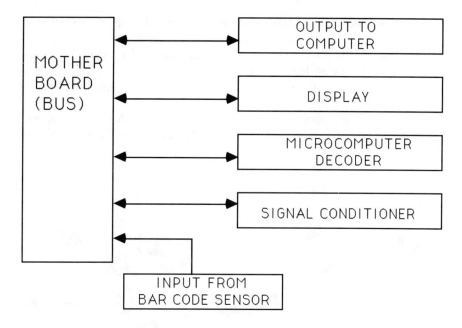

Figure 7-8. Bar Code Reading System Design.
Source: "The Market Bar Code Products: A StrategicAnalysis" by Venture Development Corp., (Natwick, MA).

access to more equipment, services, and information than ever before. More companies will be able to share databases, opening up improved vendor relationships.

GROUP TECHNOLOGY

Organization of both parts and work processes is a key element in accelerating the movement of a product to market.

Identifying and exploiting the similarity of parts and manufacturing processes can prove to be an obvious time saver for industry. Group Technology (GT) is a manufacturing philosophy that has proved successful by grouping parts into families to speed production and reduce costs.

The result of this classification process is not only improved set up and throughput time, but also effective cost reduction through improved design rationalization and better retrieval of design data. In addition, the application of GT can lead to reductions of in-process inventory and tooling costs as well as NC programming costs. Manufacturing engineers also apply GT to improve NC utilization.

In some cases, GT has also proven an essential element of Computer-Integrated Manufacturing (CIM).

THE PHILOSOPHY OF GROUP TECHNOLOGY

Group Technology's basic philosophy is to use—as fully as possible—the work already in existence to design and manufacture products.

Dr. Nancy Lea Hyer of Hewlett Packard served as Editor of the SME book *Capabilities of Group Technology*.[4] In the book's Preface, she wrote:

"GT implies the notion of recognizing and exploiting similarities in three distinct ways (1) by performing like activities together; (2) by standardizing similar tasks, and (3) by efficiently storing the retrieving information about recurring problems."

For example, applying the philosophy of Group Technology to the random collection of parts shown in *Figure 7-9* yield the "part families" shown in *Figure 7-10*.

Figure 7-9. An Organized Grouping of Parts.[5]

TOOLS TO APPLY THE GT PHILOSOPHY

To apply GT, one must have some way of identifying similarities. This can be done informally by relying on memory, for instance. However, for obvious reasons, informal approaches are not effective for complex or cross-functional GT applications.

One tool for capturing and retrieving information on item similarity is a classification and coding system. A comprehensive classification and coding system will capture and store a great deal of information that is used by multiple functions. A design engineer, a manufacturing engineer, and a purchasing agent might each require different information.

---

[4] Nancy Lea Hyer, Editor. *Capabilities of Group Technology*. Dearborn MI, Society of Manufacturing Engineers, 1987, p. iii.
[5] Arnold A. Taube, *Proceedings of AUTOFACT '90*, Dearborn MI, Society of Manufacturing Engineers, 1990, p. 16-42.

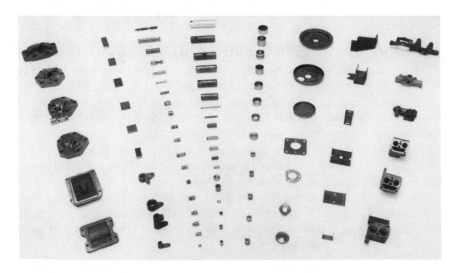

Figure 7-10. Under Group Technology, the parts may be grouped or classified this way.[6]

A coded database of part information that would be useful to the design engineer and/or manufacturing engineer might carry essential characteristics for a product such as:

- shape or geometry,
- dimensions,
- materials, raw and finishing form,
- functions, and
- chemistry.

On the other hand, customer support might require pricing substitutes, and maintainability information. A finance user would need price information, costs and vendor information.

Some commercially available Group Technology classification and coding systems come complete with programs for forming part families, analyzing manufacturing costs, calculating machine loading, and equipment utilization.

Therefore, many characteristics of the part must be retained so that each user can retrieve the information they need for effective decision making. The computer, obviously, becomes an important tool in the storage and retrieval of data to support Group Technology applications.

Some companies have found that combining GT organization principles and a relational database results in powerful tools. By using a simple question and

---

[6] Arnold A. Taube, *Proceedings of AUTOFACT '90,* "Applying GT to Improve Composite Part Manufacture." Dearborn, MI, Society of Manufacturing Engineers, 1990, p. 16-43.

answer procedure that is menu-driven, the user can specify attributes of the item wanted. The more attributes that are spelled-out, the more focused the search.

GT APPLICATIONS IN DESIGN AND MANUFACTURING

There are many informal, ad-hoc manufacturing applications for GT. For example, shop foremen or machinists organize parts for machining by looking for setup similarities. In the lab, designers can use the GT philosophy to avoid redundancy by retrieving previously completed items for re-use. This saves design time and contributes positively to Time To Market. Although applying the GT philosophy can be viewed as simply applying common sense, it makes more sense for engineering management to have formal GT systems and procedures in place for as many applications as possible.

The advent of Computer-Aided Design (CAD) presents an even more compelling reason to apply GT. It can avoid redundancy. With a CAD system, more new part designs can be produced faster. A danger, however, is that more unnecessary designs may be created.

Rick Franzosa of Prime Computer reported, in effect, in his paper *Group Technology—The Key to CIM* that an Arthur D. Little study reported only 20% of the parts made in an average manufacturing firm in any given year are truly new. About 40% are copies of existing designs and 40% more are of parts that could have been created by modifying existing designs. In other words, we don't really need all these new part designs.[7]

Redundancy savings can be significant according to Rita Feeney of Wizdom Systems Incorporated. In a paper presented at AUTOFACT '88, she said, "each time an existing design can be used instead of creating a new one, initial costs of $2,000 to $12,000 per part and lifetime design maintenance costs of over $100,000 per part are saved. The savings realized from the availability of information in a Group Technology database are less quantifiable but also significant."[8]

PROCESS PLANNING

Group Technology principles are embedded in Computer-Assisted Process Planning systems. CAPP can be variant or generative. In variant process planning, standard plans are created for a family of similar items. In generative process planning, key item features are related to specific preferred manufacturing processes. The system creates a process plan for a new part by combining only preferred standard processes.

Thus, with generative process planning, uniform manufacturing process plans can be made from information associated with engineering design. Through its

---

[7] Rick Franzosa, " Group Technology—the Key to CIM." *SME Technical Paper MS89-48*. Dearborn. MI, Society of Manufacturing Engineers, 1989, p. 4.
[8] Rita C. Feeney, *Proceedings of AUTOFACT '88*, "GT Within the Total CIM Concept." Dearborn, MI, Society of Manufacturing Engineers, 1988, p. 4-61.

use in process planning, GT provides another link between design and manufacturing and facilitates Design for Manufacturability (DFM).

MANUFACTURING CELLS

GT principles can also guide the physical organization of manufacturing through the creation of manufacturing cells. Manufacturing cells typically include a variety of machine tools and are dedicated to the efficient production of a group of similar parts.

In other instances, cellular manufacturing has resulted in better control of work-in-process, reduced setup times, shorter lead and flow times, resulted in better quality and prompted higher worker morale.[8] Most significantly, from a Time To Market perspective, adoption of cells results in shorter cycle time for parts production. This too creates faster manufacturing response times and accelerates Time To Market.

GT AT WORK

There are many good examples of GT applications in North America.

William Beeby and Phyllis Collier in their book, *New Directions Through CAD/CAM*, report one of the early examples that took place at Rocketdyne Corporation. They report:

"As a result of a five-year program, the Rocketdyne Corporation became deeply involved with implementation of GT, using the MICLASS system for coding and classification. Rocketdyne activities include common coding to link machine tools using divisions through interactive graphics—a system called MI-GRAPHICS—as well as a CADDS 4 Computervision 3-D system. These links also communicate on a stand-alone basis with the plant's management information system.

"The MICLASS Group Technology system at Rocketdyne directed batch manufacturing operations to classify and code drawings, as well as activity analysis. Such activities included the retrieval of engineering drawings, standardization of drawings, analysis of raw material requirements, production group and machine tool requirements, and their optimal routings, as well as machine tool use.

"Rocketdyne has used Group Technology as a powerful tool to identify and extract the similarities and differences in product mixes and across geographically remote manufacturing plants. Successful utilization of Group Technology requires thorough understanding of product mix and production requirements to make planning, scheduling, and manufacturing decisions. Successful utilization should suggest alternative ways of meeting such goals.

"Rocketdyne discovered that the parts must be coded accurately and uniformly to load the master data file to permit analysis for identifying manufacturing work cells, shop load, and standard manufacturing process plans. The coding programs must also provide a standardized capability and discipline so that all manufactured parts are uniformly coded. Such precautions make parts coding easier and more accurate for less experienced personnel, thereby reducing time and costs incurred for the coding effort.

"Management discovered that Group Technology is a powerful tool for accessing data and permits more effective decision making as a result of the family-of-parts capability and equipment information."[9]

Another successful example of Group Technology implementation was presented at AUTOFACT '89 by Arnold A. Taube and Gregg Malicki of Deere and Company, who said:

"There is a manufacturing transition occurring within John Deere's factories. Traditional single function and process related departments are replaced with Group Technology-related manufacturing "cells" that contain multiple machine tool types and capabilities. Where piece parts were formerly routed around a factory, through multiple "functional" departments and work-in-process (WIP) areas, they now are produced in a single manufacturing cell. And parts that used to be produced in large, seasonal production lots are now made in "line-linked" quantities on a daily basis.

"Since its beginning in the mid-1970s, this transition has resulted in substantial numbers of manufacturing cells installed in virtually all John Deere North American and European factories. Success of cellular manufacturing has led to at least one of John Deere's senior managers questioning the benefits and return on investment (ROI) of Flexible Manufacturing Systems (FMS) when compared to manufacturing cells incorporating modern NC machine tools."[10]

Deere has also used Group Technology to improve tool room efficiency, say the authors. By analyzing a pilot crib, it was discovered that there were many identical and functionally interchangeable bearings, bushings, seals, springs and inserts used for metal cutting. Potential savings were found by eliminating identical items and consolidating crib locations. Overall crib efficiency was improved.[11] *Figure 7-11* illustrates an example finding from the Group Technology analysis performed on the pilot "bearing family" at Deere.

The authors also note that: "establishment of part families is a key cellular manufacturing concept. Part families are sifted from the gross part population by segregating parts with similar features or geometry. Once identified, these part families become the fundamental building blocks of our cellular manufacturing scheme. Once established, part families can be grouped in various ways to form alternative machine cell configurations."[12]

---

[9] William Beeby and Phyllis Collier, *New Directions Through CAD/CAM,* Dearborn, MI, Society of Manufacturing Engineers. 1986, p. 49-50.

[10] Arnold A. Taube and Gregg Malicki, *Proceedings of AUTOFACT '89,* "A Successful Method for Creating GT Cells." Dearborn, MI, Society of Manufacturing Engineers, 1989, p. 6-45.

[11] William J. Dumolien, *Proceedings of AUTOFACT '89,* "Improving Tool Room Efficiency Through GT Analysis." Dearborn, MI, Society of Manufacturing Engineers, 1989.

[12] Arnold A. Taube and Gregg Malicki, *Proceeding of AUTOFACT '89,* "A Successful Method for Creating GT Cells." Dearborn. MI, Society of Manufacturing Engineers, 1989, p. 6-49.

GT is also applied by electronics manufacturers. Admittedly, development has been slow as classification systems developed for metal fabrication do not transfer readily to the manufacture of electronic parts. However, there is every reason to expect that the development of classification systems for this industry, thus locating a larger number of components for use in new designs, will reduce the effort required in new product development. Shorter lead times in product development can most certainly be expected.

One coding system is expected to save an electronics firm as much as $500,000.[13]

Another new application area for Group Technology lies in the potential for management of composite materials. The aircraft industry will most certainly benefit, since it uses many such compounds in a host of configurations. Fortunately, most can be described with complete accuracy, and so are logical candidates for inclusion in a GT database. One aircraft manufacturer now working with a GT system has already found initial applications in airframe standardization and in-factory planning.[14]

Finally, in his *Automation Encyclopedia*, author Glenn Graham sums up Group Technology this way:

"Though Group Technology and classification and coding schemes have been around for a long time, it has not been until recently that companies have shown much interest in seriously adopting the technologies. This increased interest can be attributed to:

- the number and variety of products that deluged the industry which means a need to manufacture smaller product lots.
- a growing need for more economical ways to a quality product,
- increases in product varieties and therefore, the kinds of properties of materials required,
- the need for less waste of material, or
- rapidly growing demands for better communication between design and manufacturing.

"Group Technology emerges as one of the prime forces that will integrate the engineering and manufacturing processes. Group Technology lends order to what has usually been a highly unordered collection of processes. It drastically reduces the negative phenomenon of the needlessly recreated design and improves production scheduling and control processes."[15]

Arnold Taube (Deere & Company) in his paper for AUTOFACT '90 adds: "While the United States of America is an acknowledged leader in the development of new technologies, real wealth and power come to those who effectively

---

[13] Edward D. Penfield, "A Group Technology Classification System for Electronics Manufacturing." *SME Technical Paper* MS 89-126. Dearborn, MI, Society of Manufacturing Engineers, 1989.

[14] Arnold A. Taube, *Proceedings of AUTOFACT '90.* "Applying GT to Improve Composite Part Manufacture." Dearborn, MI, Society of Manufacturing Engineers, 1990.

[15] Glenn A. Graham, *Automation Encyclopedia-A to Z in Advanced Manufacturing.* Dearborn, MI, Society of Manufacturing Engineers, 1988. p. 277-278.

KEY	BEARING NOM ID MM	BEARING NOM OD MM	BEARING BODY LENGTH MM	MFG COST $/PC	MFGRS. CODE NO. 1	MFGRS. CATALOG NO. 1
006-00-107	25.0000	52.0000	15.0000	4.17	NDH	43205
006-00-109	25.0000	52.0000	15.0000	2.05	NDH	77505
006-00-112	25.0000	52.0000	15.0000	3.22	NDH	Z99505
006-00-820	25.0000	52.0000	15.0000	.	NDH	7505
006-00-904	25.0000	52.0000	15.0000	.	NDH	Z499505
006-04-971	25.0000	52.0000	15.0000	2.07	FAFNIR	205K
006-07-547	25.0000	52.0000	15.0000	9.10	FAFNIR	205W
006-04-614	25.0000	52.0000	15.0000	3.22	MRC	205SZZ
006-07-129	25.0000	52.0000	15.0000	2.04	SKF	6205
006-06-981	25.0000	52.0000	15.0000	3.22	SKF	6205-2RSJ

JOHN DEERE GROUP TECHNOLOGY SYSTEM   USER SPECIFIED PRINT   PAGE 2

KEY	TYPE OF OF BEARING	CATEGORY OF BEARING	NOTE NO. 1
006-00-107	BALL	RADIAL	WITH SNAP RING
006-00-109	BALL	RADIAL	SHIELD BOTH SIDES
006-00-112	BALL	RADIAL	CONTACT SEAL BOTH SIDES
006-00-820	BALL	RADIAL	SHIELD ONE SIDE
006-00-904	BALL	RADIAL	CONTACT SEAL BOTH SIDES WITH SNAP RING
006-04-971	BALL	RADIAL	
006-07-547	BALL	RADIAL	
006-04-614	BALL	RADIAL	CONTACT SEAL BOTH SIDES
006-07-129	BALL	RADIAL	
006-06-981	BALL	RADIAL	CONTACT SEAL BOTH SIDES

USER SPECIFIED PRINT STATISTICS

NUMBER OF COLUMNS OF DATA	11
NUMBER OF INPUT RECORDS	10
NUMBER OF KEYWORDS SPECIFIED	9

BRGID	BRGOD	BRGLEN	MFGCOST	MFGCODE1
CATNUM1	BRGITP	BRGCAT	NOTE1	

Figure 7-11.   Examples of Findings From the GT Analysis Performed at Deere on the Pilot Bearing Family.[16]

and efficiently apply that technology. GT is a problem solving and planning approach that facilitates effective and efficient manufacturing. Further, it applies equally to design and manufacturing functions."[17]

---

[16] William J. Dumolien, *Proceedings of AUTOFACT '89,* "Improving Tool Room Efficiency Through GT Analysis." Dearborn. MI, Society of Manufacturing Engineers, 1989, p. 6-62. Sept. 1990.
[17] Arnold A. Taube, *Proceedings of Autofact '90,* "Applying GT to Improve Composite Part Manufacture." Dearborn, MI, Society of Manufacturing Engineers, 1990, p. 16-47.

CASE STUDY

USER/VENDOR RELATIONS IN FMS IMPLEMENTATION

Introduction

As a supplier of flexible manufacturing systems for almost two decades, we have learned that special organizational structuring is required by the user and vendor to accommodate the many special needs brought on by this advanced technology. *Figure 7-12* outlines the typical organizational structure that has proven itself successful over the years. This approach utilizes a central communicator in each of the organizations called the project manager. This function provides the vital link needed to keep both organizations in tune with each other and to drive and monitor internal progress of project activities to ensure the successful implementation of Flexible Manufacturing Systems.

This emphasis on planning and communication is necessary to overcome attitudinal stumbling blocks. These attitudes appear to be deeply embedded in today's organizational mentalities. It seems that user and vendor organizations alike operate under mostly outdated expectations and assumptions.

Vendors, through the benefit of repeat business over the years, have learned to adapt and structure themselves accordingly. The inexperienced prospective user of such equipment, however, still faces the problem of adjustment to a new way of doing business.

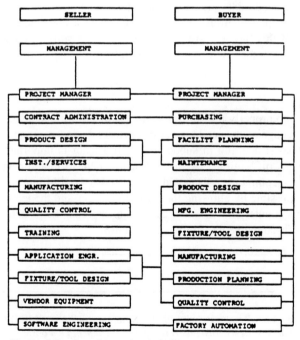

Figure 7-12. Typical Project Organization Chart.

Role of User's Project Manager—The Problem

While accepting or recognizing the necessity of a project manager, user management often underestimates the importance of this function. This is exemplified by part-time assignments, lack of organizational structuring in support of project activities, and, perhaps worst of all, lack of direct top management support for this function. Failure to correct these problems at the start is likely to cause difficulties throughout the life of the project. It often prevents relatively trouble-free implementation of manufacturing systems and the realization of mutual project goals.

Symptoms of an Emerging Problem

Symptoms of such problems are typically split responsibilities within the user organization where the project manager's role is delegated to "technical matters," while purchasing handles "contract matters." This quickly raises questions such as: who will address such important topics as system staffing, training, installation support, etc.? Lines of communication under this arrangement are unclear from the outset and require constant redefinition.

Consequences if the Problem is Ignored

The consequence of ignoring problem signals is predictable. Typically, there will be early involvement by middle management, usually from several different disciplines within the organization. However well-intentioned, this often results in meddling and contributes toward confusion rather than clarification of the issues. It also undermines the project manager's position of leadership, effectively preventing the person from performing the job in a constructive way. Other byproducts of this problem are the absence of team spirit, a tendency to point fingers at one another, and ultimately, a shifting of responsibilities and blame onto the vendor.

Conclusion

For the user to properly prepare for a successful FMS implementation, management must recognize the need for a strong project management approach. Proper organizational structuring in support of such a team is important, too, as is a mostly "hands off" attitude by management except to monitor and support all efforts. The common goal should be to make the FMS implementation as painless as possible by allowing the project manager and the team to work with the vendor's counterpart. In most cases, this approach helps achieve relatively quick and substantial benefits promised by FMS.[18]

---

[18] A. Jesswein, "User/Vendor Relations in FMS Implementation," SME Blue Book Series, *Flexible Assembly Systems: Insights Based On Experience*, Dearborn, MI, 1990, Society of Manufacturing Engineers, p. 16-18.

QUESTIONNAIRE

Answer the following questions ranking your answers from 1 to 5.
1 - represents very poor,
2 - poor,
3 - average,
4 - good and
5 - very good.

- Is your approach to automation done:
  1 - Before understanding the process,
  2 - With a little understanding,
  3 - With some understanding,
  4 - With a lot of understanding,
  5 - With full understanding.

- What is your goal for automation?
  1 - Automation for automation's sake,
  3 - To reduce dependence on workers,
  5 - To utilize resources as effectively as possible.

- CIM can include the functions of product design, order processing, process planning, cost estimating, storage and retrieval of parts, manufacturing, testing, QC, packing, shipping and customer billing. Have you applied computers to:
  1 - None of the functions,
  2 - A few,
  3 - Some,
  4 - Many,
  5 - Most.

- Using the definition of the different types of flexibility in a manufacturing system, rank your own plant from 1 to 5 in terms of:
  - Operating flexibility,
  - Changeover flexibility,
  - Process flexibility,
  - Reaction flexibility,
  - Routing flexibility,
  - Capacity flexibility.

- How have you addressed die changes to reduce time?
  - 1 - No effort made to improve die change time,
  - 2 - Minimal effort,
  - 3 - Some effort,
  - 4 - Considerable,
  - 5 - Detailed study, improvement, documentation, and monitoring of improved process.

- To what extent are you using quick part change workholding systems?
  - 1 - None,
  - 2 - A little,
  - 3 - Somewhat,
  - 4 - Considerably,
  - 5 - Extensively.

- To what extent are you using bar coding to reduce time wastage?
  - 1 - None,
  - 2 - A little,
  - 3 - Somewhat,
  - 4 - Considerably,
  - 5 - Extensively.

- To what extent are you using Group Technology to improve throughput speed in your plant?
  - 1 - None,
  - 2 - A little,
  - 3 - Somewhat,
  - 4 - Considerably,
  - 5 - Extensively.

TOTAL SCORES

- A score of 14 to 21 indicates that you have enormous potential for improvement!
- A score of 22 to 34 indicates that you are doing a poor job.
- A score of 35 to 46 indicates that you doing a reasonable job.
- A score of 47 to 58 indicates that you are doing a good job.
- A score of between 59 and 70 indicates that you have done an excellent job in applying computer technology and other time saving processes to your plant.

chapter 8

Reducing Bureaucracy

INTRODUCTION

Bureaucratic organizations stifle initiative, creativity, enthusiasm and performance. They attract people with low initiative and little concern for customers or clients. They perpetuate the past with little regard for the future.

Bureaucratic organizations take so long to accomplish tasks because their time is spent on non value added activities such as:

- enforcing rules;
- documenting policies that reduce initiative and free thinking;
- developing standards instead of promoting continuous improvement;
- excessive discipline, instead of motivation;
- meetings that focus on differences instead of commonality;
- checking other people's work, and
- supervising people closely.

This chapter examines the poor utilization of people in bureaucratic organizations and the changes needed to unlock the under utilized potential energy that exists in all people.

Industry leaders such as Procter and Gamble, Xerox, General Electric , and Northern Telecom, have long been aware of the positive effect on productivity and quality of a lean, flat organization.

THE CAUSE OF POOR PERFORMANCE

A recent poll of manufacturing managers identifies their biggest problem as poor productivity. Most blame poor performance on "bad attitudes," "spoiled workers," or "unions." The cause of poor performance seldom lies with any of these.

Similar surveys among shop people result in different responses. Employees usually will tell you that:

- n o one cares about their opinions;
- they have little or no say in reaching decisions that affect them;
- they are not supplied with useful information.
- the grapevine is their best source of information, because management doesn't communicate.
- they get little or no recognition when their performance exceeds expectations; and
- there is no financial incentive to work smarter or harder.

People Behave the Way They Are Treated

In general, shop employees say they are not treated as full business partners. In truth, most companies treat employees as children. Proponents of the Pygmalion principle tell you that when you treat people like children, they behave like children. On the other hand, organizations that have high expectations of people and treat them as adults gain far better performance from employees.

One company encouraging operator input is Northern Telecom. In many of Northern's plants, meetings are held regularly on the line. When a problem is identified, people are invited to gather around a flip chart on the shop floor to find causes. Having done so, they brainstorm solutions and develop action plans to fix the problem.

Organizations that treat people like children—either autocratically or paternalistically—suffer from:

- low productivity,
- poor quality,
- high absenteeism, and
- high staff turnover.

These organizations tend to be hierarchical in structure. A typical example was Bell Canada which, until four years ago, operated with a many-layered management structure. Getting the message from the top to the bottom became almost impossible until layers were sliced from the organization.

Other organizations have gone much further. They have moved from the triangular structure to a team structure (see *Figure 8-1*).

The trend toward team structure is gathering momentum. Problem solving teams go as far back as the 1920s and '30s, but it was not until the 1970s that they gained real momentum. This was the period when North American manufacturers tried to emulate the Quality Circle model so well developed by the Japanese.

In the 1980s however, there was a gradual decline in the use of Quality Circles and an evolution toward special purpose teams. These newly created teams involved workers and union representatives in higher-level decisions impacting on quality and productivity improvement.

The result has been that an increasing number of organizations are now trying

184

Traditional Organization Structure.

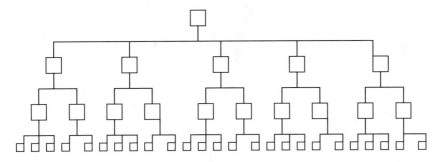

Modern Organization Structure.

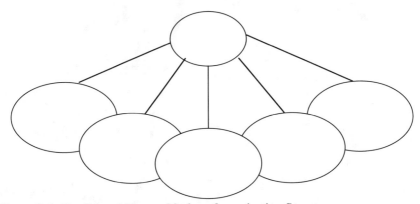

Figure 8-1. Traditional Versus Modern Organization Structure.

to replace temporary teams with permanent self-managing teams. The transition from a traditional structure to a flat team-based structure, without supervision, has been difficult for many organizations. The expectations, behavior, roles, and values of management and labor are so different that the most successful organizations have been those that took up to a decade to change or those that set up new plants where employees were hired on the basis of skills, flexibility, and willingness to assume responsibility.

Self-managing teams are the ultimate form of employee involvement (see *Figure 8-2*) because they increase employee feelings of self-worth and dignity. Above all, they encourage flexible work practices for members who tend to move from job to job. This way, companies are able to produce small-lot, customized products to meet increasing demand.

Typical of the benefits achieved are those attained at a General Electric (GE) plant in Salisbury, NC, where product configurations change a dozen times a day. Productivity at this lighting product shop is 250% higher than at GE plants making the same product in 1985.

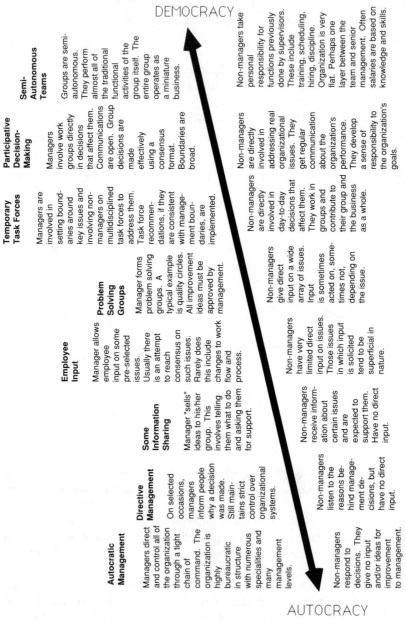

DEMOCRACY ↑

Semi-Autonomous Teams
- Groups are semi-autonomous. They perform almost all of the traditional functional activities of the group itself. The entire group operates as a miniature business.
- Non-managers take personal responsibility for functions previously done by supervisors. These include training, scheduling, hiring, discipline. Organization is very flat. Perhaps one layer between the team and senior management. Often salaries are based on knowledge and skills.

Participative Decision-Making
- Managers involve work groups directly in decisions that affect them. Communications are open. Group decisions are made effectively using a consensus format. Boundaries are broad.
- Non-managers are directly involved in addressing real organizational issues. They get regular communication about the organization's performance. They develop a sense of responsibility to the organization's goals.

Temporary Task Forces
- Managers are involved in setting boundaries around key issues and involving non-managers on multidisciplined task forces to address them. Task force recommendations, if they are consistent with management boundaries, are implemented.
- Non-managers are directly involved in day-to-day decisions that affect them. They work in groups and contribute to their group and the business as a whole.

Problem Solving Groups
- Manager forms problem solving groups. A typical example is quality circles. All improvement ideas must be approved by management.
- Non-managers give direct input on a wide array of issues. Input is sometimes acted on, sometimes not, depending on the issue.

Employee Input
- Manager allows employee input on some pre-selected issues. Usually there is an attempt to reach consensus on such issues. Rarely does this include changes to work flow and process.
- Non-managers have very limited direct input on issues. Those issues in which input is solicited tend to be superficial in nature.

Some Information Sharing
- Manager "sells" ideas to his/her group. This involves telling them what to do and asking them for support.
- Non-managers receive information about certain issues and are expected to support them. Have no direct input.

Directive Management
- On selected occasions, managers inform people why a decision was made. Still maintains strict control over organizational systems.
- Non-managers listen to the reasons behind management decisions, but have no direct input.

Autocratic Management
- Managers direct and control all of the organization through a tight chain of command. The organization is highly bureaucratic in structure with numerous specialities and many management levels.
- Non-managers respond to decisions. They give no input and/or ideas for improvement to management.

AUTOCRACY ↓

Based on a model used by Northern Telecom Canada Limited, Switching Division, Bramalea

Figure 8-2.   The Employee Involvement Continuum.[1]

[1]George Stalk Jr., & Thomas M. Hout. *Competing Against Time*. The Free Press. New York, NY 1990. p. 53

BEATING BUREAUCRACY

Considered individually, each of GE's techniques for decision making is not particularly astounding when compared with what has happened in Japan and some western European countries. Considered in total, however, the GE techniques represent a major and first-rate intelligent change. An increasing number of organizations now use some techniques learned by GE to facilitate their decision making. These ideas include:

1. Flatten The Organization Structure

Traditional organizations tend to be hierarchical. However, the greater the distance between the top and the bottom, the less the people at the bottom will know, or care, about corporate objectives.

Also, time spent in decision making will be considerable, since it expands exponentially in relation to the number of levels of management wishing to have input into the decisions.

Flatter organizations, exemplified especially throughout Japanese industry, not only get things done faster, they gain a healthier productivity advantage. The Japanese worker is no more productive than the American worker; the difference in productivity can be traced directly to the difference in the number of overhead employees. "With one-third the volume and three times the variety, the Japanese company has only one-eighteenth the number of overhead employees."[1]

One can see the crippling effect of bureaucracy in North America's automotive business. Ford Motor Co. has 17 layers between the chief executive and the shop floor people. At General Motors, the number is 21 or 22 depending on the plant. In contrast, Toyota has only seven layers between the top and bottom.[2]

Realizing this, organizations such as Canada's Northern Telecom have removed entire layers of management. Numbers of direct reports have increased, too. The tradition of looking after six or seven people is long gone, with many first-level section managers directing up to 50 people.

Jack Welch, chairman and CEO of General Electric, believes that expanding the number of direct reports stretches managers to the point where they will not be able to meddle in the day-to-day decisions of those reporting to them. At most GE plants, the number of levels between the top and bottom has been cut to three. For example, there might be only a vice-president and managers/supervisors separating the shop floor from the president.

2. Eliminate Supervision

Middle management and supervision are fast becoming endangered species. They do little to add value to the product or service. Most of their duties can be done by staff, given the proper training, at a lower cost. And people really don't want to be supervised. Given different circumstances, they prefer to work on their own, as long as they get feedback on their performance and can directly influence the system.

---

[2]James B. Treece. "A Smarter Way to Manufacture." *Business Week,* April 9, 1990. p. 62, McGraw-Hill.

Unfortunately, most supervisors put themselves in expendable positions. They could be most useful if the focus of their attention and most of their time could be spent on facilitating continuous improvement. To do this, however, requires different skills. These include the ability to:
- work harmoniously with their people,
- manage change,
- influence decision makers,
- solve problems,
- get commitment to change,
- ensure that new ideas are implemented,
- access resources,
- support new innovations, and
- support risk taking.

With these skills, they can coordinate rather than supervise a team, operating at a similar status level.

3. Use Self-managed Work Teams

A self-managing team is a group of people with total responsibility for serving a customer base or producing a product. Group members manage themselves in the absence of formal supervision, dividing responsibilities typically done by management among themselves. Typical duties of the group include:
- scheduling of work activities and flow,
- training members on multi-skilled functions,
- evaluation of one another's performance,
- discipline,
- social activities,
- goal setting, and
- continually improving the process.

Working in a self-managed team is not easy, but most workers prefer it to the alternative—being an extension of a machine, having little control and performing single skills.

Working in a team where people have equal influence requires tremendous:
- patience,
- willingness to take responsibilities,
- ability to solve interpersonal differences and conflict,
- problem solving skills, and
- flexibility.

Self-managed teams are able to compress time since they:
- work as a cell, with little or no delay as parts move directly from one operator to the next.
- uncover and save problems that cause delays,
- empower people closest and most knowledgeable about a problem to solve it right away;
- don't assume an attitude of "it's not my job,"
- focus on satisfying internal and external customer needs, and

- measure and monitor customer satisfaction and strive to continuously im
prove performance.

An effective self-managed team is multiskilled. Ideally, a group should include all necessary support people, including maintenance and engineering representatives, whose participation can be critical in eliminating needless delays and frustrations.

Self-managed work teams work best when their workstations are positioned so that team members can see each other (see *Figure 8-3*).

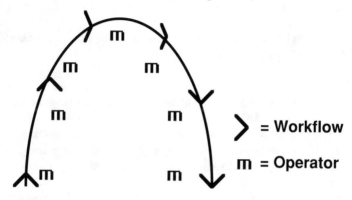

Figure 8-3. Horseshoe Layout of An Effective Self-managing Team.

Teams seeing each other will communicate best. Proximity encourages interaction and problem solving.

4. Pay for Performance and/or Knowledge

Most organizations now using the self-managing team concept have incentive programs which promote flexibility.

The benefits of having multi-skilled people are obvious. The ability to do a variety of tasks allows a worker to be moved to points that are very busy, instead of remaining at a task that is less productive. People are paid for their knowledge and skills. The more skills they acquire, the higher the pay.

Customers—internal and external—benefit, too. When information is needed, more people in the work cell will be able to deal with problems and queries. Without the shared knowledge, the customer frequently gets the "run-around" treatment, or passed from one person to another to get answers. Organizations that have successfully introduced "pay-for-knowledge" programs recommend strongly the importance of customizing a system to fit the organization. A packaged approach will not work. A lot of work needs to be done to make sure that the system meets the specific needs of the company.

Typical problems that might arise in a pay-for-knowledge implementation are:
- Dealing with people already earning more than the base rates. Take the example of someone earning $3,500 per month. Assume that the pay-for-knowledge base rate is $2,000 per month, with incremental pay increases of

$200 for each of 10 specific skills. Assuming that this employee is competent in five of the 10 skills, the compensation formula yields a pay rate of $3,000 ($2,000 base pay plus 5 x $200). It is unfair to expect this person to accept a pay cut just to implement a new program. In some organizations, this problem has been solved by offering cash incentives to acquire the additional skills.

- Introducing a pay-for-knowledge program without providing training opportunities. An important component before any changes are made is to develop all training programs and have them ready to run at the time the program is introduced. In most cases, people within the work area will be training each other. They need to be provided with time to do the training and skills to impart the information.
- Providing the knowledge without the expectation that the skill will be used. Clearly, the benefit to the organization comes from the use of the skill. Having knowledge in a person's head is of little value unless it is put to use. Take presentation skills as an example. There is no value to paying someone to learn how to make a presentation if fear prevents them from trying. Or take the case of training a person for a job which is one of the least stimulating in an area. How does one deal with the person who feels "put down" by being asked to do a very boring, mundane job?

There are a number of ways to deal with these situations. Some organizations leave it up to the team to decide who will do what job. Peer pressure usually will force everyone to take on the menial jobs when required. If people don't cooperate, the group will discipline them. In extreme cases, some members might be asked to leave the team.

Another approach, similar to the first, is to set up a schedule for regular rotation. In some organizations where tasks are quite easy, people might even change during the shift. In other cases, where technical knowledge is required, rotation may be done every six months.

- Having a subjective testing system. Many organizations allow for a peer review to confirm that a person is competent in a new skill set. Problems occur if the tester and the trainee do not agree on the trainee's competence. It is important to establish very specific criteria of what constitutes competency. This can be done in a variety of ways. One is to establish a checklist of components of the skill. The trainer can test for each item systematically. Another approach is to use an outside third party—perhaps from the training department—to administer or sit in on the test. A written test, with a specific score required for success, may be administered.

5. Throw Out Job Descriptions

Inherent flexibility in modern organizations provides a principal industry advantage. Job descriptions are either brief or nonexistent. Employees are expected to do whatever it is that benefits the customer. This could be operating one machine one day or replacing a team member on another function the next.

6. Communicate Directly with People

Because the organization develops trust among its people, employees feel comfortable communicating in all directions: up, down and sideways, often with no need to consult an immediate superior. Less emphasis is placed on written communications; instead, people communicate verbally, saving time and fixing problems on the spot.

7. Cross-train People

Having people join teams is a positive way of getting them to plan and solve common problems. Having them work effectively however, is more challenging. Weaving people into a real team with one goal is possible if they are:
- encouraged to contribute to the goals of the team;
- rewarded for doing so, and
- understand the needs of the other members.

Cross-training particularly helps to meet the last need. At Xerox, for example, newly hired engineers spend six weeks in field engineering and then nine months in manufacturing engineering. The converse is true for manufacturing people. They spend six weeks in the field, then move on to nine months in design offices and labs.

One of North America's finest examples of a high-performing organization is the Shell Canada plant in Sarnia, Ontario. This plant was set up in 1978 after eight years of research and planning by a joint management-union committee. The plant is organized to include six shift teams, each with 19 people. Multiskilling is encouraged in two ways—making training readily available and rewarding people for increasing their skills. Workers who succeed in reaching a certain level of competence in six of the plant's 10 skill classifications (known as Job Knowledge Clusters), plus two maintenance skills, earn top salaries. Each skill learned adds additional dollars to an employee's salary.

Generally, U.S., Canadian, Swedish and United Kingdom companies do a poor job in providing workers with the skills they need to be productive. In contrast, Japan and West Germany emphasize on-the-job training to develop general, as well as specialized skills. Economists from M.I.T., in a recent report *Made in America: Regaining the Productive Edge*, stated, "Workplace training makes it more likely that workers will come to understand the big picture: how context shapes the task and how contingent factors can be integrated into performance. Broader skills enable workers to make larger contributions to the productivity of the firm, and also to go on through life acquiring new skills."[3]

North American manufacturing authorities are not ignorant of the M.I.T. concern. The Canadian Labour Market and Productivity Centre, for instance, comments that workers should be more involved in decisions affecting their job, be less specialized and engage in continuous learning.

---

[3]Dertorigos, Et al. *Made In America: Regaining the Productive Edge*, Cambridge, MA, MIT Press, 1989.

C.L.M.P.C.'s own data emphasizes the poor job Canada does in training. From their surveys, 67% of full-time employees considered training and retraining as "very important" to the continued success of the organizations they work for; an additional 21% say that training and retraining are "somewhat" important.

Despite this need, Canadian workers receive little or no job-related training. Over the last two years 41% of full-time employees received no training, while 18% more received one week or less. More than half of all unskilled workers—those who need training the most—received none at all.

8. Keep Things Simple

Many organizations waste a great deal of time on needlessly complicated issues. As an organization gets bigger, the tendency to make matters more difficult grows. Why? Some believe it's because of the people who are attracted to manage bureaucratic organizations. Often, they lack personal and intellectual self-assurance that simplification would challenge. Their insecurity and nervousness cause them to plan excessively, enough to ensure against any mistakes.

Jack Welch, chairman and CEO of General Electric, feels that people overestimate the complexity of business. Business is not "rocket science." He believes that it is one of the simplest professions—and since global competitors have typically three or four major competitors, the options for strategic choices are limited.

9. Limit Corporate Staff

Decentralized organizations are able to move fast to meet local needs. The fewer people available at a corporate level, the less the amount of interference in the decisions of the people in line positions.

People in corporate positions need to change their attitudes. Their job is to assist line people, not challenge them. They need to understand that they report to line people, not the other way around.

10. Reduce the Control and Numbers of Staff People

An examination of any process within an organization will reveal involvement of a number of people who add no value to the product or service. Their involvement causes time delay. So why are they involved? Is their task necessary? If so, can it be done by a line person, or simultaneously instead of sequentially?

A common example is in the area of quality control. Inspectors on the line add no value to the product. Their presence is a delaying factor. Because *they* take responsibility for quality, each person on the line takes a little less care, increasing the chance of mistakes, which, in turn, causes rework to occur, with more delays.

Taking the inspector off the line, and giving operators the responsibility to check their own work or the work of the person before them in the process, leads to significant time reduction through earlier identification of problems, quicker resolution of problems, and less rework time.

The same lesson can be applied to other support staff. Engineers and maintenance people are helping to reduce cycle time when their reporting structure changes from responsibility to their engineering or maintenance manager, to responsibility directly to the team. As part of the team instead of being an outsider, they can facilitate collaboration and on-the-spot resolution of problems.

11. Give People the Power to Make Things Happen

Not allowing people to make simple decisions wastes time. Managers and supervisors seem to feel most needed when they constantly provide nothing more than a "yes," which is why their workplace comes to a standstill when they're not there.

Think about it. The people who work around us do all kinds of challenging tasks outside of work—they bring up families, pay off mortgages, repair televisions and automobiles, get involved in community activities and undertake hundreds of equally important tasks. Yet, we make the assumption that they've had a frontal lobotomy before they come to work! Why else would managers not allow people simple decision making authority such as the right to buy a monkey wrench for $20?

We also practice double standards. In the crunch, we give people enormous authority. One North American organization recently set up a $38 million plant in Europe. They needed to get established and capitalize on the free trade opportunities which 1992 will supposedly bring. They acted with speed. A team of 10 people put together a two-page document justifying the investment. They promptly got approval.

A team member returned recently to North America after having written checks for huge amounts of money. He now finds himself filling out three forms to justify a car rental of less than $100!

QUESTIONNAIRE

Answer the following questions ranking your answers from 1 to 5.
   1 - represents very poor,
   2 - poor,
   3 - average,
   4 - good and
   5 - very good.

Reduced Bureaucracy

- Do you have more than two levels in the organization structure separating the shop floor from the boss?
   1 - 7+ levels,
   2 - 6 levels,
   3 - 5 levels,
   4 - 4 levels,
   5 - 3 levels.

- Do shop employees make most decisions on matters affecting them?
   1 - Not allowed to,
   2 - Infrequently,
   3 - Sometimes,
   4 - Often,
   5 - Always.

- Do your managers spend more time on control functions, or facilitative activities (coaching, training, problem-solving)?
   1 - Totally control,
   2 - Mostly control,
   3 - Sometime control,
   4 - Infrequently control,
   5 - Almost exclusive facilitative.

- Do your people work in teams?
   1 - Never,
   2 - Infrequently,
   3 - Sometimes,
   4 - Mostly,
   5 - Always.

- Do you provide continuous training to your people?
  - 1 - Never,
  - 2 - Seldom,
  - 3 - Sometimes,
  - 4 - Often,
  - 5 - Regularly.

- Is your organization divided on functional lines?
  - 1 - Totally,
  - 3 - Partially,
  - 5 - Not at all.

- Does management reward and encourage a cooperative environment?
  - 1 - Never,
  - 2 - Infrequently,
  - 3 - Sometimes,
  - 4 - Usually,
  - 5 - Strongly.

- Do your operators control daily functions such as scheduling, recruiting and training?
  - 1 - No,
  - 2 - To a minor extent,
  - 3 - To some extent,
  - 4 - Usually,
  - 5 - Somewhat.

- Do you pay people for knowledge and skills?
  - 1 - No,
  - 3 - Working toward that goal,
  - 5 - Have the process in place.

- Do you provide training on a demand basis for people to become multiskilled?
  - 1 - No,
  - 3 - Somewhat,
  - 5 - Have formalized process in place.

- Do you rely on well defined, detailed job descriptions?
  - 1 - Totally,
  - 2 - Largely,
  - 3 - Somewhat
  - 4 - To a little extent,
  - 5 - Not at all.

- Does your organization encourage people to make decisions without getting unnecessary approvals?
  - 1 - No,
  - 2 - To a limited extent,
  - 3 - Somewhat,
  - 4 - Usually,
  - 5 - Always.

- Do you accept mistakes as part of the learning process?
  - 1 - No, we always scapegoat people,
  - 2 - Usually scapegoat people,
  - 3 - Sometimes scapegoat people,
  - 4 - Seldom scapegoat people,
  - 5.- Readily live with mistakes.

- Are you introducing new programs that seldom, if ever, continue?
  - 1 - Very often,
  - 2 - Quite often,
  - 3 - Sometimes,
  - 4 - Infrequently,
  - 5 - See change as part of management process, not as something different.

TOTAL SCORES

Interpretation

In relation to the element of Reduced Bureaucracy:
- A score of 14 to 24 indicates that you have a very bureaucratic organization. You are stifling your people.
- A score of 25 to 35 indicates that you are bureaucratic with a lot to do before you get "lean and mean."
- A score of 36 to 46 indicates that you are an average company when it comes to bureaucracy. You can break out from the crowd.
- A score of 47 to 57 indicates that you have done away with many of the bureaucratic impediments to quick responsiveness and flexibility.
- A score in excess of 58 indicates that you are great. Your organization is fast and flexible. You are innovative and can change at short notice.

CASE STUDY

Worthington Industries: A Bright Light In A Dark Industry

The American steel industry has been bleeding to death slowly and consistently over the past two decades. The number of blue collar workers in the industry has plummeted from 108,000 in 1978 to 31,000 in 1990.

Despite the doom and gloom of its industry, Worthington Industries in Columbus, Ohio, managed to reverse the trend. The company continues to grow through increased market share and profitability. How? Its 5,800 employees are now part of a unique work experience. Each is dedicated to the customer. Responsiveness is everything.

How did a $1 billion company continue to motivate its people to such a high degree? John McConnel Sr., the chairman, believes in a few simple principles:

1. **All facilities are kept small.**
   No facility can employ more than 100 people. By keeping units small, the organization is able to retain an intimate family-type atmosphere in each plant. A small organization ensures that each person counts. Responsibility is real.

2. **People are trusted.**
   The company has high expectations of its people. It does not have time clocks to check when people come in and leave.

3. **People are treated equally.**
   There are few distinctions at Worthington between blue collars and white collars. No one is paid an hourly wage.

4. **People have an incentive to do better.**
   A profit-sharing program promotes commitment to high quality, total flexibility and dedication to customers. The average bonus per employee is $3,000, received every quarter. Bonuses typically make up about 40% of employee salaries. 32% of Worthington's stock is owned by its people. 80% of staff own stock in the company.

5. **People have control over their environment.**
   People on the shop floor work in teams. They are responsible for such things as quality. No inspector decides what is acceptable or unacceptable. The result? A quality level that is FIVE TIMES the industry average.

Source: Tom Peters Video: "A Passion for Customers."

CASE STUDY

Beating the Japanese in Japan:
The Bare Bones of a Remarkable Motorola Strategy

One of the most remarkable success stories of the TTM strategy is Motorola's. Chief Executive Officer George M.C. Fisher will be content with nothing less than being "the best manufacturer of electronics hardware in the world."

The company's strategy has included:

- Tearing down interdepartmental barriers by involving all interested parties in the design of new products.
- An obsession with quality. Find it and fix it where it occurs *before* it gets to the customers.

- Work simplification to reduce unnecessary parts.
- Heavy investment in people, training, R & D, and capital improvements—$1.8 billion or 19% of revenues.
- Use of robotics wherever necessary.

The results are paying off handsomely. Examples include:

- Growth in sales in Japan up 70% in 1988.
- Reduction in order-to-shipment from 30 to three days over the past 18 months.
- Reduced design time since 1985 from three years to 15 months. The near-term goal is six months.
- Reduction in defects from 3000 per million in 1983 to under 200 currently.
- Savings from quality improvements of $250 million annually. This amount equals 41% of pretax income.

Source: Business Week, "The Rival Japan Respects" Nov. 13, 1989 p 108-118.

HELP	#	P	OBSTACLE	C	SOLUTION	WHEN	WHO

Figure 8-4. Project Planning Process.

chapter 9

Implementing World-Class Manufacturing

No two organizations are likely to implement an SPC (Statistical Process Control) or Just In Time process the same way. It is important to *customize* the process to fit specific needs and circumstances. However, there are 10 steps that are generally applicable to any organization.

After reviewing the steps, decide for yourself which are appropriate and in what order they should take place.

Step Number 1. Get Top Management Involvement and Support

Actions speak louder than words. People will become enthusiastic about new directions when they see tangible involvement from senior managers. Time is money. Any time spent on efforts to get products to the market quickly sends a clear signal to those in the organization who are looking for direction.

Among the most important actions that management can take are the actions on the following page:

Develop a Strategic Plan that Includes Quality

Few will disagree that the very survival of an organization depends on quality. So quality, employee involvement, and Just In Time practices need to be incorporated into the strategic plan of an organization.

In putting the strategic plan together, management should ask themselves:

- How good is our quality currently?
- Is our delivery of quality changing?
- In which direction is it changing?
- How does our quality compare to that of our main competitors?
- How can we differentiate our quality from that of our competitors?
- What role are our quality people playing in our quest for the best quality? Should it be changed?
- Are we listening to our customers?
- Is their a better way to monitor customer satisfaction?
- Do we design quality into our products or process? Or do we continually fight fires to cover mistakes?
- Are our Research and Development people playing a meaningful role in achieving quality? If not, what should their role be?
- Are we able to respond to customers' needs from manufacturing?
- Do value added activities take up most of the time for parts moving through the manufacturing process?
- Are shop employees involved in all aspects of the process that affect them?

Out of the strategic plan will emerge a vision and a mission. The vision is a picture of the organization at a future time. It describes the organization and its business in holistic terms. And it describes a desired state rather than the actual state of the organization.

An example of a vision is Northern Telecom's "Vision 2000" which sees the organization in a leadership position in the global market for telecommunications equipment by the end of the century.

In contrast, the organization's mission is more specific. It relates to the here and now. It describes in specific detail the business of the organization, who it serves, what must be done, and why this must be done.

Senior managers who are serious about strategic planning find that agreeing to a mission takes weeks or months to complete. It cannot be done over a weekend at a golf retreat. Once it is done, long-term planning is facilitated because the direction is clear.

An excellent strategic planning model has been developed by Pfeiffer, Goodstein, and Nolan[1] (see *Figure 9-1*).

This model will help executives think in terms of time, as they scan the environment and evaluate how their main competitors use time as a competitive weapon.

Ensure that Every Department and Person Has Clear Time-Based Goals

A goal is a very precise target that needs to be met within a specific time. Developing a strategic plan to focus on quality management will set targets that must be achieved.

---

[1] *Applied Strategic Planning: A How to Do It Guide,* University Associates Inc., 1985

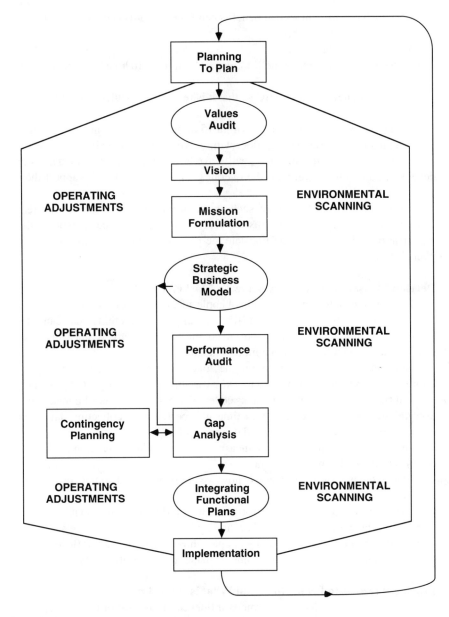

Figure 9-1. The Strategic Planning Model.

Examples could be:
- To deliver custom-designed products to the customer within two days of the order by June 16.
- To reduce manufacturing cycle time by 75% within the next six months. These might be macro goals. They need to be translated into micro goals

201

for each department so that benefits can flow upwards and ensure that macro goals are reached.

Examples could be:

- To reduce cycle time in the XYZ department from 16 hours to two hours by December 15.
- To design new product ABC so that it is ready for manufacturing by January 1.
- To process customers' orders within 15 minutes and have the manufacturing instructions on the shop floor within five minutes thereafter, by June 16.

To achieve this, senior managers will have to involve all middle managers in developing a comfort level with the overall goal, so that they will support their portion of the plan.

The most important benefit of such an extensive process, must be that real changes take place. The plan must be relayed to each area and person in the organization, who in turn must translate the plan into personal goals and action plans.

Develop Measurement for Key Time To Market Variables

Measurement is the tool that helps people identify whether they are getting better or worse. It is extremely difficult to improve something that can't be measured. Measurement allows people to communicate effectively since all minds can be focused with the use of a common language—data.

Senior management needs to set the tone for effective measurements by limiting its own measurements to a few key variables. Using the Pareto principle, one will find that 20% of the yardsticks cover 80% of the business. So measuring everything is really wasteful. More time will be spent on collecting data than interpreting it, communicating it, and dealing with it!

A useful start regarding what to measure (and what data collection to discontinue) is to be guided by these principles:

- Does the measurement identify how we are serving a customer (internal or external)?
- Does it measure the group effort more than it does the individual?
- Can it be collected easily and accurately?
- Will it be easily understood by people whose performance it reflects?
- Will a change in it affect customer satisfaction and profitability?

Provide Rewards to People to Signal What is Important

The reward system has an enormous influence on the corporate culture, as it sends clear signals of what is really important and what is not. For example, if supervisors are sent to acquire the skills to do performance appraisals, they will often sit back and not use the skills unless encouraged to do so. If they are rewarded for conducting effective performance appraisals through verbal compliments, written pats-on-the-back and the like, they will continue. On the other hand, if rebuked for not using the skills, they will react to the criticism and start to use the acquired skills. But if they get back to work, are not questioned about the training and never encouraged to put it into practice, they will more likely channel their energies into other efforts which do yield personal benefits through tangible recognition.

Only senior management can change the reward system. The compensation system should be modified so that it rises or falls directly in relation to the departmental or individual achievement of the quality goals. The reward system is like the fuel in a gas tank. A performance-driven compensation system will be like high-octane gas; lack of such a system might cause the vehicle to sputter along as it would on low-octane fuel.

Provide Adequate Resources

As people look for new and better ways to meet their customers' goals, they will have to change equipment, methods and materials. Some will require capital spending while others will not.

Since the payback of Time To Market improvements tends to be substantial, one would expect approvals to be easily forthcoming. Unfortunately, this doesn't happen too often.

When time drags between proposals and approvals, people become skeptical about management's willingness to improve quality.

Perhaps the most important resource that management can provide is time. Time is needed for training, for meetings, to collect data, to experiment with new ideas, to implement new processes, to attend team meetings, and so on. Changing to a time-driven organization will initially add time requirements for people, as they refocus their energies on team activities whose purpose will be to save time later.

Deal with Employee Apprehensions

A comprehensive strategy that takes time out of activities will naturally lead to apprehensions about job losses. Reality is that in a fast and flexible organization fewer people are needed. To deal with this, management should not wait for concerns to grow to the boiling point. They need to keep people informed about their plan and the impact it will have on jobs. Bad news is often better than no news. At least people can deal with a bad situation by developing plans to overcome problems that are approaching.

By facing and planning for a reduced staff complement, management can use a variety of methods of addressing the problem. These include:
- not replacing people who leave as a result of retirements and resignations;
- retraining people to fill vacancies in other areas of the organizations;
- networking with other organizations in the community to help relocate people;
- providing attractive early retirement packages for senior people; and
- providing a "golden handshake" to those remaining people for whom there is no alternative but termination.

Another source of apprehension is the skepticism that a change in direction will bring. Which organization hasn't gone through the "flavor of the month" syndrome? When employees hear about a change in direction, their reaction will vary from total disbelief to skepticism, apprehension and enthusiasm. Experience shows that most people will distrust management. Only time and sincere and consistent actions will overcome negativism. Senior management should learn from past mistakes—No more T-shirts, buttons, hats, and streamers. No more posters and slogans before actions have proved the sincerity of management's direction.

Senior Management Must Delegate

Senior management must provide the vision, mission, and goals, and it must provide the rewards and resources. It must also be visible in its involvement with efforts to improve Time To Market responsiveness. But at the same time, it must confine most of its time to strategic issues and the big picture. The implementation of the nitty-gritty plans at the lower levels must be left to the troops. That requires delegation, but these terms do not mean abdication. Abdication is the process whereby a task is passed down to someone lower on the totem pole, who is left to sink or swim with no clear direction, no help, and no follow-up. When these people fail, as frequently they do, they must live with the consequences.

Senior Management Must Provide the Structure

A major change in the focus of an organization often necessitates the formation of a steering committee to help plan for and phase in the necessary transformation. Only senior management can set up a committee that has real authority. The committee should be given a clear mandate and the time and money to get the job done.

Step Number 2. Set Up a Steering Committee

Before a program can become fully operational, it must be sponsored and nurtured. A group of people from various parts of the organization should act as initial guardians for as long as it takes to get line management to take responsibility. People from manufacturing, purchasing, quality assurance, manufacturing engineering, design engineering, materials, and scheduling should be included.

The steering committee should also include representation from the union, if one exists. Such inclusion should be made in the beginning, before key decisions are made, so as to prevent workers feeling manipulated and without real influence.

To help promote understanding about the new direction, the steering committee should develop a policy document that is circulated throughout the company. Inside it should state:

- the corporate mission, vision, and values,
- who is responsible for continuous improvement on time-based issues,
- the role of the steering committee,
- the goals of the process,
- major milestones that are part of the plan,
- the function of a coordinator, and
- the implementation process.

Choosing a Champion

The steering committee should also appoint a *coordinator*. This person's function will be to make sure that the new focus toward TTM becomes an integral part of the corporate structure.

Converting to a time-based organization can amount to a revolution. Some revolutions fail and others succeed. Those that succeed do so primarily because of the passion and determination of a leader.

Ideally, the leader should be the chief executive. Realistically, the person waving the flag on a day-to-day basis will be lower down in the hierarchy. But it is important that the leader not be too low in the hierarchy as this would create the perception that the swing to time-based strategies is not important. Also, having direct access to the President or a Vice-President would allow the champion to enlist help when roadblocks appear in the path.

The personality make-up of the champion should be considered before making a choice. While not essential, it is important that leaders enjoy working with people, and present themselves professionally. They need to be able to inspire people, so that their presentation skills—formal and informal—need to be well developed. And their communications need to be done with a real sense of enthusiasm. They also need to be subject-matter experts. While they should have a solid understanding of the nature of the business, they should also have an excellent grasp of the most important elements of time-based strategies.

Step Number 3. Get As Much Information as Possible

The steering committee should find out as much as possible about the key components of time-based manufacturing techniques. This gathering of information might include:

- subscribing to technical magazines,
- joining associations that deal with Quality, Manufacturing, JIT, EI (Employee Involvement) and so on,
- attending conferences,
- buying appropriate books,
- visiting other organizations, and
- meeting with consultants.

Probably the most useful of all the methods is visiting other organizations that have adopted a similar strategy. This may sometimes be difficult, as direct competitors may be unwilling to divulge information that could be of direct benefit to a competitor. So visits to organizations with different products or services should be undertaken, since the lessons learned can always be translated back into the context of one's own organization. Much can be learned from the mistakes of others. For a variety of reasons, most organizations fail to reach their objectives the first or even the second time around. Finding out "why" helps to prevent making the same mistakes.

Using an outside consultant can be extremely useful. Choosing a person who has been down the same road many times before can help the organization to get going faster and with fewer mishaps. Because many of the changes required may shake an organization right down to its foundations, it can be useful to have an objective outsider help the process, free of infighting or territorialism.

Choosing a consultant is not easy. While price might be a factor, it is worthwhile to evaluate closely what he or she can bring to the organization. It is important too, to ask the consultant for a statement of consulting philosophy. The best consultants are those who will:

- act as facilitators,
- aim to make the organization independent of outside help,
- listen and respond to the client's needs, and
- offer a customized approach.

Above all, the consultant should have worked in a variety of organizations and delivered on commitments. Reference checks would be a source of information needed before deciding who to hire.

Step Number 4. Develop a Time-Based Manufacturing Plan

The steering committee should document its plan. The plan should set out key actions, milestones, and people who will need to take responsibility for those actions and milestones.

The plan will detail how each work area will be impacted and how changes will be made. Because of the enormity of the project, early milestones will be very detailed, although milestones that need to be achieved after two or more years might require less specific action items. As the process unfolds, more specific details can be documented and delegated for action.

In this planning phase, it is *vital* to remember that SPC, JIT, and EI are interwoven, and that they should proceed simultaneously. For example, an early task of JIT activities will be to reduce buffer stocks on the line, so operators will have only the parts that they need to complete that shift's production. This will require that all the parts available to the operator are perfect. There is no room for defective parts. And for this to happen consistently, it is important to have an SPC program in place which would guarantee zero defects.

It is equally important to remember that each process is multifaceted, and that they cannot be introduced all at once. Patience is required. It is easier to plan for small achievements than to go for broke in a short time. Small gains will build enthusiasm and confidence, which will then provide the platform for greater achievements later.

Drawing up a plan is not an easy task. It is important that the plan be comprehensive. Implementing the Total Quality program, as an example, requires that a variety of key questions be addressed. These include:

- Product Development. What and who determines which products are developed? To what extent do efforts reflect market demands?
- Purchasing and Materials Management. Do you have many vendors? Are you buying on the basis of price? Do you have to inspect incoming materials? Do you have a vendor certification program?
- Inspection and Test. Who checks products? At what stage? Who is responsible for quality? Is the focus on the product or the process? How

accurate is your data collection procedure?

- Marketing. Do you stress quality? Can you sell for more if quality is superior? Who determines quality? How does the customer know the difference between a quality product and a poor product? What are the key characteristics? Do you get customer feedback? If so, how do you use the data? Does it lead to continuous improvement?
- Organization Effectiveness. What organizational roadblocks might prevent success? Which areas are most ready for projects? What are the key issues preventing the highest level of motivation in your organization? With what degree of enthusiasm are your people likely to react to a change in management style? How capable are your managers and supervisors of implementing a continuous improvement process? What training do they need? Are there any other training needs that you have? What is the relationship with your union? How can we solicit its help in the process?

The strategic plan should set out goals for the whole organization and dates by which they need to be achieved. Since many of these goals will be ambitious, such as reducing delivery time by 90%, mini-goals should also be established with realistic but challenging time deadlines. A useful method of setting out this plan is to use the *Performance Indexing* system described in *Chapter 10*.

Step Number 5.   Set Up a Pilot Project

Having developed a sound knowledge of the issues, the steering committee should decide where to set up its pilot program. Depending on the readiness of an organization, the committee might decide to start in more than one area.

Picking the right area can be difficult, although there is sometimes a clear choice. Should you start in the area where change is needed most—rework, inventory or scrap management—or should you start in the area where you need it least, but where you are sure of success? The latter area is likely to be the best managed. The supervisor probably has excellent people skills and is already working in a team environment.

After choosing the pilot area, a joint meeting should be held with the people in the area to explain:

- the objective of the initiative,
- goals,
- resources,
- training, and answer any questions.

It is critical that support groups are included in the pilot team. Excluding engineering and maintenance people will have disastrous effects on the project. Each group will be fighting to protect its own turf rather than working toward a common goal.

Step Number 6.   Provide Education and Training For Everyone

It is difficult to decide whether to educate everyone, or only those that will be involved in the first projects. Experience suggests that a compromise is the best solution. An overview of what is happening should be provided to everyone, but it should be done in such a way that it does not raise expectations. The presenter should provide cautious estimates about the program timetable. And no grand claims should be made about how people's lives will be changed for the better! Change is threatening to a lot of people, so many will experience stress and not jubilation as they are asked to make significant changes to their work habits.

The training plan should be carefully thought out. *Table 9-1* shows how the first cut of a training plan might be developed.

Table 9-1.
Education and Training Plan by Management Level.

	Awareness Sessions	General Training Sessions	Skill Building Sessions
Senior Management	X		
Middle Management	X		
Lower Level Management	X	X	
Support Staff	X	X	X
Direct Labor	X	X	X

This plan will need to be amplified further. The awareness session, for example, might include the following:
- competing in a global economy,
- case studies of successful competitors,
- changing demands in the marketplace,
- the consequences of not improving performance continuously,
- the cost of inefficiency,
- broad principles of world-class manufacturing, and
- implementation steps and timetable.

A few notes of caution. First, there is a real temptation to consistently show Japan and Japanese companies as the model. Don't. It doesn't help to put local organizations and people down although some case studies from foreign countries can prove effective if used in moderation.

Experience suggests that it is better to use an outsider to present to awareness sessions. Ironically, consultants will be able to engage people more readily, even though they may have less ability and less knowledge about the business. They often bring an important ingredient to the session—credibility. If they have walked down the same path before, they can recall examples of success and some of failure. And when they detect skepticism, and see people rolling their eyes when they discuss the new initiative, they can draw people out and listen without being defensive. Often these sessions can get rowdy, but a skilled presenter will find it possible to turn people's hostility into positive energy, simply by agreeing with the points made by people and then asking them how the problem can be solved. In this way, trainers and participants often find themselves on the same side of the line, and that differences are largely semantic.

A last consideration for the awareness session is the presence of senior management. Again, there are two schools of thought. One says that senior management must be present to show their commitment. The other school suggests that people will be so intimidated that it is better not to have senior management present. Perhaps the answer will be determined by the amount of trust that exists between staff and top management. If the organization has a history of punishing outspoken people, then management should probably not sit in on the sessions. But, they should still go through the sessions on their own, to familiarize themselves with the content. In addition, they should attend the beginning and end of each session in which they are not involved. The introductory part should be used to indicate their commitment while the end session should be devoted to questions and answers.

In the general education sessions, you are dealing with people who need to be either directly supportive or involved in the day-to-day activities of the changes. Their task will be made easier if they learn how to work together and manage change. Specifically they could benefit from training in:

- teamwork,
- problem solving,
- decision making,
- cost/benefit analysis,
- communication skills, and
- project management.

Those people that might take a leadership position need more detailed training. For example, a workshop covering teamwork, problem solving, and decision making might cover five days for supervisors and only three days for operators.

A long-term view is necessary, because a crash program doesn't stand a chance of being retained or even used. A modularized approach works best with each module customized for each area. There is no point in training purchasing people in preventive maintenance, and there is no value in presenting anything but a brief overview of vendor certification for people from the shop floor.

The knowledge that end users might need could include the following:

Quality
- an overview of TQC (Total Quality Control),
- what quality is,
- the cost of quality,
- the importance of the customer,
- internal versus external customers,
- the concept of variation,
- the value of data,
- the normal curve and standard deviations,
- sampling,
- construction and interpretation of control charts, and
- who is responsible for quality.

JIT
- housekeeping,
- pull versus push system,
- uniform plant loading,
- Quick Die Change and setup reduction,
- role of suppliers,
- preventive maintenance.

Support people from engineering, scheduling, and purchasing will need extensive education, too. Their training would probably include:
- how to do a make versus buy analysis,
- production scheduling, and
- new vendor relationships including:
  - daily deliveries,
  - certification analysis, and
  - negotiating skills.

There are two different views regarding awareness education across the board. Some people feel that the information can lead to raised expectations that cannot be met in the short term. This will sometimes lead to skepticism, negativism, and cynicism. But withholding general information can lead to problems, too. Providing training to a select group in isolation can lead to resentment and accusations of favoritism. It can also create rumor mongering that may send the wrong messages through the grapevine. Is the company making these changes because it has no interest in other products? Are jobs going to be lost? Will we be forced to do things we're not trained for? Could we be fired if we refuse to join in? Is our department out of favor with management?

An example of the layout and content of a JIT/TQC/EI training program is shown in *Table 9-2*.

There has never been a successful JIT/TQC implementation without extensive education. People need to be aware of the concepts; they also need the skills to do the job.

Everyone in the organization needs education to create an awareness of the direction in which the company is moving, and how it intends to get there. But only those involved need the actual skills to be able to make and maintain meaningful changes.

Training and education should never be seen as a "program" because they never end. Training is an ongoing and evolutionary process. There are always new ideas and new methods of achieving objectives. And new training programs and concepts are continually made available in the marketplace.

Any effective training process in a reasonably sized organization will continue indefinitely, the only thing changing will be the attendees.

Step Number 7. Develop a Pilot Plan

The pilot team needs to develop its own plan for change. This will ensure that they have ownership of the implementation phase. The coordinator can facilitate

Table 9-2.
Time-Based Manufacturing-Training Plan.

WHAT	WHO & WHEN				
	Sr. Mgmt.	Middle Mgmt.	Supervisors	Shop	Engs.
Overview					
TTM-What & Why	2/91	3/91	4/91	5/91	4/91
TTM-How	2/91		4/91		
Importance	2/91				
World Class	2/91	3/91	4/91		4/91
JIT					
Overview	3/91	3/91			
Techniques			4/91	5/91	4/91
SPC					
Overview	3/91	3/91			
Techniques			4/91	5/91	4/91
Problem Solving			4/91		4/91
Teamwork					
Meetings			4/91	4/91	4/91
Managing Conflict			4/91		

the process.

The plan should include such details as:

- who will be trained,
- what they will be trained to do,
- who will do the training,
- which process to begin with,
- what will be measured, how it will be measured and who will do it,
- goals for improvement,
- a new inspection plan, including who will inspect, how it will be done, how often it will be done, and
- changes in layout.

An example of a plan is shown in *Table 9-3*.

Table 9-3.   Example of JIT/SPC/EI Implementation Plan.

ITEM	GOAL	HOW	WHO	WHEN
Housekeeping	Clean up twice daily	Get individual brooms	Dave to order	15/1
Preventive Maintenance	Have operators do lub.	Training by Maintenance	John	18/1
Improve Problem Solving	Daily Meetings	Build meeting facility in shop	Peter	1/2
Review Progress	Monthly	Monthly review meetings	Peter	1/2
Inspection	Self Inspection	Training on S.P.C.	Training Dept.	10/2
Inspection	Self Inspection	Start on machine #3 & 4	Mary/Sue	18/2
Review and change layout	Produce U shape and extend all	Integrating three functions	Team	30/2
Pull System	Change to Kanban	Meet with sales people and change system	Team	15/3
Set-Up Reduction	Reduce by 75%	Study existing system	Team	15/4
Set-Up Reduction	Reduce by 75%	Recommendations/Review	Team	30/4
Set-Up Reduction	Reduce by 75%	Document New System	Mavis	15/4
Set-Up Reduction	Reduce by 75%	Train all teams	Mavis	30/4

Step Number 8.   Review the Plan

The pilot team should inform the steering committee of its plans. This will force the team to clearly think through their most important decisions. Specifically, they will need to do a cost/benefit analysis related to any capital expenditures.

The presentation of the plan should be formalized, with the team and senior management going through the details step by step. It is important that management show enthusiasm and support for ideas and that they follow up on their commitments.

Step Number 9.   Implement the Pilot Program

The team should be given the green light to go ahead, but it is critical to realize that things seldom go according to plan. Reality and theory often differ dramatically. Expect the worst. Anticipate problems.

As the plan unfolds, it is really important to be flexible. If something doesn't work, it should be reviewed and tried again. Each failure is a learning experience.

In the first 12 months of implementation, some of the more important changes made are described on the following pages.

Improve Housekeeping

One of the first items on the team's agenda will be to improve its housekeeping. The old saying "clean up your own back yard before you ask others to do so" applies. The first principle of housekeeping is obvious—cleanliness. Working in an immaculate setting helps people feel a sense of pride and promotes the type of work habits that produce quality products. Workers need to ensure that they have enough trash bins around, have their own brooms to sweep up, and keep their machines clean of excessive oil. But better housekeeping goes beyond shiny floors and an absence of garbage. It requires that all tools and materials should be readily accessible and visible. Storage of the items should ensure that they cause no safety hazard and can be obtained by each operator with a minimum of effort and movement.

Set up a Preventive Maintenance Program

Another early task for the group is to implement a plan for preventive maintenance. This is a good opportunity for a team approach, since both involve the operator and the maintenance person.

Based on historical information of breakdowns, downtime, etc., the team should establish the most frequent causes of breakdown. The 80/20 rule often applies: 80% of the breakdowns are caused by 20% of the problems. Once the 20% problems have been established, they need to be further analyzed to determine who has the knowledge and ability to fix or prevent them. Some can be attended to by the operator. Others, requiring more technical knowledge, may be left to the mechanic. Many times, the operator can do a number of fairly routine tasks not previously done, freeing the mechanic to do a better job on more difficult tasks.

Generally, there can be two types of preventive maintenance:
- scheduled maintenance, and
- monitored maintenance.

Scheduled maintenance occurs according to a systematic plan. It is conducted after a certain number of hours of operation. These hours will vary, but will be influenced by the age of the machine.

The benefits of a comprehensive preventive maintenance program will be:
- fewer breakdowns,
- greater throughput,
- improved cycle times,
- fewer serious, costly repairs, and
- improved customer service.

Promote Teamwork

Putting a group of people together will not make them into an effective team. A team needs to work toward a common objective and constantly find new and improved ways of getting there. Fundamental to the process is communication.

Communication in a JIT/TQC cell needs to be done constantly. It needs to be formal when significant improvements need to be made, and informal when small daily changes are required.

In a sports team, people might plan their strategy in the locker room, or in a huddle on the playing field. So it is in an effective JIT cell. The members need to review the progress toward their goals at least once a month. This should be done in a meeting room off the shop floor. But the team should also get together on a daily basis to ensure that they operate as a cohesive unit

A more effective way of achieving better communications is to build a meeting place in the work area (see *Figure 9-2*).

Figure 9-2. Communication Center in the Shop.

The team should meet for five to 10 minutes at the start of every shift so that everyone is on the same wave length.

A typical meeting has four parts:

Part One - Information. The meeting leader provides information of a general nature.

Part Two - Feedback. The next few minutes should be devoted to reviewing the performance of the cell in the previous work period. For example, the P-chart could be commented upon as it would reveal the number of defective units or parts that were made. An analysis of the defects on a Pareto would increase the value of the information. It can reveal the major cause of problems and where they occur most.

If previous results show an improvement in performance, it is a time for congratulations. If not, the group needs to get into the next phase.

Part Three - Problem Solving. If there is a function that is causing immediate problems, it must be resolved by those who have the knowledge and who will be involved in its resolution. This is a time to gather people's ideas and record them on the flipchart. The ideas must be narrowed down to identify the cause before a solution is established.

Part Four - Decision Making. The group must decide on an action to take to resolve the problem. This must be agreed to by all (consensus) and then documented. It is advisable to record the action plan on a white board so it is visible. When the action item is completed, it is removed.

To make these meetings effective, they should include a maintenance person, someone from engineering, a representative from the next shift, the supervisor and his/her staff. Having all the players present will improve decisions and problem solving significantly.

Take Responsibility for Quality

The responsibility for producing defect-free products must be transferred to the operators. This cannot happen overnight. It starts with information, and continues with education. But putting the knowledge into practice is the most difficult stage. It is important that quality professionals help the operators construct and use their SPC charts until they become comfortable with the chart's use.

An important lesson of almost every SPC installation is to limit the number of charts in use. Documenting a process initially will usually reveal a very undisciplined process, one that is frequently out of statistical control. A lot of work will be needed to get the process operating within statistical control *and* within customers' specifications. Achieving this improvement will require the collaborative effort of the operator, maintenance people, and engineering. Many of the documented causes of out-of-control conditions will be outside of the operator's control. It will take time, effort and sometimes money to fix problems. Resources will be stretched to the limit. The more effort that is made in a few areas, the quicker changes will occur. Dissipating resources, over a large area and many problems, will guarantee that little or nothing will be accomplished.

Change the Physical Configuration

The cell will want to rearrange the physical layout to:
- improve communications, and
- reduce the need for transportation of items between operators or equipment.

If operators are checking one another's work, they need to communicate quickly and effectively with each other when problems arise. This is often best achieved in a U-shape setup. This allows more than one operator to communicate with others as opposed to a straight-line flow where only two people can communicate effectively at one time.

An effective layout can reduce cycle time and work-in-process, if independent operators are joined to one another. Two independent processes that are joined become a cell. Adding a third machine extends the size of the cell. As the cell grows, throughput will improve, inventory will go down, and cycle times will fall.

Each new cell created will reflect a product flow rather than a function. Whereas many factories separate functions such as machining, welding and assembly, the equipment in these areas is best moved into a cell to take over the production of an entire product. At that point, the cell becomes a focused factory or a factory within a factory.

Convert to a Pull System

As efficiencies begin to improve and setup times are reduced, the cell will be better placed to meet a fluctuating daily demand. A cell will plan its own production rather than be part of a centralized planning system based on expected rather than actual demand.

At a cut-off point, the cell will respond only to the needs of its external or internal customer. The demand will be established by a Kanban or signal. The signal can be in many forms—an empty tray, a card, or even a phone call.

Reduce Setup

An important task of the JIT cell is to increase its flexibility so that it can produce a lot size as small as one, if necessary. This appears difficult, particularly in factories that have a history of mass production. While producing long runs might appear to have worked in the past, it no longer works now. Quick-response times to varying customer needs require an immediate response, which is not possible if parts spend more time in a queue than in processing. In fact in a typical factory with little or no JIT application, parts can spend as much as 20 minutes out of process for every one minute of processing.

Quick setups will help increase responsiveness. And the opportunity exists to reduce setup times by at least 50% in most factories. According to Peter Kreppenhofer,[2] considerable time wastage originates from a variety of nonvalue-added activities. They include:

- looking for tools, material handling equipment, and setup parts;
- traveling back and forth to the setup parts storage area;
- filling out paperwork;
- waiting for inspection to qualify the setup;
- interruptions while attending other machines;
- looking for information regarding machine settings;
- waiting for components to heat to operating temperatures, and
- preparing setup parts (cleaning, setting dimensions, installing, lifting dies, etc.).

Sometimes it is difficult to see our own mistakes. But having learned some of the theory behind quick setup, it becomes easier to apply when objectively studying our own work patterns. Experience has found that cell members can do their best by watching a videotape of their activities. This should reflect activities that are as close to typical as possible.

The team should observe the videotape, documenting each activity and how long it takes. Next, each activity should be classified in terms of when it was done. Finally, those activities done during downtime should be analyzed as to whether they could be done during production time. For example, a die can only

---

[2] Peter Kreppenhofer. "Time is Money," *Plant Engineering and Maintenance*, April 1990, p. 54.

be removed during downtime, but all preparatory activities should be done before the machine is stopped.

The group should brainstorm for as many ideas as possible to make changeovers more quickly. These, when agreed upon, should be documented and communicated to everyone concerned. Documented procedures should be followed through regular appraisals to ensure that old habits don't creep back into the system.

Quick setup improvement is not a one-shot deal. The cell members will always find additional methods of improvement. These may include:

- Finding quicker or better fastening methods.
  It is possible to reduce a variety of motions to set up parts and safety covers. "Another aspect of better fastening is to develop common damping heights for interchangeable setup parts. This eliminates the need to obtain various lengths and widths of bolts and spacers and also allows the use of toggle clamps without having to adjust for different sizes of pieces to be clamped." [3]
- Using more people.
  It is possible that a concerted effort in a short period of time, by more than one person, will save time. But care must be taken not to compromise safety by having a number of people in a limited space.
- Avoiding measurement and relocation of parts.
  The cell may find the use of templates, locating blocks and fixtures will help them get parts to the correct position the first time.
- Avoiding adjustments.
  A little more care to make sure that the equipment is set up exactly as it was before can help to get the machine producing quality parts right away and avoid continuous adjustments. Scrap and rework are the result of poor adjustments.
- Automating where possible.
  As a final step, and with a thorough knowledge of the process, it will be possible to automate some setup procedures. These may include hydraulic clamping, automated die and mold handling, and programmable controls.

Step Number 10. Do a Post-Mortem on the Pilot Project and Write a Case Study

It is astonishing how mistakes are continually repeated in organizations. It is equally surprising that so few successes are acknowledged. Learning and recognition can both be achieved if the pilot group documents its experience in a case-study format.

The case study need not be elaborate. It should state the nature of the opportunity, the goals set, and the goals achieved. It should describe problems

---

[3] Peter Kreppenhofer. "Time is Money," *Plant Engineering and Maintenance*, April 1990, p. 56.

that occurred and how they were overcome, so that future groups can undertake similar projects with fewer problems. Finally, the group should comment on the training. Was there enough? Was it effective? Was it practical? How could it be improved?

The documented case study can be used in many ways. First, it can form part of the education for new team and projects. It will help motivate the team to reach its goals, because no one likes to document failure. Next, it will provide a focal point for recognition by management. Finally, it will help to change the attitudes in the organization, since greater visibility is given to people who are getting things done.

Step Number 11. The Pilot Team Reports Back to the Steering Committee

All issues reviewed in the post-mortem should be fed back to the steering committee.

This is a time for learning, but it is also a time for celebrating. No doubt there have been some gains; it is important that the pilot team members are acknowledged for their efforts. This can be done in the form of a recognition lunch or dinner. Certificates, pens or other items such as calculators may also be awarded. It is vital that senior management be involved in the recognition process.

Step Number 12. Do It Again Until the Whole Organization is Involved

The lessons learned from the first program will provide invaluable insights into future management of the process. Having learned what to do and what not to do makes it possible to expand the program more aggressively. For example, if the organization started with a single pilot group, it may be possible to launch two more after the post mortem.

The program will continue to expand until all areas in the organization are involved. In fact, each work area must subject itself to an overhaul, since all are interlinked.

Expand the Process to Service Areas

Now that we have discussed the changes that might be made on the shop floor, we will turn our attention to some of the changes that must take place in the design, order entry, production planning, production scheduling, purchasing, and distribution areas.

As service departments, each must be examined for its:
- understanding and contribution to a faster and more flexible organization;
- provision of value added services;
- cost of doing business;
- activities that cause delays, and
- throughput.

A systematic study should be made, involving as many members of the department as possible. The process will be easier if it is facilitated by a skilled outsider, because the potential for conflict is great. A significant number of non-value-added activities are sure to become the subject of heated debate. Staff will find it difficult to let go of work habits that have been established for a long time, even though they prove to be of limited value. Typical of these will be reports that have no value, distribution of memos and documents to people with little interest, collection of statistics that no one analyzes, and meetings about issues that could be handled much quicker by the right people informally.

The steps that need to be taken to streamline each work area are similar. They are:

Step One–Determine the Mission of the Area. The members should think about who their customers are—internal or external. Then they should consult with those customers to find out exactly what they want, how they want it, and when they want it.

The answers might come as a shock to some people who, on reflection, might find that little of their daily activity has anything to do with customer service.

Step Two–Identify All Functions and Services Currently Provided. A list of activities should be drawn up and evaluated against the mission. What are the activities? Are the activities service-oriented? Do they add value?

Step Three–Do a Flow Diagram of Activities. This diagram will identify each activity, its time and delays. It will also reveal nonvalue-added activities and waste.

Step Four–Find Ways for Improvement. The group should develop a list of improvements in an action planning format. The savings in the plan should be summarized.

Step Five–Present the Plan for Approval. The department members should present their ideas to management for approval.

Step Six–Implement the Plan. The action items should be put into effect. The group should meet regularly to monitor progress.

Step Seven–Develop a Measurement System. To ensure that benefits continue to take place, each department should have a number of key measurements that will keep track of the quality of its service, how cost effective it is, and its time responsiveness. This can usually be done by using a Performance Index (see *Chapter 10*), an excellent system that will allow them to track progress on a variety of issues (indexes) simultaneously.

The training will not only provide the skills to do the job, but the enthusiasm to move ahead. It is important that the training be customized to the needs of the plant. A proper needs analysis will:
- identify the existing skills of the trainees,
- take account of their literacy levels, and
- identify any roadblocks that might prevent people from using the skills.

CASE STUDY

THE REWARDS OF JIT AT ELECTROMOTORS LIMITED

Electromotors Ltd., a subsidiary of Brook Crompton Parkinson Limited and owned by the Hawker Siddeley PLC group of companies, is a major European producer of electric motors for various industries. One of its manufacturing businesses is Squirrel Cage Motors (SCM) which produces small AC motors.

Previous to the JIT implementation program, the motors were predominantly manufactured using a process functional layout. Shafts and cast cores were manufactured in the Shaft & Rotor Department, machining of endshields and frames in other departments, winding and motor assembly in yet another department. These components were produced to a forecast inventory control system which resulted in high safety levels and a poor response to customer change requirements.

Components, after manufacture, were shipped to a central store. The rotor and shaft, bearing and endshield were then kitted and issued to be subassembled. The remaining components were kitted, issued, and brought together with the subassembly to be assembled.

Purchased components were stored in a warehouse. Material handling was in the form of a considerable number of fork-lift trucks transporting material from stores and between operations. Manufacture of components was largely achieved using conventional machine tools with long setups, causing large batches to be produced to achieve EBQ returns. Overall control of stocks was achieved using several MRP modules.

This type of manufacturing caused long lead times and poor customer response, and produced vast amounts of Work In Progress (WIP) and inventory.

During 1987, it became apparent that a revision of the manufacturing methods was needed primarily to ensure that the business survived and secondly, to forge ahead and become a world-class manufacturing unit and meet future objectives stated in the company strategy.

JIT appeared to offer the solutions, with its effect of reducing waste, particularly inventory and nonvalue adding operations, for a relatively small investment compared with other options.

A preliminary target of 10,000 motors per week was set and the effects were forecast for direct and indirect labor, machine investment, and total inventory.

Other benefits which were not costed but favored the introduction of JIT manufacturing were:
- increased motors per worker day;
- a reduction in floor manufacturing area due to reduced WIP and the adoption of cellular manufacture;
- reduced "overdues." Overdues are those motors which are late to their program for manufacture;
- improved control of manufacture due to simplified workflow and improved information systems; and

- a reduction in manufacturing lead time.

The feelings expressed at the time suggested that automation would further complicate manufacturing by introducing yet more procedures and computer systems. The requirement was for a simplification of the existing processes and procedures, so that the underlying principles could be established before proceeding with further refinements.

Kanban systems were designed and implemented. The systems operated with customers, both internally and externally. Internal Kanban systems were designed to operate using dedicated containers with part numbers, quantities, and part descriptions detailed on them. The internal Kanban system was broadly divided into two systems, one for the more expensive items and another for the cheaper items (e.g., screws, labels, etc.). The system operating with the cheaper items utilized a two-bin system. One bin was filled at a central store while the other was utilized on-line.

The Kanban system operating with external suppliers used containers with Identification Tags attached (Kanbans). The number of containers within the system was based upon previous usage of part numbers, with the suppliers' lead time also taken into account. Containers emptied on the production line are taken to a specially prepared area and the Kanbans placed in a cabinet mounted on the wall. When the supplier delivers the following batch of part numbers, empty containers are loaded on the vehicle to be taken back to the supplier with the Kanbans. The system repeats itself with the supplier delivering up to twice per week.

The Kanban systems have "mechanized" many of the internal transactions and deliveries of part numbers. The advantages include:
- The production of internal Kanban part numbers is signalled using identified empty containers, eliminating the use of internally written paper orders and computer transactions.
- Parts are no longer shipped to and from stores, as all operations, including assembly, now occur consecutively down a balanced JIT line.
- The frequency of the purchasing department transactions has been considerably reduced. Part-number prices are negotiated once per year and revised if necessary. Part numbers are no longer on blanket order, thus eliminating the constant revision of orders with suppliers as a result of variations in the production plan.

While some housekeeping problems were encountered, overall workflow was more organized. So, too, was planning by the Line Managers. The manufacturing lead time was reduced from as much as six weeks to four days. The production area was reduced, together with the manufacturing path length. The reduction of area improved teamwork and communications.

The number of stock models was reduced from 76 to 37. Overdues have decreased to less than one day as a result of the high availability of Kanban parts.

The overall quality of the product improved as problems were highlighted before dispatch. This was achieved by ensuring that operators had responsibility for their own quality and for other operators' quality further along the line.

Because operators no longer see large batch buildups in front of them, psychologically they have felt less hurried and are therefore less likely to produce errors.

Electromotors Ltd. has been active in reducing the Order Processing lead time, that is, the time from customer inquiry to receipt of an order in the manufacturing department.

Source: M .G. Conway et al, "JIT in the UK Electric Motor Industry: A Case Study," *SME Technical Paper*, MS 90-845.

QUESTIONNAIRE

Answer the following questions ranking your answers from 1 to 5.
1 - represents very poor,
2 - poor,
3 - average,
4 - good, and
5 - very good.

- Do you have a strategic plan?
  1 - No,
  2 - In the boss's head,
  3 - Some senior managers have a plan,
  4 - Have a plan, not well documented ,
  5 - Have a plan, known to
      all that need to know.

- Does your strategic plan include Time To Market considerations?
  1 - No,
  3 - Somewhat,
  5 - Clearly.

- Do all areas of the organization have time-based goals?

1 - None,	4 - Most,
2 - Very few,	5 - All.
3 - Some,	

- Are the Time To Market goals measured and monitored at all levels?

1 - No,	4 - Mostly,
2 - Very little,	5 - All.
3 - Somewhat,	

- Do you have a steering committee that nurtures and promotes change to world-class manufacturing strategies?
  - 1 - No,
  - 3 - Yes, but not totally effective,
  - 5 - Yes

- Do you have a full-time resource person promoting change to world-class manufacturing techniques?
  - 1 - No,
  - 3 - Part-time,
  - 5 - Yes

- Have you researched the full implications of world-class manufacturing techniques before moving ahead?
  - 1 - No,   4 - Fairly well
  - 2 - A little,   5 - Extensively
  - 3 - Somewhat,

- Do you have a documented plan, with milestones, actions and people identified to do tasks?
  - 1 - No,   4 - Fairly well done,
  - 2 - Poorly done,   5 - Well done
  - 3 - Somewhat,

- Has everyone in your "pilot" area been adequately trained?
  - 1 - No,   4 - Fairly well,
  - 2 - A little,   5 - Extensively
  - 3 - Somewhat,

- Does the pilot team have a plan?
  - 1 - No,
  - 2 - Not well articulated,
  - 3 - Somewhat,
  - 4 - Fairly well articulated,
  - 5 - Well articulated and documented

- Have you dedicated support staff to the pilot team to ensure that they have all the help needed to make changes?
  - 1 - No,
  - 3 - Some full-time,
  - 5 - Dedicated

- Has responsibility for quality and other performance indicators been passed to line people?

1 - No,	4 - Largely,
2 - A little,	5 - Totally
3 - Somewhat,	

- Are shop people measuring their own quality on SPC charts?
  1 - No,
  2 - A little,
  3 - Somewhat,
  4 - Mostly,
  5 - All where applicable

- Have machines been moved closer to each other, increasing sized cells?
  1 - No,
  3 - Some,
  5 - Extensive changes

- Do you have a team evaluating how to reduce setup times?
  1 - No,
  2 - Thinking about it,
  3 - Informally,
  4 - Somewhat formally,
  5 - Formal teams

- Do you evaluate your projects after a reasonable period?
  1 - No,
  2 - A little,
  3 - Informally,
  4 - Formally
  5 - Formally including doing a case study

- Do you incorporate ideas from previous experiences in expanded projects?
  1 - No, don't learn,
  2 - Learn a little,
  3 - Use some ideas,
  4 - Learn quite a lot,
  5 - Use a great deal of experience

TOTAL SCORES

Interpretation

- A score of between 18 and 32 indicates that you have no plans to implement world-class manufacturing, and are unlikely to be successful.
- A score of 33 to 47 indicates that you have little clarity about what you are doing, and need to think clearly about where you are going, why and how.
- A score of 48 to 63 indicates that you have taken some steps to implement world-class manufacturing, and may be modestly successful.
- A score of 64 to 78 indicates that you are doing a fairly good job of implementing world-class manufacturing techniques.
- A score of 79 to 90 indicates that you are doing an excellent job of implementing world-class manufacturing techniques.

chapter *10*

Building Speed Techniques Into Day-to-Day Management

INTRODUCTION

Most people find it difficult to think of a time when everyone pulled together over a continuous period to meet customer needs. Or, if they can remember such occurrences, they would admit that those times were rare.

Even so, getting consistently high performance from people can be done. We do it all the time. Just stroll to a local baseball diamond and watch a group of adults get together for a game. Witness the change in behavior when they divide into groups. All kinds of new behaviors occur. The group becomes focused; they want to win. They cheer one another on. They delight in one another's accomplishments. They lift each other's spirits if plays don't go their way.

So, if we're capable of performing with such high enthusiasm on the sports field, why can't we perform equally well back in the shop? A challenging question!

The truth is that there is no good excuse for not getting people to perform as if they were a sports team. Learn about the makings of a good sports team and then apply the principles to the people at work .

So think about having the opportunity to be a sports coach. What would you do to motivate your people? If you drew up a checklist it would probably resemble this:

- Provide players with ongoing training.
- Provide players with continuous feedback on their level of performance.

227

- Compensate people for exceptional performance.
- Recognize excellence.
- Encourage people to work as a team since they will sink or swim together.
- Provide specific, clear goals.
- Monitor performance with appropriate measurement tools.

To what extent do you do these things? The more you do, the more likely your people will behave like a sports team. It can become almost a self-fulfilling prophesy; if you treat people as team players, they will behave like a team.

How can you make this a reality? How can you ensure that Time To Market issues predominate in people activities?

Part of the answer lies in setting up a measurement system that will:
- Monitor performance.
- Incorporate the opinions of the team members (to get commitment to the process).
- Focus on continuous improvement.
- Take all key aspects of performance into account, specifically those relative to customer service (internal or external).

Riggs and Felix[1] designed a matrix measurement system which meets these criteria. We call it *Performance Indexing*.

A completed index or scorecard appears as *Figure 10-1*.

Such an index chart should be set up in a permanent place in the work area of a team, allowing the members to:
- Monitor their progress,
- Plan for improvement,
- Celebrate improvements, and
- Solve problems when scores decline.

STEP BY STEP

Step 1 - Define the System

Navel gazing is the first step. Some questions that members of the work unit need to answer as they begin the process of bringing speed to the organization include:
- Who are our customers, internal or external?
- What are their needs?
- How are these needs being measured?
- How should they be measured?
- What products or services are we currently supplying (outputs)?
- What resources are we using to meet our customers' needs (inputs)? A description of the primary resources should be documented (people, materials, methods, equipment, and capital).

---

[1] James L. Riggs, Glenn A. Felix. *Productivity by Objectives*, Prentice Hall Inc. , Englewood, N. J. 07632 1983.

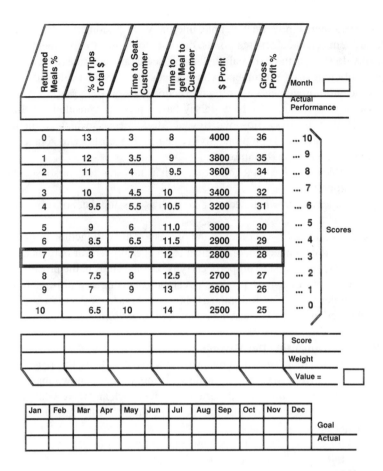

Figure 10-1. Example of a Completed Plan Using A Performance\Index.

The second step is to design a flow diagram to help highlight how the process operates as opposed to how it should function. A flow diagram shows the steps that are taken in a process and how they relate to one another.

When people get together to map out a process, they derive significant benefits.

Understanding the total system. People understand their portion of the total but rarely have knowledge about the whole. When they get together and share this information, the process becomes a revelation.

Finding opportunities for improvement. Since circumstances change much quicker than systems, an evaluation of procedures invariably leads to questions such as, "Why do we do this? " "Do we need to do it at all? " "Isn't this a better way? " "How long have we done this? " Answers to these and other questions lead to improvements.

Better customer service. It is widely assumed that all employees understand who their customer is. While most people understand the concept of the external customer, they rarely treat people internally as customers. But unless each department sends defect-free goods, on time, to the next department, the system breaks down and the external customers' needs are not satisfied. A flow diagram often reveals customers whose needs have been neglected, leading to significant improvements as corrective action is taken.

Geary A. Rummler, a New Jersey-based process consultant, believes that documenting the work flow will reveal "disconnects," which result in slower times, poor quality, poor productivity, and higher costs. The sources of these problems are categorized into:

1. Problems with what's going out, such as missing, late, or substandard outputs.
2. Problems with what's coming in, such as missing, late, or substandard inputs.
3. Flaws in the logical order of the process. This will include missing, redundant, unneeded, or illogical sequences of steps or bottlenecks.
4. Problems related to properly carrying out the steps in the process.

An example of a new product development using a multi-functional team approach developed by Rummler is shown in *Figure 10-2*. Flow diagrams can be enhanced when they use standard symbols (see *Figure 10-3*).

Step 2 - Documenting the Mission

The work group should agree why they exist. It is the reason for their existence. Anyone who has been through this process knows that it typically takes weeks or months. At a departmental level such an effort, while praiseworthy, is unnecessary. A simpler approach would be for the group to answer six simple questions:

1. **Who** are we? Describe the number and types of jobs.
2. **What** are we? State the name of the organization.
3. **What** do we do? Describe the product or service offered.
4. **Whom** do we serve? Describe the customers, specifying their market segments if necessary.
5. **How** do we serve them? Describe key product or service dimensions such as time, quality, or cost effectiveness.
6. **Why** do we exist? State the reason for the existence of the organization, such as profitability.

Once these questions are answered, "plug" them into the following framework.

The _____ are _____
         (1)   (2)

that _____ for _____
          (3)   (4)

by _____ to _____.
        (5)   (6)

Some wordsmithing and massaging of the information will be required to get it into an acceptable format.

Step 3 - Identify Key Performance Indicators

The work group needs to identify key indices in the most important categories of performance. These categories typically relate to quality, cost effectiveness (profitability), timeliness (including speed), utilization, and health and safety issues.

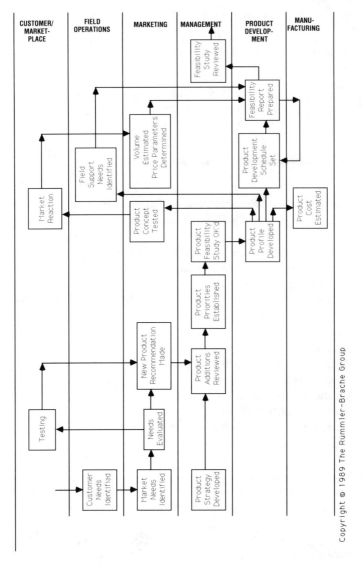

Figure 10-2. Cross Functional Process Flow (New Product Development).

231

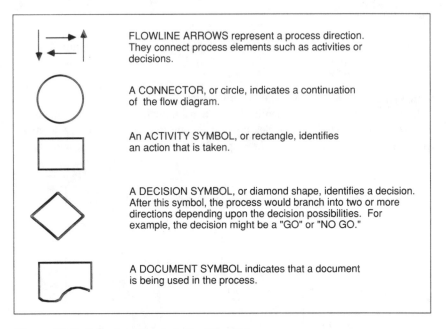

Figure 10-3. Standard Symbols for Flow Diagrams.

Members of the group should reach consensus on what these indices are. Their input and agreement will build commitment that focuses on these key issues.

Performance measures are best defined by ratios or fractions, although they may not always be. Three to seven indicators are generally sufficient to measure a unit's performance adequately.

They should account for inflation and, where possible, their indicators should:

- Already be generated through the existing management information system,
- Be accurate,
- Measure what is intended to be measured,
- Reflect customer needs,
- Accurately represent the service,
- Be easy to understand, and
- Account for inflation in constant dollar terms (i.e. in both numerator and denominator).

Here are some examples of indices:

a) Quality - These will measure the extent to which the unit is meeting customer obligations each time, every time, the first time.

Re-worked documents   Re-work hours
Total documents released   Total hours

Customer complaints	Number of changes to documents
Projects completed	Number of documents produced

Customer satisfaction index	Proposals won
Target index	Proposals submitted

Returns	Staff turnover
Deliveries	Total Staff

Scrap
Amount Produced

b) Cost Effectiveness - This index measures the extent to which the unit's resources are used effectively. At a higher level in the organization, it may
relate to profitability. Typical indicators for a work unit include:

Hours expended	Overtime hours
Documents completed	Total hours worked

Training cost or hours	Documents completed
Employee cost or hours	Number of employees

Documents completed	Computer downtime
Documents scheduled	Available time

Units produced	Projected costs
Total costs	Actual costs

Documents accepted	Inquiries answered
Documents released	Inquiries received

Inquiries received	Labor-year experience
Number of employees	Target-level experience

At the top of the organization, typical indices are:

Monthly cash flow	Gross profit percentage
Monthly profitability	Net profit percentage

Net income
Share holders equity

c) Timeliness and Speed - This index measures the unit's ability to meet
its time commitments. Typical indicators include:

Documents overdue	Actual response time
Total documents	Standard response time
Projects completed on time	Turnaround time
Projects complete	Target turnaround
Project elapsed time	Current cycle time
Actual elapsed time	Previous cycle time

d) Health and Safety - These indicators would measure the unit's ability to conduct its affairs in a manner not determined by the physical well-being of its members:

Number of accidents	Hours of lost time due to accidents
Total labor hours	Number of employees
Lost time accidents	Number of incidents reported
Number of employees	Number of employees
Number of accidents	Current H & S audit index
Total work hours	Previous H & S audit index

For our example, let us assume that the unit members identified six indices. These are written into the top of the index chart which, for the chapter's example, is a restaurant.

Step 4 - Determine the Existing Performance Levels

Unit members need to find out how they are currently performing as indicated by the chosen indices.

Rather than take one month's data, the unit should average the performance of the previous three months. A moving average of some previous period might be appropriate too.

The exercise of gathering data will give the unit a   reference regarding the suitability of that index. If, for example, it becomes extremely costly to collect — as is the case with some customer surveys—then its value might be questionable.

If no data is available, but it is easy and inexpensive to get, the group can start with their best estimate of current performance.

Current performance levels are entered in the boxes at the level of the score of three in the matrix. This allows future performance levels greater room for improvement than for decline on the zero-to-10 rating scale.

The existing levels for our restaurant are entered on line three of the Performance Index (see *Figure 10-4*).

Step 5 - Establish Goals

The unit must next set up realistic goals. They must define a specific time period, usually one to two years, within which they will attain these goals. This is

234

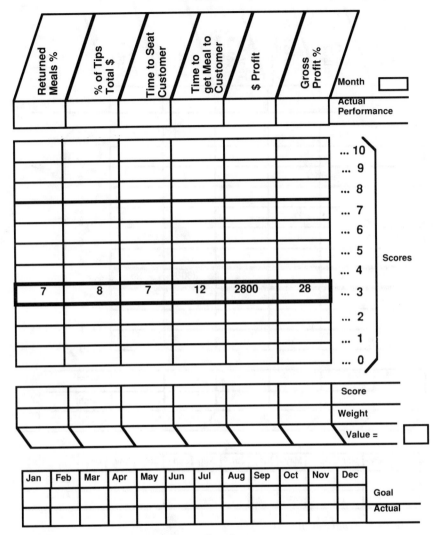

Returned Meals %	% of Tips Total $	Time to Seat Customer	Time to get Meal to Customer	$ Profit	Gross Profit %	Month ☐
						Actual Performance

						... 10
						... 9
						... 8
						... 7
						... 6
						... 5 Scores
						... 4
7	8	7	12	2800	28	... 3
						... 2
						... 1
						... 0

						Score
						Weight
						Value = ☐

Jan	Feb	Mar	Apr	May	Jun	Jul	Aug	Sep	Oct	Nov	Dec	
												Goal
												Actual

Figure 10-4. Existing Performance Levels.

the time frame for the completed matrix. Much discussion and good judgement will be required to select the right goals at the highest performance level.

Criteria for good goals are that they should be:

- Specific,
- Realistic,
- Challenging,
- Attainable, and
- Measurable.

The goals are then entered in the matrix at the level corresponding to the score of 10 (see *Figure 10-5*).

235

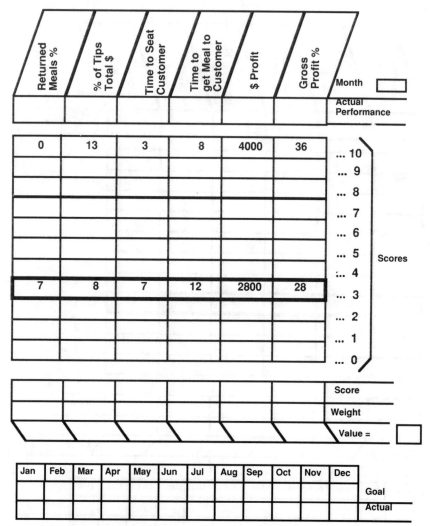

Returned Meals %	% of Tips Total $	Time to Seat Customer	Time to get Meal to Customer	$ Profit	Gross Profit %		
						Month	☐
						Actual Performance	

0	13	3	8	4000	36	... 10	
						... 9	
						... 8	
						... 7	
						... 6	
						... 5	Scores
						... 4	
7	8	7	12	2800	28	... 3	
						... 2	
						... 1	
						... 0	

						Score	
						Weight	
						Value =	☐

Jan	Feb	Mar	Apr	May	Jun	Jul	Aug	Sep	Oct	Nov	Dec		
												Goal	
												Actual	

Figure 10-5. Goal Setting.

Step 6 - Determine Mini-Goals

The work unit will not go from a level of three to ten overnight. It may take a year. It is important that their efforts are recognized and recorded in the interim, so that they see improvement, and are recognized accordingly. That is the value of having milestones.

The intermediate performance levels four to nine can be thought of as mini-goals. Each succeeding score should relate to the preceding one and define progress towards the ultimate goal. This progress is expressed by the numerical distance from each intermediate score to the next.

The mini-goals are entered in the matrix at the levels corresponding to the scores of four, five, six, seven, eight, and nine (see *Figure 10-6*).

236

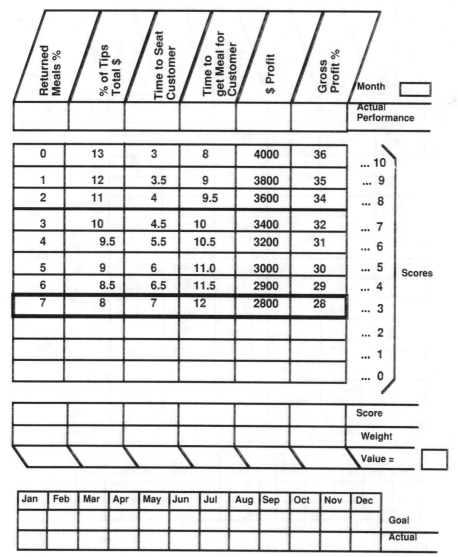

Returned Meals %	% of Tips Total $	Time to Seat Customer	Time to get Meal for Customer	$ Profit	Gross Profit %	Month
						Actual Performance

						Scores
0	13	3	8	4000	36	... 10
1	12	3.5	9	3800	35	... 9
2	11	4	9.5	3600	34	... 8
3	10	4.5	10	3400	32	... 7
4	9.5	5.5	10.5	3200	31	... 6
5	9	6	11.0	3000	30	... 5
6	8.5	6.5	11.5	2900	29	... 4
7	8	7	12	2800	28	... 3
						... 2
						... 1
						... 0

						Score
						Weight
						Value =

Jan	Feb	Mar	Apr	May	Jun	Jul	Aug	Sep	Oct	Nov	Dec	
												Goal
												Actual

Figure 10-6. Setting Mini-Goals.

Step 7 - Establish the Lower Performance Levels

This determination establishes a base at which the group does not choose to perform. Realistically, however, performance might go below current levels.

After determining the lower levels, they should be entered in the matrix at a level corresponding to a score of zero. Finally, the group should suggest two intervening scores that would link the worst possible performance (zero) with the current level (three), and insert these scores at one and two (see *Figure 10-7*).

The range of possible scores is now complete.

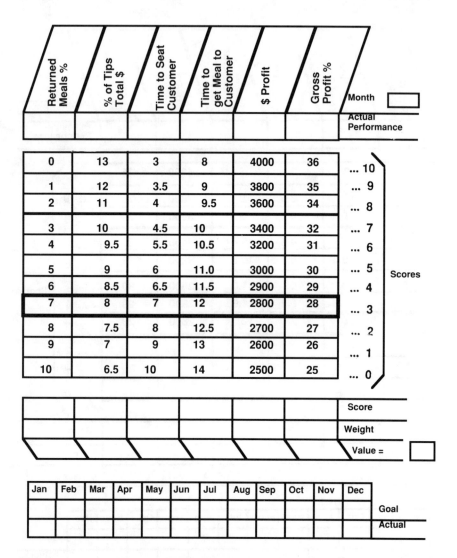

Returned Meals %	% of Tips Total $	Time to Seat Customer	Time to get Meal to Customer	$ Profit	Gross Profit %	
0	13	3	8	4000	36	... 10
1	12	3.5	9	3800	35	... 9
2	11	4	9.5	3600	34	... 8
3	10	4.5	10	3400	32	... 7
4	9.5	5.5	10.5	3200	31	... 6
5	9	6	11.0	3000	30	... 5
6	8.5	6.5	11.5	2900	29	... 4
7	8	7	12	2800	28	... 3
8	7.5	8	12.5	2700	27	... 2
9	7	9	13	2600	26	... 1
10	6.5	10	14	2500	25	... 0

Month

Actual Performance

Scores

Score

Weight

Value =

Jan	Feb	Mar	Apr	May	Jun	Jul	Aug	Sep	Oct	Nov	Dec	
												Goal
												Actual

Figure 10-7. Establishing Lower Performance Levels.

Step 8 - Assign Weights to the Indices

The work unit will need to have a sense of how it is doing overall, since the scores achieved each period will change at different rates for each index.

A consensus must be negotiated providing a weighting for each index, the sum of which must equal 100. This is a critical step since it signals what issues are of greater importance.

Deciding which indices have the greatest weight determines how quality, speed, and costs stack up together in relation to the performance mission of the unit.

238

The weight of each indicator is entered in the appropriate box on the "Weight" row (see *Figure 10-8*).

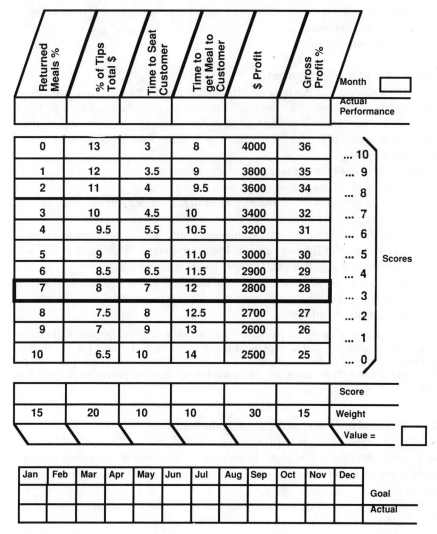

Returned Meals %	% of Tips Total $	Time to Seat Customer	Time to get Meal to Customer	$ Profit	Gross Profit %	
						Month ☐
						Actual Performance
0	13	3	8	4000	36	... 10
1	12	3.5	9	3800	35	... 9
2	11	4	9.5	3600	34	... 8
3	10	4.5	10	3400	32	... 7
4	9.5	5.5	10.5	3200	31	... 6
5	9	6	11.0	3000	30	... 5 Scores
6	8.5	6.5	11.5	2900	29	... 4
7	8	7	12	2800	28	... 3
8	7.5	8	12.5	2700	27	... 2
9	7	9	13	2600	26	... 1
10	6.5	10	14	2500	25	... 0
						Score
15	20	10	10	30	15	**Weight**
						Value = ☐

Jan	Feb	Mar	Apr	May	Jun	Jul	Aug	Sep	Oct	Nov	Dec	
												Goal
												Actual

Figure 10-8. Weighting.

Step 9 - Development Period

As a first go-around, it is very possible that the group will make some less-than-satisfactory choices. If the system is "cast-in-stone" and cannot be changed, it will lose its value. A development period of up to three months should give the group time to:

- Confirm current performance levels.
- Establish that data can be collated for related indices.

- Devise the simplest and easiest way of collecting accurate data.
- Develop an appropriate weighting system, bearing in mind the relative importance of each index.
- Develop a plan for responsibility for the maintenance of the system and data collection, and
- Plan for improvement.

Step 10 - Plan for Improvement

This index alone will not lead to performance improvement. Some benefit is bound to be experienced with raised awareness of the importance of each performance index, but this will be short-lived as the excitement associated with the new system wears off. The real benefit will come from implementing well thought-out plans.

Simple guidelines for any operating unit to follow are to:
- Focus on problems that members have control over.
- Work on problems where other people can provide support or knowledge. Ask for their help. Bring them into unit meetings.
- Break the problem down into component parts. Tackle them one at a time.
- Prioritize plans. The unit has only limited resources. They need to do whatever will give them the biggest "bang for their buck. "
- Work as a team. With involvement of members comes commitment and better solutions. Also, teams tend to produce more creative solutions than any one individual can.

There is a variety of excellent planning tools which will allow the unit members to identify all roadblocks that will prevent the achievement of goals. One of these is the project planning process at the end of the chapter. After doing this, plans are put in place to remove these obstacles, while the action items are passes on to those who have control of them.

Step 11 - Tabulate Scores and Calculate the Index

After all adjustments are verified and completed, the work unit should make these results the final action plan. From now on, the basis of the matrix should not be changed, because comparisons between periods would then become meaningless.

At the conclusion of each monitoring period—weekly or monthly—the unit should gather the data and plot the results. The steps to follow are these:
a) Calculate the actual measure for each productivity indicator and enter it on the performance line of the matrix.
b) Circle the actual performance of each indicator on the scale. If a mini-goal is not achieved, the lower performance level should be circled. Any performance lower than a score of zero should achieve a zero for the period.
c) Score the corresponding performance (zero to ten) and enter it on the score line of the matrix.
d) Multiply the weighting factors by the score to get a weighted value. These totals are entered into the value line of the matrix.

e) Add the weighted values together. The sum equals the performance index for that monitoring period (see *Figure 10-9*).

Over time, the movement of the index provides excellent tracking of the results of productivity improvements. In general, at the beginning, the index is 300. The goal is 1000.

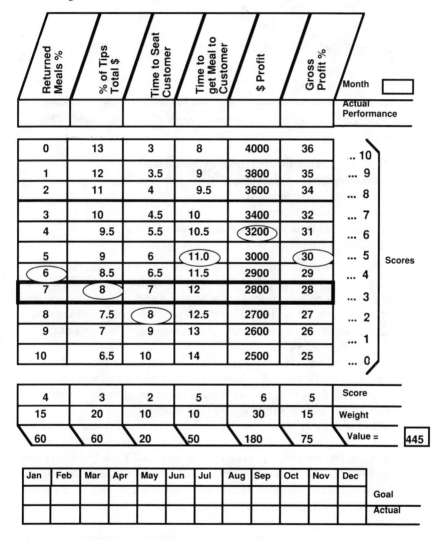

Returned Meals %	% of Tips Total $	Time to Seat Customer	Time to get Meal to Customer	$ Profit	Gross Profit %	Month [ ]
						Actual Performance
0	13	3	8	4000	36	.. 10
1	12	3.5	9	3800	35	... 9
2	11	4	9.5	3600	34	... 8
3	10	4.5	10	3400	32	... 7
4	9.5	5.5	10.5	(3200)	31	... 6
5	9	6	(11.0)	3000	(30)	... 5 Scores
(6)	8.5	6.5	11.5	2900	29	... 4
7	(8)	7	12	2800	28	... 3
8	7.5	(8)	12.5	2700	27	... 2
9	7	9	13	2600	26	... 1
10	6.5	10	14	2500	25	... 0

4	3	2	5	6	5	Score
15	20	10	10	30	15	Weight
60	60	20	50	180	75	Value = 445

Jan	Feb	Mar	Apr	May	Jun	Jul	Aug	Sep	Oct	Nov	Dec	
												Goal
												Actual

Figure 10-9. Calculation of Performance Index.

Step 12 - Plot the Results

The actual Performance Index should be plotted on a graph against a target curve which should start at 300 and end at 1000. A three-month moving average may be used and plotted to accommodate variations (see *Figure 10-10*).

241

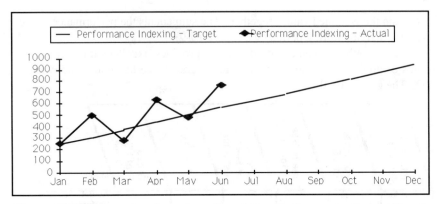

Figure 10-10. Example of an Actual and Target Composite Index That Is Plotted Monthly.

Step 13 - Manage the Unit for Increased Performance

Whatever the objective — speed, quality or cost reduction — performance improvement will happen if people are:

- Empowered to make changes,
- Given regular feedback on performance, and
- Rewarded for achievement.

Empowerment comes from managers and supervisors who respect the technical knowledge and sense of responsibility of their people. It takes place in an environment where people are valued. It works best where people are continuously trained to perform better. But it also allows people to make mistakes so that they can learn from the experience, grow and progress to new levels of performance.

Feedback on performance levels is an important ingredient too. A measurement system such as *Performance Indexing* allows performance levels to be available to all. This knowledge—considered confidential in some organizations —makes each person feel important and part of the team.

Recognition and Rewards are closely linked to feedback. What people are rewarded for sends a clear signal to others about what is important in the organization. It helps define the values of people at the top. So if Time To Market is to be the strategy of the '90s, then anything that will help the organization respond quicker than it did before, or quicker than its competitors, should be rewarded. Then other people will want to do the same, or better, so that they can be rewarded too.

Reward systems need to be created for the specific environment. Some organizations don't have a culture that appreciate people informally, so they introduce a formal system. Examples include:

- Employee of the Month recognition,
- Suggestion Award Programs, and
- Long Service Awards.

242

Linking performance to the reward system is vital. The Performance Indexing system can be linked to a tangible reward system, cash or otherwise.

SUMMARY

The focus on getting to the market quickly can be translated from a mission into reality only by management action. Specifically, speed will become part of the corporate culture only if it becomes one of the key measurements by which people's performances are judged, and

- People are rewarded and recognized if they achieve Time To Market goals.
- Departmental meetings keep Time To Market on the agenda, and
- Problem solving groups devote time to removing roadblocks which inhibit Time To Market strategies.

The Performance Indexing system is an excellent tool to help people in every part of an organization focus on meeting client expectations for quality, speed, and cost effectiveness. It involves people in defining key indices and rewards them for attaining continued improvement in these indices.

APPENDIX 1

Planning for Improvement
Using the Project Planning Process

The Project Planning Process most commonly ensures that projects are implemented. To do this, it identifies possible obstacles, ensuring that these are dealt with effectively.

Construction of a Project Planning Process

Like all effective tools, the Project Planning Process works best when it is used systematically. The steps are as follows:

Step I. Construct the appropriate figure (shown next)

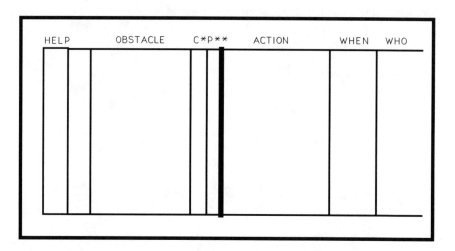

* **C** stands for control.
** **P** stands for priority.

Step II. List all possible obstacles that can or might prevent the project's success. List items that can help you.

Step III. Decide who has control over the obstacles.

HELP	#	OBSTACLE	C*P**	ACTION	WHEN	WHO
support Training programs Budget $	1	Untrained people	1			
	2	Lack of time	1			
	3	Little mid-management support	2			
	4	Downtime	2			

Problems you have full control over are given as 1.
Problems you have partial control over are given as 2.
Problems you have no control over are given as 3.

Step IV. Prioritize items in terms of their impact on the problem or project. Get a consensus.

HELP	#	OBSTACLE	C*	P**	ACTION	WHEN	WHO
support Training programs Budget $	1	Untrained people	1	2			
	2	Lack of time	1	1			
	3	Little mid-management support	2	3			
	4	Downtime	2	4			

Step V. Make a judgement whether or not to continue. You may decide to abandon the project or solution if there are important obstacles which are outside of your control. If not, proceed.

Step VI. Develop actions to deal with all obstacles. Utilize the resources listed in the "Help" column. Follow these simple principles:

- Start with the most important obstacles first.
- Involve people outside the group for Type Two problems.
- Don't try to do everything at once. Work on the obstacles one at a time, being realistic about your resources (time, money).
- Get commitments for activities and completion dates from the people involved.

HELP	#	OBSTACLE	C*	P**	ACTION	WHEN	WHO
support	1	Untrained people	1	2	Provide training program in problem solving	July 1	Mac
Training programs	2	Lack of time	1	1	Time management program	June 5	Pete
Budget $	3	Little mid-management support	2	3	Presentation to middle management	June 18	Group
	4	Downtime	2	4	Preventive main-tenance schedule	July 19	Marsha

chapter 11

Even the Giants Can Adapt To Speed

Northern Telecom is the world's leading supplier of fully digital telecommunications systems. Controlled by Bell Canada, the company operates in more than 70 countries in North and South America, the Caribbean, Europe, the Middle East, the Far East, and the Pacific Rim. Northern operates 40 manufacturing plants in Australia, Canada, France, Malaysia, the Peoples Republic of China, the Republic of Ireland, and the United States.

In the international telecommunications field, Northern Telecom is large, but by no means the biggest (see *Figure 11-1*).

But Northern's aspirations are high. Its "Vision 2000" is to be the leading global player in a market that is expected to grow to some $300 billion (from $75 billion in 1987).

Speed Has Been a Key to Success

Northern Telecom's ability to pioneer new technology and quickly bring it to the market quickly has paid off handsomely. In 1976, Northern launched a range of new office telephone switches which used digital signals, as opposed to conventional analog signals. The new systems helped slash maintenance costs, multiplied network capacity, and paved the way for further innovations such as voice mail and call forwarding. The timing couldn't be better. The breakup of AT&T in the U.S. in 1984, saw the birth of a number of independent telephone

247

companies who looked away from AT&T's Western Electric to more progressive suppliers. The result was a sales bonanza; Northern's total income ballooned to $5.8 billion in 1985 from $3 billion in 1982.[1]

Northern Telecom enters the 1990s with declining sales and growth. But the organization remains confident in the future, as it has again surpassed its competitors in bringing new technology to the market quicker. Fibre World — a range of high-speed fibre optics based switches — will give Northern's customers almost unlimited capability to carry telephone signals, sharp, high-definition TV (HDTV), and an array of high-tech services into homes and offices.

CORPORATION	COUNTRY	%
AT&T	U.S.	24.0
Siemens West	Germany	15.6
Alcatel	France	14.4
NEC	Japan	9.3
Northern Telecom	Canada	7.5
L.M.Ericson	Sweden	5.8
Fujitsu	Japan	4.1
Other		19.3

Figure 11-1. International Competitors in Telecommunications Equipment.

Significantly, Northern Telecom (NTI) will be about six months ahead of arch rival — AT&T — a significant amount of time in a market where the window of opportunity is shrinking dramatically with each passing day.

Among major North American manufacturing conglomerates, Northern Telecom's grasp of meeting the Time to Market challenge is a little short of inspirational. The trigger for the company's gradual and now whole-hearted embrace of the TTM approach was the realization in 1985 that a new manufacturing philosophy and strategy was needed. After an eight-year, 1200% increase in annual sales volume to $2.5 billion, sales to the telecommunications industry of the firm's innovative fully digital switches were decreasing. The company's early monopoly was ending.

Mounting global competition and the need to meet customer demands for better, more sophisticated products, and at lower costs, were viewed by management as immutable forces that could only increase. The time had come, the company said, to rethink its entire approach to operations. In the words of NTI's President Roy Merrills, "We discovered that all of the things vital to our long-term competitiveness had one thing in common: time. Everything we wanted to do to improve operations had something to do with squeezing time out of our processes."[2]

---

[1] *Financial Post.* July 30, 1990 issue, Toronto, Ontario.
[2] "How Northern Telecom Competes on Time." *Harvard Business Review*, *July-August 1989, p. 108.*

- Operations planning and scheduling.
- Product delivery costs.
- Installation and field service.

Results of the implementation of the first three core programs are outstanding (see *Figure 11-2*).

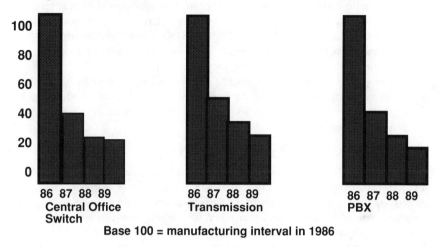

Base 100 = manufacturing interval in 1986

Figure 11-2. Reduced Manufacturing Cycle Times.

To improve its procurement process, the company worked closely with vendors to set up totally understood quality standards. Each vendor was scrutinized closely and, if found up to the standards, received "certification" from NTI. The goal, however, was to sharply reduce the number of vendors from its 1984 peak of 9,300. Competition among vendors was fierce and each strove mightily to gain and retain certification.

Now, company wide, NTI's divisions pull inventory from suppliers directly to the shop floor. Nearly 85% of materials come from single-source suppliers, with the result that the receiving cycle has been cut 97% — from three weeks to four hours. Incoming inspection staff has been halved and production problems related to defective supplies all but eliminated.

By 1988 the number of vendors was reduced by 2,500, and NTI was enjoying the benefits of not having to invest in large inventories and incoming inspection, not wasting time waiting for components, and not having anything approaching the volume of rework necessary before the program.

Manufacturing process improvement began with introduction of TQC — Total Quality Control. By using simple statistical charts to monitor key variables of a manufacturing process, people began to understand the interaction and roles of people, materials, the equipment, and methods. By noting the circumstances that occurred when output did not conform to a desired outcome, people were able to eliminate problems systematically.

After initial training, line employees were given authority to shut down their line whenever they spotted a problem, and it stayed down until the issue was

DEVELOPING A PLAN

Probably the most significant example of the cost of time to NTI came with management's early realization that some 20% of manufacturing overhead costs resulted from the need to make engineering changes to existing products at least once every two hours, at each of the company's plants. Even with generous use of Just In Time production, fast-flow and Computer-Integrated Manufacturing, automation and cross-training, the company grew to appreciate that the benefits from this sort of band-aid help would be only short term.

The company's major worry, according to Merrills, was that internationally generated technological change and the resultant shorter and shorter product life would place the firm in deepening jeopardy. A plan was needed to make the company more competitive.

U.S. Plants

Early in 1985, NTI assembled a 12-person Operations Council, drawn from all divisions and from the head office. It was a diverse group. Although basic technology was common throughout the firm, products, customers and division priorities were often dissimilar. To arrive at a workable company-wide operations strategy seemed illusionary, even to the most optimistic members. However, by seeking a wide consensus, keeping people informed, and listening to feedback, the group finally was able to define three strategic five-year objectives.

The three objectives were easy to state, but represented nearly a year's tough argument, sometimes angry negotiation, and much compromise. But all three were agreed upon by Council members, and in the spring of 1986 they became the basis for the company's future efforts.

First, said the Council, the company will boost customer satisfaction by 20% using its established annual customer survey as the measuring stick. Second, inventory days will be slashed by 50%. Third, manufacturing overhead, as a percentage of sales, must be cut by half. The result, for NTI, would be to double the speed of product throughput but not at the expense of boosting inventory or overhead costs. The Council added that there was to be no deviation from these objectives. They would apply to all 13 manufacturing facilities and 14 R&D establishments.

To reach the goals, added the Council, it will be necessary to chop manufacturing cycle times from months to no more than two weeks, yet maintain quality that meets customer demands.

The Council designed six core programs and directed that each division implement them to best suit their individual needs. It was made clear that time improvement was wanted eventually in each of the six programs, but it was also recognized that it would be best to start the TTM process with only three:

- Procurement practices.
- Manufacturing process improvement.
- New product introduction and change.

The remaining three core programs were not launched until 1989, after time-based operations became the norm and the necessary infrastructure to support the concepts was functioning. The final core programs are:

resolved. Production certainly suffered in the early days, but in a matter of weeks, production quality leapt ahead with a dramatically reduced defect rate.

Superior quality helped to reduce manufacturing lot sizes so that rather than push a week's inventory to the production line, the line now pulled material from inventory as needed with a target lot size of one. This was made possible because of the simultaneous progress with improvements in procurement.

A result of the successful adoption of TTM techniques for NTI's manufacturing people has been that the time needed for new product introduction has dropped by 20%; in some cases by 50%. Manufacturing process time improvement is even more impressive. One interval dropped from nine to 2.4 weeks, another's from 4.2 to 1.4 weeks, and yet another from 16 to 6 weeks. Corporately, the firm reached 50% of its five-year improvement goal in about two years.

In a company with some 22,000 employees, introducing change wasn't easy. Rivalries and pride engendered early resistance at the divisional and functional level, and this had to be addressed. Management gained cooperation in stages. Middle managers, in groups of 25, were given a full one-week course in the strategies and fundamentals of time-based operations. Two-day courses for first-level managers and professionals were introduced. Nearly 8,000 employees are involved in the training effort. As well, customers were invited to tour NTI plants and encouraged to give frank performance appraisals of what they saw and how the company's products met their needs.

Line employees, too, have been involved in NTI's TTM process. Having a highly motivated, flexible work force was critical. So, a "pay for skill" program was introduced. Employees are given pay increases for each new task they master. Their new and rewarding flexibility frees them from performing single task jobs and allows them movement among a variety of assignments. Staff morale improved, and employees now understand how their actions fit the corporate objective of being responsive to customers.

Because time-based operations work only if there is instant information where it is needed, the company reduced the internal "secrecy" level dramatically. For instance, production workers were encouraged to pull schematics and other drawings on display screens without having to wait for hard copies, thus eliminating any worries about whether or not the information is up-to-date. Internal "absorption accounting," which prompted the burying of many costs in the nebulousness of inventory, was done away with and replaced by an expense-based system that discloses real cost sources. The system highlights problems and pressures managers to fix them quickly.

Capital expenditure authorization procedures were altered, too. The single criterion of how-soon-will-there-be-a-financial-payback was expanded so that now managers can justify capital spending if they can show it will improve quality or result in time savings.

And In Canada

In Canada, world headquarters for Northern Telecom, the company's domestic operating subsidiary, Northern Telecom Canada Limited, operates some 20 plants in seven of the ten provinces. With nearly 22,000 employees, Northern manufactures a wide range of telecommunications and other high-technology products. Among other interests, the company also enjoys 70% ownership (with Bell Canada) of Ottawa-based Bell-Northern Research (the country's largest R & D organization) which employs some 6,000 scientists and technicians in several Canadian and U.S. centers and the United Kingdom.

Included in the family of NTCL plants is the company's Calgary-based *Business Products Divisions* (BPD), an operation that demonstrates again how Northern Telecom is meeting the Time to Market challenge and reaping substantial rewards.

The Calgary plant opened in 1980 when BPD was moved from London, Ontario as part of the company's contribution to help diversify western Canada's economy. It was to refine, manufacture, and market the NT Vantage analog key system, a product intended for providing a range from two to 50 telephone lines for the small business market.

Sales were reasonably good at first, but within a few years, BPD was in difficulty.

There were more than a few problems:

- Technological superiority dissipated.
- Costs rose to the point that Vantage was pricing itself out of the market.
- Quality levels sagged with commensurate increases in servicing costs.
- Employee morale was low.
- Surveys showed increasing customer dissatisfaction.
- Industry deregulation encouraged mounting competition from Japan, Korea, Taiwan, and AT&T in the United States.
- Low-end Vantage systems simply had too many expensive unused features of no appeal to price-sensitive prospects.

The result was that a division able to supply all of North America was left with only a shrinking slice of the Canadian market. Massive effort did bring costs down by about 40%, but the division's dwindling financial resources reduced redesign efforts and there was little effort to improve attitudes toward customers. For instance, if a dealer or telephone company asked for service, BPD would respond only to technical concerns. No other problem could be addressed, said the division.

By 1985, the company was ready to close the division. But a last ditch effort to do "something" was handed to a new vice-president and general manager, Michael Ennis. He proposed what some of his fellow executives thought could be a $40-million throwaway. He proposed to build on Northern Telecom's significant technology base and replace Vantage with a new open, distributed call processing system that would act as a slave to any system terminal that negotiated a connection. The new product's design and development would be an immediate step to be taken while he tackled other aspects of BPD's problem.

Critical to the success of the division, believed Ennis, would be a clear understanding that everybody had to be responsible for the quality of his or her outputs and that individual ownership of quality would be essential for success.

The second part of the proposal focused on customers. BPD personnel were directed, urged, and encouraged to get closer to them, but not necessarily on the golf course or at lunches, and to ask about the performance of competing products. The idea was to appreciate how Northern Telecom's products could be improved and function more usefully in terms that customers could *recognize*. Instead of making and sustaining customer contact solely through marketing and sales personnel, other functional personnel — from all departments — were prompted to develop and report on their contacts.

Ennis also encouraged the viewpoint that everyone was a customer. In many cases, this customer was internal to the business. It was critical to identify the next person in the process and do everything to help that person by delivering problem-free products, or services, on time.

Internally, the customer focus led to dismantling walls, as different groups looked at how they could help each other rather than compete. Externally, the obsession to help customers quickly was reflected positively in the customer satisfaction surveys showing over 90% expressing satisfaction in the 1989 survey (see *Figure 11-3*).

Next, key personnel were sent to project teams with varying mandates such as resolving new product design problems, improving supplier performance, improving yields, and cutting defects in both production and scrap. The players were drawn from marketing, design, engineering, manufacturing, purchasing, operations, and inventory. An essential corporate goal was that each of the functional representatives should come to understand that internal cooperation and support would be decisive in the division's survival. Product production cycles had to be cut dramatically.

Northern uses a "gating" system to manage its introduction of the Meridian Norstar. Each gate is a significant milestone. Achieving a "gate" is not only important to the project, but it is linked to individual objectives and rewards through Northern's performance appraisal system.

Norstar's Gate 0 took place when the concept of the Meridian Norstar was described in general terms, including a timetable for the design and manufacture of the product.

Gate 1 took place six months later than planned since it proved to be extremely difficult to reconcile the commercial and product specifications, because each group promoted its own interests. But once the business case was agreed upon, the design process was facilitated. This was because management refused to extend the last gate and expected the project team to play catch-up instead.

The third gate was the field trial which proved effective because of the attention to detail by the team.

The final gate was the point at which the product was released to the market, on time and ahead of the competition.

The gating process has put a lot of intelligent discipline into the launch of a new product, says Mr. Ennis. It provides needed knowledge of the practicality of a new venture. It assigns priorities, determines capital needs, and indicates staff and employee responsibilities, all at a minimal cost. It also encourages internal cooperation and fosters extensive team effort, not to mention the teaching of

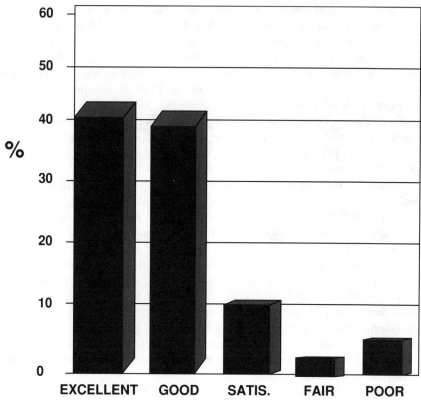

Figure 11-3. Customer Service Survey.

negotiating skills among the people involved. A variety of techniques were developed to make the manufacturing process fast and flexible. BPD did not make the mistake of using robots just for the sake of automation. They studied each process, simplified it, and then automated it with equipment that they had custom made for them. The use of bar coding on each order enabled the flexible manufacturing system to produce as little as one, without any problem. Inspection of products on the line was eliminated wherever possible; this mundane task was taken over by the equipment itself.

The most up-to-date technology was used in design too. Using CAD to automate design functions, it became possible to integrate functionally separate operations. At the time that the Norstar was being designed, the building instructions — details of the equipment, tools, parts, and production steps — were generated too.

As changes were made, lead times dropped dramatically (see *Figure 11-4*).

Information gained by the division showed that product simplicity — in stocking, installation and use — would be essential to survival and growth with absolute collaborative design, engineering, and manufacturing effort pivotal to

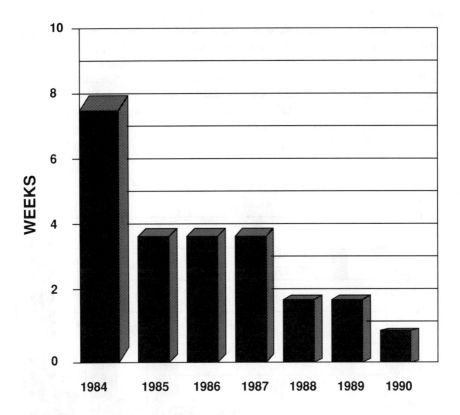

Figure 11-4. Published Lead Time.

any growth of BPD. Even more essential would be the design and production of a communications system that would complement, rather than obsolesce any future system improvements. The hope was to gain on-going windows of sales opportunity with customers, so that users would use BPD sales calls as opportunities to gain added value for their system investments.

With the dedicated joint support of Bell Northern Research, BPD was finally able to come up with a business telephone system that includes features that users say they want and that is competitive against the best available from anywhere in the world. Aside from the earlier features of Vantage, which included speed dialing, paging, hands-free speaking, intercom, re-dial, and conference calling, the new Calgary team accepted incorporation of one added feature that now gives the company a major advantage in the market. The added feature is a small-screen user display which details how to use the system. Further, the system was designed to provide over 100-line capacity, a doubling of the Vantage capability broadened the division's overall market potential.

Producing a superior product in the fastest possible time did not happen easily. Especially since it took six months longer than expected to write a business plan and have it accepted. But the goal was firm: to be on the market quicker than

Toshiba, who was believed to be designing a product aimed at the same market. BPD avoided the temptation to involve research people in different parts of North America. Instead, Ennis insisted that all research — system, hardware and software — be done under one roof, so that the coordinator "could stand on his desk and see everyone working on the product" at the same time. Now named the Meridian Norstar system, BPD's new product is experiencing outstanding success. Sales continue to soar (see *Figure 11-5*).

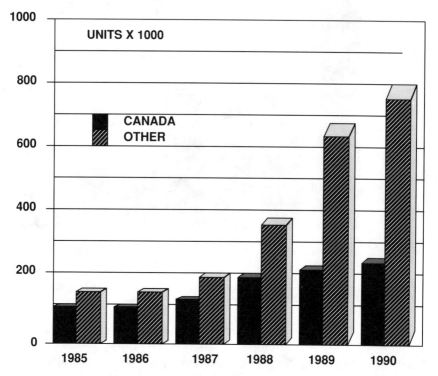

Figure 11-5. Sales.

From a Canadian market share of 21% in 1986, the division by 1989 gained first place with 41%. In the U.S., market share has gone from less than 1% to about 8%, which represents a solid hold on fifth place. (Note that the North American 2-100-station market in 1991 is estimated at U.S. $1.1 billion, and the global market at $3.2 billion by 1994.)

As the world's first digital key telephone system, the Meridian Norstar's alphanumeric user display screen has undoubtedly contributed significantly to its success. Among the advantages it gives users, the display:

- Enables the user to verify the number being called and to see the names of people calling from other Norstar terminals on the system.
- Notifies the user of changes in the status of a call — showing, for instance, if a call is being forwarded, or that two calls have been conferenced.

256

- Provides promptings to guide the user through the operation of any feature.
- Confirms correct use of a feature or identifies error causes.
- Reminds users if features such as do-not-disturb or call forward are in use.
- Simplifies system-programming activities for the installer and system co-ordinator.

The launch of Norstar demanded intense simplification for the Calgary plant. No longer could the plant tolerate vast stores of inventory. Such overhead costs would kill them. By encouraging and educating suppliers and vendors about Kanban (simply a series of signals to replace only what is consumed in the manufacturing process), Calgary became a model of how to "pull" materials and components, rather than an extensive example of how a "pushed" plant can go out of business.

One example is illustrative. BPD gained a 60% cut in the storage space requirement for pallets of plastic terminal castings. Before Kanban, the plant maintained an inventory of 150 pallets. By the end of a year, production had doubled, but on-hand storage amounted to only 60 pallets at any one time. Today, the Kanban system is self-governing and responds only to production demands.

In meeting the Time To Market challenge, Vice-president Ennis also gives credit to the plant's reduction of administrative complexity. Examples:

1. The division had 45 telephone lines, mostly for test purposes, with each invoiced monthly — a total of more than 500 transactions a year. BPD now pays annually with a single transaction and an annual labor savings of several hundreds of dollars.
2. Earlier invoicing and payment for single shipments from a single plastics molder once demanded 60 transactions a week, and the division's total amounted to a staggering 25,000 transactions annually. Monthly invoicing arrangements now permit only 1,600 transactions annually, a drop of 93%.
3. Repetitive entry of shipments received and inventory-consumer data has been all but eliminated with the use of bar coding.
4. Engineering *Change Notice* documentation had previously demanded up to 75 pages per authorization. New procedures have cut the documentation to two pages with the attendant time savings for high-priced senior management.
5. Linked computer modems (on a need-to-know basis) permit suppliers to reconcile their invoices against division receipts before anything is committed to paper. Paper communications are now precise and enormously time-saving.

Northern Telecom's new Norstar product also exhibits the real rewards of a cooperative effort by design and manufacturing people. In spite of having two locations, designers in Ottawa and manufacturing people in Calgary had one burning ambition — to bring the most up-to-date technology onto the market before Toshiba. Len Smith, Director of Product Line Management and a key team member, recalls many bitter debates. "But at the end of each day, we would get together and have a beer. Our friendships grew from a mutual respect. By the end of the project, the bonds became unbreakable."

Even though Norstar is a sophisticated product, it is still simple to stock and maintain. Part of the reason is that it is complete enough that few accessories need be stocked by dealers or telephone companies. Standard system components already include a headphone jack and extra-length coil cords, and units can be readily converted from desk-standing to wall-mounting with a simple base-plate turn. Telco and dealer buyers need only a minimum of inventory.

As a result of continuous customer probing, the division also learned that standard telephone touchpads, which lack "q" and "z," also prompt consumer unease. Norstar now incorporates both missing letters, which, not incidentally, allows the system to be uniquely computer-adaptable for many functions including word processing.

Installation of Norstar has been streamlined. For an 18-station system, for instance, expensive technician time is about one-third less than for competitive systems. For a 10-station system, BPD now needs less than half the time needed by the competition.

Streamlining of the new Norstar product itself, of course, led to the savings in installation. Components are silicon-intensive, a concept first made practical by BPD and Bell-Northern Research. Several discrete components could now be combined as a single intensively tested reliable component with a resulting cut in manufacturing complexity and overhead costs. Overall, only about one-tenth the number of components of a Vantage system are needed for the vastly superior Norstar system. The reduced manufacturing complexity has led to "enormous" savings in equipment, space, and time for both operators and engineers. In addition, extensive in-plant testing, which adds no product value, has all but been eliminated. Quality management is focused on component manufacture whether in-house or from vendors.

The quality of Norstar has led also to a major reduction in after-installation service. Technicians can usually identify a customer problem over the telephone so that if a customer warranty or service call is necessary, they can go fully prepared to correct any fault.

The changes within BPD that led to the division's turnaround also included a major shop floor effort. Operators were invited to explore ways of delivering zero-defect product to each of their customers — the next work station or the next department. So successful are the shop employees that they now set their own targets, consistently raising them to levels thought unattainable by management.

An example of increased employee dedication came with their writing of a new manual for auto-insertion machine operation. It is more comprehensive and consistent than the machine builders. Not to be left out, a group of quality inspectors eventually decided that they added no value to Norstar because their skills had now been transferred to the people doing the work they used to inspect. The group re-assigned themselves as troubleshooters and became absorbed into line functions on the floor.

258

As each change in the order-to-delivery process has been made, efficiencies have materialized and time-to-delivery has dropped (see *Figure 11-6*).

Today, European customers are getting 24-hour delivery. In the U.K., for example, BPD operates on a Kanban system at Heathrow, where a minimum buffer stock is kept. As each unit is sold, it is replaced within 24 hours from Calgary.

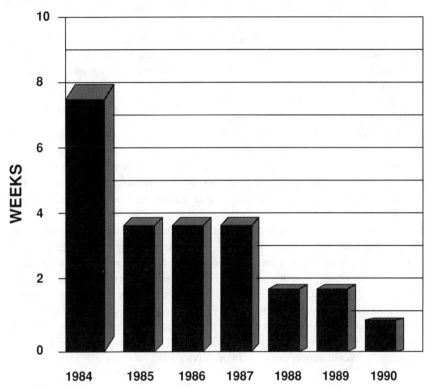

Figure 11-6. Published Lead Time.

The performance of the Business Products Division of Northern Telecom Canada Limited in the period 1985-90 speaks for itself:
- Product costs dropped from nearly $500 to less than $200 — a 60% cut.
- Yield improvement teams chopped component assembly and soldering defects from 3000 parts per million to a minuscule 200.
- Vendor partnership programs have resulted in a reduction of rejected lots from 20% to 2%.
- Published lead times in 1984 were eight weeks. In 1990, the published time is one week and most customers now face just 48-hour lead time before delivery. (This compares with the lead times of up to seven months demanded by some Pacific Rim competitors.)
- BPD's delivery promise of 48 hours is working. By 1992, the division

will be able to promise a lead time of 48 hours to any place in the world connected with a direct air flight from Calgary. (More-than-single-stop air shipments now face time delays by customs officials which are greater than the time it takes Calgary to manufacture the product.)

- Customer satisfaction surveys show the division with 90% + indicating "excellent" or "good."
- The division can now produce a one-only product in ten variations just as profitably as it can build 10 copies of the same product.

Now operating with a "Culture of Commitment," in the words of Mike Ennis, the Business Products Division is a turned-around enterprise. From an operation threatened with closure in 1985, the division is now regarded as one of the jewels in Northern Telecom's 40-plant world universe. Divisional annual sales in 1990 are expected to exceed $200 million, up from only $40 million in 1988. The now high-morale 700-employee workforce could double by 1993.

One mark of BPD's turnaround is its recent first sale to Korea, gained in mid-1990. It is a reflection of the steadily building international business the division is beginning to enjoy, reports Ennis, who also notes it would not have been possible without realization of the goal of serving customers with products they can use, at a cost they can afford, and doing it right the first time, in the shortest possible time.

According to Ennis, "Time to Market, as it is understood by the Norstar team, is not simply an acceptable interval in which a consignment of product may be delivered to a customer, but an all-encompassing frame of reference whose clock starts with the conception of a customer need and ends with the customer enjoying the use of the product. Between those two events lie product development, a flexible production system that delivers quality product to short order intervals, a responsive delivery system, and an intrinsic level of service reliability that customers can count on from their specified installation date until the system is replaced." World supply is no problem, says BPD.

chapter *12*

Conclusion

AN AIM TO THE FUTURE

For many chief executives, the information explosion has led to migraine-sized concerns. It has become truly impossible to keep pace with so much that is new and exciting. This is particularly so for those trying to master or manage a number of functions, skills, and business disciplines. It means that industry and business leaders need to lift themselves above the fog and clearly see opportunities and problems in a global perspective. If they do so, they will see these trends:

THE WORLD IS MOVING FASTER

In some respects, the world is becoming an easier place in which to trade. Barriers are dropping and economies are integrating faster and faster. In less than a year Germany became one; Europeans will integrate their economies by 1992; Free Trade between Canada and the United States is already partially operational (with Mexico sure to join the process in the foreseeable future). Political barriers now have more consequence for historians than they do for business people and industrialists.

Being out of touch with current events, as on a remote vacation, can be almost dangerous because circumstances change so quickly. A refinery can be buying crude oil for $16 a barrel one week, paying $28 the next, and up to $40 a week after. Crises on one side of the globe send tremors around the world.

The World is Getting Smaller

Modern technology allows things to get done in a split second rather than days or weeks. Direct dealing, conference calling, faxes, and cellular telephones are some of the tools that are making geographical location more and more irrelevant. Travel between countries is more routine and commonplace than before. Executives who speak more than one language and who have working experience on different continents command a premium.

Design of new products can be done in Toronto, Toledo, or Tokyo. It doesn't really matter, since drawings can be transferred instantly and reviewed at any time, anywhere in the world.

Distributing products over great distances more often than not has ceased to be a disadvantage, as transportation costs on giant ships have kept unit costs sufficiently low. Transportation methodologies will continue to improve significantly, making the location of manufacturing sites an all but academic decision.

Competition is Becoming More Cut-Throat

The 19th century belonged to Europe. The 20th century to the United States. And predictions are that the 21st will belong to the Pacific Rim countries such as Japan, Korea, and Taiwan. North American and European organizations may not agree with this assessment, as nobody wants to lie down and play dead. After all, there is a need to protect product volumes (and jobs) as domestic consumption falls. Research and development costs are so significant today that cost recovery on major items such as drugs or new cars, is possible only in a global market.

Offshore Manufacturing Opportunities will Become More Attractive

Social pressures in the western democratic countries will continue to influence wage rates. The disparity between have and have-not countries will not narrow, but will increase.

Already, many businesses have found it impossible to compete against low-wage developing nations, where labor is conditioned to working 10 to 12 hour days, six days a week, for a fraction of North American pay scales.

Dinosaurs Will Disappear. . . Quickly

Large, fat, bureaucratic organizations will no longer bleed slowly to death. Instead, they will die quickly or become victims of hard-nosed managers. The changes that will be made to them will be significant. They will be cut to fighting size. Uneconomic units will be sold or shut down. Those that remain will be downsized and flattened. A significant proportion of middle managers will disappear. First-level supervision will lose power and authority over workers and spend more time coordinating activities, problem solving, and coaching.

The Focus of Competitive Advantage will Emphasize Time

Cost and quality increasingly will be taken for granted. Response time will become an important factor in the determination of who wins and who loses. In the area of high-technology particularly, organizations able to introduce new

262

products to the market significantly ahead of competitors will own a major share of niche markets. In manufacturing, those organizations able to supply almost instantly, from production rather than stock, will be the most profitable, lowest cost producers. They will devour their competitors.

STRATEGIC CHANGES WILL REAP LONG-TERM REWARDS

As timeliness and responsiveness become critical competitive weapons in this last decade of the century, it is important to examine prospects of making such a major transition. There are at least two attitudes that can prevent most North American organizations from making it. First, there is an obsession with short-term gains. Rewards in most organizations are based on the here and now. People with vision and long-sightedness tend to be in staff rather than line roles. The movers and shakers have been glamorized and immortalized much more than the visionaries and builders. Deal making is far more profitable than producing, or so goes the perception. The best and brightest of our business schools head for Wall Street and Main Street rather than the side streets where hard work takes time to pay off. Decision making is based on financial ratios, not futures. And decision makers are number-crunchers, not builders.

The second attitude is really a consequence of the "here and now" mentality. It is the need to find instant solutions. Resorting to quick fixes is far more acceptable than fundamental change, since they can be made often with little pain or discomfort.

No organization can emerge as a serious time-based competitor without changing itself fundamentally. As with any organizational change, conversion to time-based operations is not an easy task; it is much more difficult than most other change. However, some companies have made the transition and alot can be learned from their experiences. For example:

Lesson Number 1 - There is No Gain Without Pain

Time-based competitiveness means root-level shakeups. Few systems will remain intact, and few people will avoid some adjustment. Even though humans are remarkably adaptable, changes are disliked immensely, especially when they can't control it. Today's challenges, the number and size of adjustments that people are called on to make, are getting bigger and bigger and becoming more and more frequent.

Under such conditions, stress in the workplace will increase. Smart organizations will be responsive to people who struggle. They will:

- Involve people as much as possible in decisions that impact them.
- Keep them informed about changes that will affect them, as soon as it is known.
- Provide counselling services to those who develop dysfunctional behavior in the face of too much change.
- Provide out-counselling for those who can function effectively only in a more sedate environment.

Lesson Number 2 - Deal with Changes from a Systems Standpoint

Any organization is a system. It has a number of parts, each of which impacts others with change. When change is implemented, it is important to take the whole organization into account, and this includes suppliers and distributors.

Peter Goldsbrough and Philip Deane, of the Boston Consulting Group, see the change process in three distinct steps[1]. First, they recommend an evaluation process during which staff document existing systems. In such an exercise, it is inevitable that a number of non value-added activities will show up (see *Figure 12-1*). These need to be challenged. Do they need to be done at all? Can they be done simultaneously with other activities, instead of sequentially? Can they be done quicker? Can they be done by front-line people?

Second, they recommend looking at how existing systems can be modified to reduce time. In this phase, decisions regarding a lot of "sacred cows" need to be made. It takes real courage, because the decisions taken will change the work area. Third, time-based change could mean reducing or eliminating entire departments — quality control or stock control, for instance — or some layer of supervision, or even an unnecessary layer of management. All decisions will be based on the same three principles:

1. Tasks must be done faster.
2. Tasks must be performed simultaneously rather than sequentially.
3. The number of interfaces between activities and people must be reduced to a minimum.

Lesson Number 3 - Changes Must Start with Top Management

Converting an organization into an extraordinary market-responsive unit requires fundamental changes in internal and external outlook, structure, and reward. These changes can begin only in the executive offices. Too often they do not. And the results are easily observable. There is continuous introduction of new programs, few of which benefit the organization; programs overlap, previous ideas are duplicated. Change is sabotaged, never fulfilled, perpetuity reigns until corporate death.

THE CHALLENGE

Having arrived at the end of this book, you might feel like congratulating yourself. Don't be too effusive. The real challenges have yet to come. They will be met and conquered only if you put into practice some or all of the powerful tools, manufacturing ideas, and techniques described in this book.

So what will it take for you to make a difference? To reduce manufacturing times by half? Or reduce design times by 90%? Certainly these are daunting challenges, but they can and must be met. Your organization, no matter how

---

[1]Peter Boldsbrough and Philip Deane, "Time is Money." *Management Today,* September 1988, p.132.

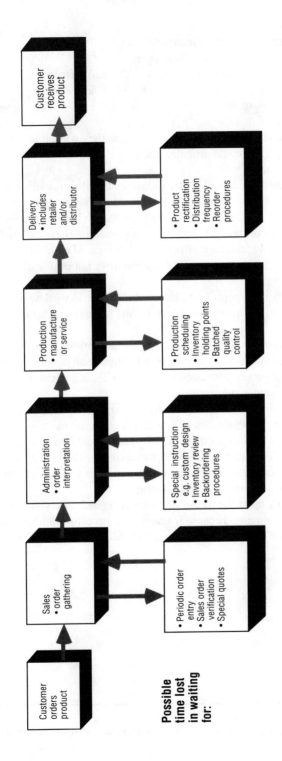

Figure 12-1. The Objective is to Minimize Cycle Time from Order to Delivery.

good, still needs to take a quantum leap to survive, let alone thrive. And you must grasp the challenge and become a change agent.

Perhaps some wisdom from one of the world's most effective change agents can help. Rosabeth Moss-Kantor in her book *"The Change Masters"*[2] describes some of the attributes of executives who have successfully transformed their enterprises. She found that they:

- **Have a clear vision.** All knew exactly where they wanted to take their organization. They could articulate the future state and get others to buy into their dream.
- **Are persistent.** There isn't a major change effort that doesn't bring with it many roadblocks and minefields. But effective change agents are not easily deterred. Instead, each time they fall flat on their face, they get up, dust themselves off and get right back into the fire. They don't quit. They are passionate. In fact, their efforts can be compared to drops of water on a rock. It seems to make no impact for some time, but eventually it makes a hole in the rock.
- **Network.** Change agents find like-minded people to work with. They create a subculture that expands as more and more converts buy into the new ideas.
- **Work in teams.** Change agents know their limitations. They cannot be in all places at once. Nor can they be all things to all people. So they attract capable people with complementary skills and talents to share the load of the daunting task ahead.
- **Take risks.** Finally, change agents have courage. All organizations are difficult to budget because there is so much conventional wisdom around. People who try to change conventional wisdom seldom win popularity sweepstakes. They can be chastised, ostracized, or even fired. But they are still prepared to take risks because of the importance of the idea to them. They commit themselves, right or wrong.

How do you stack up to the model of a change agent? Are you ready to take the plunge? I hope you are; because if you do, the benefits, both personally and organizationally, will be considerable. You will still be in business 20 years from now.

---

[2]Rosabeth Moss-Kantor, *The Change Masters,* Touchstone, Simon and Shuster Inc., New York, 1983.

INDEX

267